GEOGRAPHIES OF ENGLAND

To what extent has a North–South divide been a structural feature of England's geography during the last millennium and to what extent has it been especially associated with, and recognised during, particular periods in the past? These are the central questions addressed in *Geographies of England*, a pioneering exploration of the history of a fundamentally geographical concept. Six essays treating different historical periods – 1971–2000, 1918–1971, 1830–1918, 1750–1830, 1550–1750 and 1066–1550 – are integrated by their common concern with two geographical questions: first, to what extent is it possible for us today, as observers, to detect with historical hindsight a material or tangible North–South divide in England in those periods in terms of regional differences in, for example, population, economy, society and culture; and, secondly, how important was the idea of such a divide to the geographical imaginations of contemporaries, of the actors, in those periods? A concluding essay by the editors reviews the social construction of England's geography and history and the significance of the North–South divide as a cultural metaphor.

Geographies of England provides a learned and sustained examination of a theme of perennial interest. It will appeal to geographers, historians, sociologists, political scientists and all those seeking to understand the cultural composition of England today.

ALAN R. H. BAKER is a Fellow of Emmanuel College, Cambridge, General Editor of Cambridge Studies in Historical Geography, and the author of numerous books and articles on historical geography, most recently *Geography and History: Bridging the Divide* (Cambridge, 2003).

MARK BILLINGE is University Lecturer in Geography and a Fellow of Magdalene College, Cambridge. Dr Billinge was the co-editor (with Alan Baker) of the very first book in Cambridge Studies in Historical Geography, *Period and Place* (Cambridge, 1982).

Cambridge Studies in Historical Geography 37

Series editors:
ALAN R. H. BAKER, RICHARD DENNIS, DERYCK HOLDSWORTH

Cambridge Studies in Historical Geography encourages exploration of the philosophies, methodologies and techniques of historical geography and publishes the results of new research within all branches of the subject. It endeavours to secure the marriage of traditional scholarship with innovative approaches to problems and to sources, aiming in this way to provide a focus for the discipline and to contribute towards its development. The series is an international forum for publication in historical geography which also promotes contact with workers in cognate disciplines.

For a full list of titles in the series, please see end of book.

GEOGRAPHIES OF ENGLAND

The North–South Divide, Material and Imagined

Edited by

ALAN R. H. BAKER
Fellow of Emmanuel College, Cambridge

and

MARK BILLINGE
University Lecturer in Geography and
Fellow of Magdalene College, Cambridge

CAMBRIDGE
UNIVERSITY PRESS

PUBLISHED BY THE PRESS SYNDICATE OF THE UNIVERSITY OF CAMBRIDGE
The Pitt Building, Trumpington Street, Cambridge, United Kingdom

CAMBRIDGE UNIVERSITY PRESS
The Edinburgh Building, Cambridge, CB2 2RU, UK
40 West 20th Street, New York, NY 10011–4211, USA
477 Williamstown Road, Port Melbourne, VIC 3207, Australia
Ruiz de Alarcón 13, 28014 Madrid, Spain
Dock House, The Waterfront, Cape Town 8001, South Africa

http://www.cambridge.org

© the editors and contributors 2004

This book is in copyright. Subject to statutory exception
and to the provisions of relevant collective licensing agreements,
no reproduction of any part may take place without
the written permission of Cambridge University Press.

First published 2004

Printed in the United Kingdom at the University Press, Cambridge

Typeface Times 10/12 pt.   *System* LATEX 2$_\varepsilon$ [TB]

A catalogue record for this book is available from the British Library

ISBN 0 521 82261 0 hardback

Contents

Figures

Tables

Contributors

ALAN R.H. BAKER is a Life Fellow of Emmanuel College, Cambridge

MARK BILLINGE is Lecturer in Geography at the University of Cambridge and a Fellow of Magdalene College

BRUCE M. S. CAMPBELL is Professor of Geography at the Queen's University of Belfast

DANNY DORLING is Professor of Geography at the University of Sheffield

PHILIP HOWELL is Lecturer in Geography at the University of Cambridge and a Fellow of Emmanuel College

JOHN LANGTON is Lecturer in Geography at the University of Oxford and a Fellow of St John's College, Oxford

RONALD L. MARTIN is Professor of Geography at the University of Cambridge and a Fellow of St Catharine's College, Cambridge

Preface

The specific origin of this book lies in the fact that one of us was struck some years ago by the broad similarity between the geographical distribution of wealth in England in the early-fourteenth century and that in the late-twentieth century. Developments in between, including the Industrial Revolution, appeared puzzlingly not to have upset that fundamental pattern. More generally, the concept of a North–South divide has featured hugely in the political and popular imagination but hardly at all in studies of the historical geography of England. This book seeks to address that puzzle and to correct that neglect. We are grateful to the individual authors for participating in a workshop to discuss the issues and for engaging in this collective project. The final stages of this book have benefited immensely from the meticulous copy-editing of Jacqueline French, whose help we have warmly appreciated.

ALAN R. H. BAKER
MARK BILLINGE

1

Material and imagined geographies of England

ALAN R. H. BAKER AND MARK BILLINGE

Two themes

Scholarly accounts of the historical geography of England since the Norman Conquest have tended to focus upon systematic changes in its population, economy, society and landscape. Although addressing 'geographical' issues, their organisational structures have led them to place more emphasis upon chronological (temporal) changes than upon regional (spatial) differences. By contrast, popular accounts of the changing geography of England in modern times have tended to emphasise a basic divide between North and South. To some extent, this difference in emphasis might be because the former have tended to focus upon material geographies and the latter upon imagined geographies of England. There is, therefore, a case for combining these two perspectives in an examination of both the material and the imagined geographies of England since the Norman Conquest. The central questions to be addressed in this book are: To what extent has a North–South divide – in diverse forms – been a structural feature of England's geography during the last millennium and to what extent has it been especially associated with, and recognised during, particular periods in the past?

The concept of a North–South divide has surfaced in recent political debates about regional contrasts in wealth and welfare in England but aspects of the concept can be traced in literature for almost two centuries. Famously, Benjamin Disraeli (1845) in his novel *Sybil, or The Two Nations* portrayed the existence of 'two nations; between whom there is no intercourse and no sympathy; who are as ignorant of each other's habits, thoughts, and feelings, as if they were dwellers of different planets; who are formed by a different breeding, are fed by different food, are ordered by different manners, and are not governed by the same laws'. This social rather than spatial concept of two nations was reinforced geographically in Elizabeth Gaskell's (1855) novel *North and South* and has since then become part of English popular and political culture. For example, a historical account of the idea of Englishness written by an Australian, Donald Horne, identified

1

two regionally specific variations, what he terms 'an ambivalence caused by the industrial revolution':

> In the *Northern Metaphor* Britain is pragmatic, empirical, calculating, Puritan, bourgeois, enterprising, adventurous, scientific, serious, and believes in struggle. Its sinful excess is a ruthless avarice, rationalised in the belief that the prime impulse in all human beings is a rational, calculating, economic self-interest. In the *Southern Metaphor* Britain is romantic, illogical, muddled, divinely lucky, Anglican, aristocratic, traditional, frivolous, and believes in order and tradition. Its sinful excess is a ruthless pride, rationalised in the belief that men are born to serve. (Horne 1970: 22)

Beryl Bainbridge (1987), in her book *Forever England*, set out to examine the roots of what she called 'that evergreen assumption, the notion that England is two nations'. Distrusting of historical scholarship, and doubting the reliability of fragmentary historical evidence, Bainbridge preferred to call partially upon literature but principally upon the memories of six families – three from the North and three from the South – to testify to the character of the concept. Two more academic accounts of the North–South divide were published in 1989 by professional geographers: David Smith explored in his book *North and South* what he saw as a growing economic, social and political divide in Britain since the end of the Second World War; and Jim Lewis and Alan Townsend edited a collection of eight essays on regional change in Britain during the 1980s, under the general title *The North–South Divide*. More recently, Helen M. Jewell has provided a scholarly, historical examination of one aspect of this duality in her book *The North–South Divide: The Origins of Northern Consciousness in England* (1994). Fundamentally although not exclusively a geographical concept, the North–South divide both as a 'reality' and as a 'representation of reality' clearly had a history.

But it is a history neglected by geographers. For example, in Robert Dodgshon and Robin Butlin's (1990) second edition of their synthesis of the historical geography of England and Wales, the North–South 'problem' featured only in the essay by Brian Robson on the interwar years and even then only occupies a few lines of its introduction and of a section on regional disparities in employment structures (Robson 1990: 546 and 557). That chapter included a reference to Robson's own rarely cited essay on the North–South divide (Robson 1985). Richard Lawton and Colin Pooley (1992) rightly emphasised the persistence of regional cultures in their historical geography of Britain between 1740 and 1950 but they said nothing about any North–South divide. In the recently published, pioneering, historical geography of Britain in the twentieth century, the editors – David Gilbert, David Matless and Brian Short – refer briefly to Horne's northern and southern metaphors arguing both that they can be overplayed (ignoring or sidelining other significant regional differences in Britain) and that a more culturally and historically informed story of those metaphors awaits detailed elaboration, because the North–South divide is not addressed further in their own collection of essays (Gilbert, Matless and Short 2003: 10–11).

The concept of a North–South divide in England will be approached in this present book in two ways. First, there is the task of identifying the broad, regional differences in the *material* or 'tangible' geography of England. This involves describing and explaining the geography of England in terms of the broad, regional differences in, for example, its population, economy, society, culture or landscape. Such studies are reconstructions undertaken by *observers* with historical hindsight using evidence of a variety of kinds from different historical periods. The aim here is to delineate the broad geographical structures which have underpinned England's history during the last one thousand years. Emphasis will be placed on the economic contrasts between North and South, because they have constituted such an important component of the concept, but appropriate attention will also be paid to demographic, social, political and cultural characteristics (such as language and religion). The second approach is that of historical geosophy, of reconstructing the geographical ideas, the geographical *imaginations*, of peoples in the past. The task here is to identify the nature of geographical ideas held by *actors* in the past, to determine the importance of a sense of place and in particular to assess the significance of the idea of the locality, of the region, of the province and of the nation at different times in England's history. Just how has England's geography been imagined through the centuries? Here the book draws upon a wide range of economic, social, political and cultural sources, which differ from period to period. Geographical conceptions in both popular and elitist culture are derived from literary sources, such as topographies, newspapers and novels; from graphical sources, such as maps and paintings; and from statistical sources, such as censuses and surveys.

Our book focuses on the North–South divide in England, because it is to England that the concept has been most specifically applied. But, where appropriate, reference will be made to that division within the broader context of Great Britain (or the United Kingdom). The six substantive essays, while treating different historical periods, are integrated by their common concern with two fundamentally geographical questions: first, to what extent is it possible for us today to detect a North–South divide in England during specific periods in the past; and secondly, how important was the idea of such a divide to contemporaries in those periods? Of course, there is a certain arbitrariness about the time periods selected for study – the periodisation of history, like the regionalisation of geography, is as much art as science and often more so. The periods chosen provide a framework, a historical grid, through which to examine the material character and the imagined content of the North–South divide. Unusually, a modified retrogressive approach has been adopted. The book 'retrogresses' chapter by chapter from a later period to an earlier period, beginning in the late-twentieth century and moving backwards period by period into the eleventh century. This approach has been adopted in part because the concept of a North–South divide in England is undoubtedly of popular and political significance today and it has enabled our contributors to ask in turn how significant the divide was both in material terms and in imagination in a series of increasingly remote historical periods. A retrogressive approach has been adopted additionally because it has permitted contributors to proceed from the better known to the less-well known, from the better understood to the less-well understood, aspects of the North–South divide. Discussion within each chapter, however, is not necessarily chronological: it is often thematic, because the book's approach is fundamentally geographical and it is not attempting to present a narrative history of the North–South divide.

Few geographical concepts have become deeply embedded in popular and political culture. Perhaps in recent years that of 'globalisation' has become so, throughout the world, but that of the North–South divide, nationally within England, has been so for more than a century. While the *idea* of a North–South divide in England undoubtedly has deep historical roots, the existence – or non-existence – of such a divide in reality has become a significant geographical component of popular culture and of political discourse especially in post-war Britain. As debates about devolution, about the possibility of regional assemblies in England and about geographical inequalities in work and welfare become more pressing, claims to the legitimacy of more localised autonomy will surely seek to draw upon the histories and cultural identities of localities and regions within England. The concept of a North–South divide thus has both contemporary importance and historical significance. The essays presented here endeavour collectively to reveal that dual role but they do so in individually distinctive ways. Discussion of their common threads is best deferred until the essays have been read, but their singular contributions may usefully be highlighted at this stage.

Six essays

During the last quarter of the twentieth century and through to the present day, the North–South divide in British social and economic life became a prominent topic of political, academic and popular discourse. Not only has debate raged about the existence and significance of the divide, but this has also provoked discussion of its history, origins and evolution. Ron Martin (Chapter 2) does not present a detailed catalogue raisonné of the numerous indicators and measures that could be, and have been, used to prove or contest the existence of the divide. He does use some empirical evidence to argue the case for a divide (marshalling information on regional GDP growth, employment, class, incomes, health and social welfare), but he accepts that the basic facts and figures relating to the issue have already been assembled elsewhere. Instead, Martin's primary aim is to address some key questions surrounding the divide. Why did a distinctive North–South divide – both material and imagined, both economic-political and sociocultural – (re)emerge so prominently from the mid-1970s onwards? Why has it proved to be such a contentious issue? Why does the divide matter? Martin argues that the (re)assertion of the divide since the mid-1970s is inextricably bound up with Britain's progressive shift from an industrial socio-economy to a post-industrial, and increasingly globalised, form. While the process of post-industrialisation can arguably be traced back to the 1950s, it was not until the late-1960s that it began to be evident in terms of its geographical consequences. Up until then, during the so-called 'long post-war boom', regional disparities in socioeconomic welfare had been minimal (especially as compared to the marked inequalities of the interwar period). In the late-1960s, large-scale de-industrialisation set in, which then accelerated sharply during the 1980s at precisely the time that the growth of services, high-technology and the 'knowledge economy' took off.

Martin argues that, like earlier phases of British capitalism, the upheavals and transformations of the past quarter-century have been inherently uneven geographically, in both form and impact. The main brunt of de-industrialisation since the 1960s has been borne by the old industrial urban regions of the north of England, Wales and Scotland (but also the Birmingham and London conurbations), where it has undermined not just the economic bases of those areas – with serious consequential effects on employment and incomes – but also their associated industrial cultures, social networks and traditions. In contrast, the growth of the post-industrial economy, with its different social structures and cultural politics, has developed disproportionately in south-east England (including London). During the 1980s, the Thatcher governments' policies of monetarism, deregulation and privatisation gave added impetus to these divergent trends between the 'north' and 'south' (and 'west' and 'east') of the country. Indeed, Martin argues, the 'post-industrial, internationalised, enterprise-orientated and consumerist-individualist south' was actively promoted as the social, economic and cultural exemplar which the ailing 'industrial, labourist, and welfare-dependent north' should seek to emulate. Thus, while on the one hand the Thatcher governments persistently denied that a North–South divide existed, on the other the South was repeatedly used ideologically as the model of a modern, post-industrial society for Britain as a whole.

This portrayal, Martin contends, whilst rooted to a large degree in stark socio-economic realities – a prosperous south-east and a lagging rest of England, Wales and Scotland – was also founded on, and has served to reproduce, two key structural aspects of the divide. The first is the concentration of economic, financial and political power in London and the south-east, a concentration which not only itself is an integral component of the divide, but which also imparts a distinct southern bias to perceptions and conceptions of the 'British' socio-economy, its problems and solutions. This London-based nexus has been playing an instrumental role in shaping the geography of capital accumulation in post-industrial Britain. The second is the political and cultural significance of the southern electorate, which is perceived (even if in slightly different ways) by both the Conservative and New Labour political parties as representing the 'core values' of a modern post-industrial society, a 'new Britain', and whose vote, therefore, is essential to electoral success. For the Tories, this was less of a problem, since the south of England has long been their main socio-spatial heartland. For Blair's New

Labour government, however, it meant abandoning the old industrial values of its socio-spatial heartlands in northern Britain in order to appeal to those of the service-dominated south. In this sense, Martin suggests, since the late-1970s, and unlike earlier decades, the north–south geography of sociopolitical legitimation has correlated closely with the north–south geography of economic accumulation. At the same time, he argues, the notion of a North–South divide is both complicated by, and tends to obscure, the existence of more local intra-regional disparities, or what some refer to as 'north–north' and 'south–south' divides. Notwithstanding their importance, however, these other dimensions of economic, social and political disparity do not undermine the existence or significance of the basic North–South divide.

In the final part of his essay, Martin turns to an examination of some of the tensions generated by these uneven geographies of post-industrial Britain at the end of the twentieth century. He argues that the continued concentration of economic growth, wealth, power and population in the south and east of England relative to the north and west, has not only generated negative effects there (for example, congestion, rising house costs and environmental pressures), but poses problems for the running of the national economy. In the mid-1960s, overheating in southern England undermined the then Labour government's National Plan. Similarly, during the second half of the 1980s, overheating in the south-east brought Chancellor Lawson's boom to a halt. In the late-1990s the Bank of England's high-interest-rate policies attracted considerable criticism from the northern business community, angered by the Bank's view that higher unemployment in the north of England (caused by high interest rates) was a 'price worth paying' to keep the south from overheating. Meanwhile the Labour government denied the existence of a divide. The policy response has not been so much one of seeking to promote growth in the north, or deliberately redistributing wealth and prosperity northwards from the south, in order to close the divide, but rather a strategy of political devolution in the case of Scotland and Wales, and regional policy devolution to new Regional Development Agencies in the case of the English regions. At the same time, the government is pushing through plans to allow the building of an additional one million homes in the south of England by 2020 in order to accommodate and maintain economic growth there. Martin opines that, in the early years of the twenty-first century, there are few signs that the North–South divide, whether material or imagined, will disappear.

The central decades of the twentieth century are the focus of Danny Dorling's essay (Chapter 3), which argues that it was in this period that the North–South divide in England both became most acute in reality and paradoxically went largely unrecognised by people at the time. He argues that within the period from 1918 to 1940, a North–South divide, which can now be readily identified by observers with historical hindsight, was off-stage for most of the actors in that dramatic period of England's history. He suggests that revelation of the divide's existence had to await both detailed analysis of the 1931 census and a new social welfare agenda developed during the 1950s and 1960s that then continued to underpin political discourse and academic writing through the 1970s, 1980s and 1990s. Dorling is convinced that a line from the Severn to the Wash delineates a metaphorical cliff between North and South, a cliff which he claims was at its steepest in the 1920s and 1930s.

This conviction is based not on the views of writers and commentators from that period but on tabular and geographical analysis of its statistics and their interpretation with the benefit of historical hindsight. In order to identify the North–South divide *c*.1930 and to compare it with the situation some forty years later, Dorling examines the infant mortality data for 1928 and 1971, and unemployment and social class data for 1931 and 1971. Massaging the earlier data in that manner and comparing the *c*.1930 data with that from a later period enables Dorling to view the information in a way that was not available to contemporaries and to identify a North–South divide of which he claims they were not aware. Placing little credence in what he calls 'travelogues' as historical evidence, and emphasising the limited cartographical techniques available to researchers and commentators in the 1920s and 1930s, Dorling prefers a more rigorous and sophisticated analysis of the numerical data collected in those decades. Given that contemporary observations of the North–South divide were either made or interpreted by an intellectual elite, Dorling essays a more systematic discussion of how the divide might have been experienced and then expressed by the public at large in voting behaviour. His examination of voting patterns in ten general elections between 1918 and 1951 leads him to conclude that, from the point of view of political expression, there were no stark regional divides, and that during this period support for the Conservatives strengthened in the North while that for Labour weakened. He claims that voting behaviour depicted local rather than regional patterns. The pattern of voting behaviour did not, Dorling argues, show evidence of a North–South divide and, he implies, it must therefore have been of little consequence to, or in the consciousness of, voters.

In his concluding remarks, Dorling acknowledges that local and regional planning came to be much debated during the 1940s and 1950s but he claims that the North–South divide of the 1920s and 1930s was itself narrowing during those decades and only came to be fully recognised later. Unable to find convincing verbal testimony to a contemporary recognition of a North–South divide in that earlier period, Dorling is nonetheless sure from his handling of numerical data from the period that a highly significant divide did indeed then exist. As Dorling puts it, we find what we are looking for.

A central assumption in discussions of a North–South divide in the modern period has been the rise and fall of the North as an industrial region: the supposition of industrial prosperity in the North has even led some to suggest that there was no 'regional problem' before the symptoms of industrial decline became apparent in the early-twentieth century. Philip Howell (Chapter 4) examines the myths and realities of a North–South divide in what he claims has to be considered a crucial period – after the achievements of the first industrial revolution but before the acknowledged era of British industrial failure. He accepts that caution is necessary about such easy periodisations, not least because although industrialisation must be viewed as being central to any assessment of the North–South divide, regional divisions are a complex admixture of material and discursive realities. In reaching this conclusion, Howell's argument proceeds in three stages: first, he examines critically the broadly econometric conclusions of the new economic history; secondly, he considers the social and political status of regionalisation; and, thirdly, he maps the contours of what Patrick Joyce has called the 'geography of belonging' in the field of popular culture.

Howell begins by discussing the various attempts by revisionist historians to downgrade the impact of industrialisation in the nineteenth and early-twentieth centuries, to trace the persistence of a London and south-east dominated service and commercial economy throughout this period, and also (thus) to identify the symptoms of economic decline as early as the 1840s. Howell notes that the conclusions of the new economic history for the idea of a North–South divide are at best ambiguous: if, for example, one accepts the notion of an economic climacteric in the 1840s, with a decisive downturn in the growth rates of industrial output thereafter, then the shift in gravity to a non-industrial/non-manufacturing South would appear very early; on the other hand, the shift from untransformed to transformed sectors could be read as industrial maturity rather than decline, and the notion of a later climacteric and pronounced industrial dominance in the North would still be apposite. But even the most avid proponents of revisionism concede the importance of both regional and sectoral economic differentiation, and Howell argues that geographies of wage differentials, unemployment statistics, and of fixed and circulating capital broadly confirm the existence of a significant regional divide. He argues that recognition of the differentiated regional and sectoral patterns allows us to reconcile the claims of continuity and discontinuity nationally. Howell contends that patterns of industrialisation, decisive at the local and regional scales before 1840, endured into the twentieth century, acting as constraints to the economic developments that would produce the national patterns so emphasised by the econometric revisionists. The industrial roots of a North–South divide in England from the 1840s can therefore be generally accepted. Nonetheless, it is the continuing economic strength of London and the South-East and their persistent advantage over the North which is most apparent for Howell. He argues that this version of a North–South divide, uncoupled from what he considers to be a misleading emphasis on industrial hegemony, is established as arguably the critical feature of Victorian economy and society. Towards the end of the nineteenth century the pivotal shift towards finance and the metropolitan economy appears to Howell to have widened decisively the divide between North and South.

The second section of Howell's chapter, however, contests any notion of a uniformly prosperous North in contrast to an undeveloped South, whatever the period under review. Broadening his perspective to questions about society and politics,

Howell suggests that besides a picture of the autonomy of the provinces – illustrated by the evolution of vibrant and innovative bourgeois public spheres in the provincial towns, itself the legacy of the earlier urban revolution in northern England – should be set a recognition of the importance of core-periphery relationships that instate the priority of London and the South, particularly given the accelerating growth of London after 1841. Howell's wide-ranging discussion here includes urban networks, the growth of provincial municipal culture and the strength of localism within the nation. Coupling this with an examination of social policy and the reach of the state, Howell is critical of a view of regional differentiation which disregards the continuing and even growing significance of central authority. While social and political life was locally organised and concentrated, it was also nationally connected and coordinated. Howell accepts the interdependence of regional differentiation and national integration. In this section, then, the North–South divide is treated with more caution and scepticism. Howell sees the industrial North as being in this period more independent of London's influence than it had been at any time in the previous two centuries. Nonetheless, while becoming different from the South, the North remained to a degree dependent upon the metropolis. But the decades leading up to 1914, Howell argues, saw a growing challenge to localism and a reassertion of the importance of London, in the process transforming the relation of North and South from one that was essentially symbiotic to one that was fundamentally oppositional.

In his final section, Howell moves from material economic differences that divided the nation to consider the representation of North and South in the cultural imaginations of Victorians and Edwardians. While recognising the North–South divide as being in part a space-myth created by a literary elite, Howell also insists on the significance of the concept in the popular imagination as a way of enabling people to identify themselves, to comprehend their social reality and to express a geographical belonging. The 'North' and the 'South' were thus cultural constructions, populist metaphors (or, as preferred by Howell, synecdoches) for two different versions of Englishness. Moreover, Howell suggests that 'southern' populism ultimately became more powerful than its 'northern' counterpart, affirming the centrality and 'superiority' of London and the South-East over the marginal and 'inferior' North. That process of denigration, Howell suggests, was fully worked out only after 1918.

Each of the periods addressed in this collation has its own particular significance but in the next essay Mark Billinge (Chapter 5) claims that the period between 1750 and 1830 can legitimately be considered the most transformational in Britain's written history. It witnessed at home the triumph of machinofacture, the end of the old organic dependencies and the explosion of urbanism, while it also saw the consolidation of overseas trade and, as an idea at least, the apogee of empire. Responsibility for these developments (as well as for their recursive and co-lateral domestic effects) was not, Billinge emphasises, evenly distributed amongst the English regions, for this was also an era in which the basic relationships between an industrialising North and a still largely agricultural South were in the process of crucial renegotiation. As Britain industrialised and its perspectives internationalised, North and South both contributed to and benefited unevenly from the development process. Significant as these material transformations were (not least in their impact on the English landscape), Billinge stresses that increasingly radical changes were also afoot in the realm of ideas; for the period's significance lay as much in its determination to rethink the status of people and their relationship with nature, the purpose of civil society and the expectations of a modernising state as in any of its more practical accomplishments. Billinge argues that it was the rich elaboration combined with the uneven acceptance of Enlightenment, secularist and scientific critiques which lay at the heart of the process of regional differentiation. Simultaneously, Billinge argues, London's metropolitan dominance gave way to provincial regeneration and the economies of the regions were progressively freed from the rigid control of the London-based mercantile monopolies. Underpinned by the new turnpike and canal networks, these decentralising forces promoted the burgeoning growth of the northern and midland cities and a pattern of demographic redistribution which would create, in the minds of many contemporaries, a clear sense of northern vitality and southern stagnation: a reversal of historic fortune as startling as it was novel. As such progressive ideas and their impacts spread, they were subject to definition both by geography and by social position. Billinge considers that as a result, the advance of a 'northern' (essentially bourgeois) prospectus did much to entrench a 'southern' mentality grounded in tradition, propriety and natural superiority. Billinge seeks to establish the nature of these developments and to assess their differing impact – 'actual and perceived' – on the English regions.

Billinge begins by examining the 'reality' of North and South: the materiality of such conventions broadly described as a developing (industrial) North and a relatively lethargic (agricultural) South. Reviewing the demographic and economic changes of the period leads Billinge to argue that industrialisation produced greater regional diversity but within a framework of a broadly homogenising national culture. His general impression is of a buoyant North and a readjusting South, concluding that the late-eighteenth century began to witness a fundamental reversal of the long-standing fortunes of North and South. Such an economic transformation also saw a decisive shift in the social realm, for whereas the old society of the South had been based upon a moral economy that of the emerging society of the North was based on a new political economy.

While accepting a broad impression of a North–South divide and of a pattern of diverging fortunes on either side of it, Billinge then confronts that generalisation with some detailed issues which sit uncomfortably within it. For example, the role of London and the relation of the capital to the provinces do not fit easily into a simplified North–South picture. Nor, Billinge argues, do the Midlands: just as the county society of Warwickshire was eclipsed by the rise of industry in the Midlands' towns, so the claims of the Midlands to belong to the heartland of the aristocratic rural past were superseded by its industries' increasing association with the developing industrial economy of the North. He also argues that economic restructuring between 1750 and 1830 created a dichotomy of country and city which was at least as significant as that between north and south. Thus in this period, Billinge both establishes the 'reality' of a North–South divide and also sets out other perspectives on its economic development.

The next, even more difficult step, taken by Billinge is to establish the weight of a North–South divide in the public consciousness and within particular cultures in this period. But this is not a straightforward matter. No ideas or attitudes set 'the North' unambiguously apart from 'the South'. Furthermore, information circulated only slowly, unevenly and often inaccurately down the social hierarchy at the end of the eighteenth century, so that any conscious perception or systematic thinking about a North–South divide would have been limited to a small segment of the population, mainly to those with a vested interest in any such divide and to those with the leisure to intellectualise such a situation. Nonetheless, Billinge considers that a feeling of North–South and of a perceived difference between them seems to have become an abstract commonplace, a commonsense notion, in the late-eighteenth century and he seeks to find out how and why. He explores a range of possible answers, including the emergence of two different cultures in Georgian Britain in the late-eighteenth century and the expansion of geographical knowledge and opportunities to travel and thus to become aware of geographical differences, of geographical 'others'. Billinge argues that a distinction which could not be mapped precisely developed as a perception of difference, as a metaphor of otherness.

Stepping further back, into the two preceding centuries, John Langton (Chapter 6) emphasises that although economic, demographic, political and cultural development had been quickening between 1550 and 1750, there remained some significant continuities in this period of early modernisation. Langton argues that human existence in this period remained fundamentally dependent on annual harvests, through which incoming solar energy was harnessed via plant and animal converters, supplemented only marginally by energy derived from wind, flowing water and minerals. Geographical variations in the expression of such an organic economy clearly reflected environmental conditions, so that within the broad contrast between sheep-corn and wood-pasture regions were embedded many local variations. To these agricultural differences were added others linked to, for example, the uses made of timber, of minerals and of water, both for energy and for transport. Furthermore, the expansion of exchange, the rise of secondary and tertiary activities, and the growth of towns within a developing national space-economy being linked increasingly to a world system all contributed to an accentuation of geographical diversity. Within this growing geographical complexity, Langton asks, what evidence is there of a real or an imagined North–South divide?

Recognising that a dearth of systematically collected and comparative statistical information makes it impossible to construct completely reliable maps of the human geography of England between 1550 and 1750, Langton nonetheless engages a suite of maps to examine the problem of areal differentiation within the country during that period. He examines in turn the distribution of wealth, of population and population growth, of urban populations and growth, and of some economic variables. Langton concludes that, rather than revealing broad contrasts between northern and southern areas of England, his maps portray a more complex, dominantly agricultural, mosaic reflective of environmental circumstances, particularly soils. They also indicate that the geography of wealth and population were changing in response to greater exploitation of non-agricultural resources. But perhaps most significant of all the maps provide clear evidence of the central role of London's consumers, producers and merchants in the spatial organisation of early modern England. Langton argues that core and periphery relationships that might have created a North–South divide in material terms did not do so because of coastal shipping and because of the way in which intricately patterned resource endowments underpinned England's economic geography. That conclusion is reinforced when Langton turns more briefly to a consideration of cultural and political issues. It is the detail and complexity of England's human geography in this period that Langton emphasises, rather than any broad and simple contrast between two large areas.

In his final section, Langton considers how 'this seething space of contrasts and changes was envisioned and depicted at the time'. Both historical and geographical writings about England are abundant in this period, which also saw a great flowering of cartographical description at a variety of scales. Langton argues that the principal message being conveyed collectively by the written texts was that of a singular idealised England. The role of cartography was more ambivalent, with maps of the nation and of counties as components of the nation standing alongside those of estates. Defoe's *Tour* is seen by Langton as a 'paean to the national harmony brought about by trade, unified into a single entity by London'. But when examining public administration, Langton finds that the theory of a unified nation was far from the practice of a massive and incoherent fragmentation. There was, Langton admits, a contemporary recognition of difference between North and South that was institutionalised in some administrative arrangements, such as the existence of two Chief Justices for the Forests, one for those north of the River Trent and one for those to the south. But Langton doubts that, in the face of the complex geographies of the period, a simple North–South dichotomy could have been maintained or even given much credence by administrative practices.

Langton argues, nonetheless, that contemporaries were aware of the geographical restructuring of England taking place between 1550 and 1750. But, like Defoe, he considers they tended to see the harmonisation brought about by spatial integration rather than a process of areal differentiation. Langton contends that spatial integration was compounded as central government created a modern polity. An increasingly powerful and centralised bureaucracy created and then dismantled structures such as the Councils of the North and of the Marches, as it deliberately integrated and then homogenised national space for political, administrative,

economic and cultural purposes, legitimising itself through an increasingly stri-
dent nationalist ideology. This process spread cultural values, statute laws and
privatised property rights, administrative and religious structures, and economic
influences from the southern metropolitan core into the periphery. They were
vigorously resisted. The revolts and rebellions of the period, the Civil War and
contention within the Parliamentary army, were agencies of or reactions to this
spreading southern hegemony; but they were not simply patterned into a North–
South divide.

The objective of political nation building was an ideologically unitary realm,
focused on parliament, the Crown, its court and its national church, and eventually
also on other institutions based in London. Langton considers that the stress by contemporaries on sameness from place to place was inevitable given the biblical intellectual structures of the time, and the consequent inability to accommodate the deep
political fractures caused by the Reformation, Civil War, Restoration, Glorious
Revolution and Hanoverian succession. He suggests that the 'other' against which
the southern national stereotype was given definition was not dialectically contained, but safely pushed away outside England, first in the pastoral fecklessness
of 'heathen' (i.e. Catholic) Ireland, then in the uncivilised aboriginal inhabitants
of overseas colonies. In England only the South existed, except in so far as other
regions were compared to colonies where the civilising metropolitan mission had
not yet been fulfilled. The nation that was being mapped and written was different
from the England that actually existed; but it did not contain a North–South divide
either.

The roots of any such divide are sought in an even more remote past by Bruce
Campbell (Chapter 7), who argues that medieval England was a land of contrasts,
even of multiple dichotomies. The most conspicuous were those between upland
and lowland, between dispersed and nucleated settlement, between enclosed and
open fields, between weak and strong lordship, between free and customary tenants
and tenures, between remoteness and proximity to major markets, and between
the marches and the metropolitan core. While Campbell recognises that many of
these dichotomies had a strong north–south dimension, he argues that this does
not necessarily mean that there was such a phenomenon as a North–South divide
or that distinctions between north and south should be privileged above other
spatial and regional differences. He also argues that the strength and nature of
these dichotomies varied through time, depending upon whether centripetal or
centrifugal forces were dominant. He sees shifts in the balance between these two
tendencies as being likely to heighten the tensions between core and periphery,
agreeing with Jewell (1994) that this would thereby give rise to expressions of
northern and southern consciousness.

Campbell looks at popular protests as potential expressions of tensions between
the North and the South but he examines more closely the development of lay and
ecclesiastical administrative structures and boundaries. In the case of the state,
these included shires, escheatries and forest courts with arrangements north of the

Trent often differing from those to the south. The same spatial dichotomy is echoed in the ecclesiastical division between the provinces of York and Canterbury and the differences in diocesan and parochial structure with which these were associated. These structures shaped thinking about the geography of England. During the medieval period the northernmost counties were incorporated into the English realm, in a complex process of spatial and social contestation that also involved conflict between Scotland and England for the control of territories.

The geographically uneven development of the economy between the late-eleventh century and the mid-sixteenth century in England is then explored by Campbell in some detail. Throughout this period, the area to the south and east of a line from the Humber to the Severn, and thence to the Tamar, was consistently wealthier and more economically developed than the area to the north and west of that divide. Within each of those two broad areas there were, of course, significant local variations which did not, however, negate the wider regional picture. Rural settlement patterns, agricultural systems and common rights were also broadly contrasted on either side of that divide, although eventually Campbell argues here not for a bipartite but instead for a tripartite division which recognises a northern and western province, a central province and a south-eastern province.

In effect, Campbell argues, differences between North and South are not hard to find but whether they divided more than they united is, in his view, more difficult to determine. Campbell is, however, convinced that there is no evidence of a contemporary concept of a North–South divide in the Middle Ages. On the contrary, the period is, he claims, marked by the emergence of a growing national consciousness and a corresponding diminution of regional identities. This period saw the production of the first national maps and a growing recognition of a differentiation between the English and the non-English Welsh, Scots and Irish. Campbell contends that within England itself divisions based upon class and gender were more significant to contemporaries than any based upon regional alliances. In terms of government and administration, it is the precocious unity of medieval England that Campbell finds most striking, notwithstanding the persistent usage of, for example, local and regional customs, mensuration systems, dialects and building materials. Campbell considers that more important than an awareness of any North–South divide would have been a growing recognition of the increasing impact of London on England's society and economy. Campbell concludes that, in medieval England, core and periphery would have loomed larger in the popular geographical imagination than North and South – although not, of course, in those terms.

It will be evident already that the identification of a North–South geographical divide at any period in England's history is fraught with difficulties. There were, it would seem, many divides and many ways of imagining them. But we will defer any further general reflections to our concluding essay.

2

The contemporary debate over the North–South divide: images and realities of regional inequality in late-twentieth-century Britain

RONALD L. MARTIN

Introduction

In the period since the Second World War, and especially since the 1970s, the unity and meaning of the United Kingdom, virtually unchallenged for two hundred years, has come increasingly into question. One by one, the very forces and assumptions that helped to forge a sense of national identity and common unity, have disappeared. The spell was broken by the Suez debacle in 1956, which compelled the British people at last to begin the painful task of reassessing their sense of themselves and their position in the world. From the mid-1960s onwards, a growing awareness of national relative economic decline – of a progressive slippage of the nation down the international league table of living standards – fuelled the process, and stimulated a flood of jeremiads on the causes and consequences of Britain's economic failure (Manser 1971; Barnett 1972; Kramnick 1975; Allen 1976; Eatwell 1982; Pollard 1982; Roderick and Stephens 1982; Smith 1984), a literary genre that continued into the 1990s (Coates 1994; Hutton 1996; Clarke and Trebilcock 1997). A surge of Scottish and Welsh nationalism in the early 1970s, and the public debate on federalism and devolution this activated, merely compounded the sense of gloom surrounding the state and unity of the nation. Little wonder that political commentators talked of the 'break up of Britain' (Nairn 1981). Margaret Thatcher's attempt in the 1980s to recover a sense of national unity and pride by appealing to the public and private virtues of a bygone Victorian era, and the brief welling up of national sentiments by the Falklands and Gulf Wars, failed to stem the rising tide of disillusionment. And as the 1990s wore on, the seemingly ineluctable march of European economic and social integration, accelerating multiculturalism, and political devolution for Scotland, Wales and Northern Ireland, all threatened to undermine the notion of a United Kingdom still further.

Perhaps not surprisingly, then, at a time when the meaning of the United Kingdom appears to be in question, when many of the customs and institutions that gave its people a sense of national identity and common purpose are being dismantled, there has been an outpouring of laments and memorials of what has been lost. Given the pulling away of Scotland, Wales and Northern Ireland, the ideas of England and Englishness have become the focus of fervent commentary (Osmond 1988; Proud 1994; Barnes 1998; Paxman 1998; Hitchens 1999; Redwood 1999; Scruton 2000). Much of this literature is itself valedictory in tone, concerned with the fate of England and the passing of this or that aspect of what it is claimed historically made England what is was. (Perhaps the recent veritable flood of TV programmes on British and English history is another expression of this concern to rekindle a sense of our past and common heritage.) Some accounts are nakedly nostalgic. Yet others attempt to pick up the pieces (or a few of them at least), while pieces remain. It is as if the on-going weakening of the notion of a United Kingdom has stimulated an urge to discover – even to recover – the meaning of English identity, of English unity.

But events over the past quarter of a century have also revealed that the idea of a united England is itself something of a myth. For since the mid-1970s, and especially since the mid-1980s, an uninterrupted and heated debate has rumbled through academic, public and political circles as to whether and to what extent the country has become a 'divided nation', a society split between rich and poor, between the employed and the unemployed, between those living in comfortable suburbia and those entrapped in impoverished inner city communities, between those included in the economic mainstream of work, wealth and prosperity, and those excluded. One of the most contentious dimensions of this debate is the claim that a major geographical fault line has opened up in England's (and Britain's) economic and social landscape, a 'territorial divide' separating one nation of 'have-nots' residing in an economically depressed 'North' of the country and another nation of 'haves' in a much more economically dynamic 'South'.

Not unexpectedly, the idea of a 'North–South divide' has proved highly controversial, on several counts. For one thing, there has been dispute about whether the divide really exists. While some argue that it captures a real and substantive boundary in the geographies of wealth, well-being and welfare across England, and across Britain as a whole, others consider the divide to be a grossly simplified and generalised representation of reality, little more than a misleading caricature. Still others view it as an imagined boundary invented on the basis of – and serving to reproduce – stereotypical and even prejudicial characterisations of 'northerners' and 'southerners'. A second area of dispute is why the notion of the North–South divide (whether real or imagined) surfaced so suddenly and dramatically in the 1980s. Is the divide something entirely new, or the re-emergence of a longer-standing geographical division or image that can be traced back much earlier, but which until recently was less visible, less significant? Many saw its (re)emergence during the high years of Thatcherism as far from coincidental, as the direct result of the politics and policies of the Thatcher governments, and the term became closely associated with critiques of those policies (Jessop *et al.*, 1988; Martin 1988, 1992). Thirdly, there has been debate over whether and in what sense the divide, if it does indeed exist, matters, and what should be done about it. On the one side are those who argue that the existence of the divide is both socially inequitable and economically inefficient, and that its elimination should be a central aim of policy-makers. On the other are those who, downplaying the significance of the divide, argue that a combination of market forces and local initiative, and not government intervention, is the only viable basis for prosperity, whether in northern or southern Britain.

My aim here is to try to make some sense of these debates surrounding the existence, causes and consequences of the divide in the late-twentieth century. I begin by exploring some of the myths and realities of the North–South divide, and then move on to argue that while the divide is certainly not new, its marked reassertion over the past twenty-five years – both as a material reality and as an idea – is inextricably bound up with the historical transformation that is underway in Britain at the present time. Not only is the divide caught up in a wider discourse of a much-vaunted shift from an 'old' to a 'new' Britain, but the South itself is seen by many as the economic, social and cultural exemplar of what this 'new' Britain will (or should) look like, and thus what the North should seek to emulate.

The contemporary North–South divide: myth or reality?

During the course of the 1980s, and into the 1990s, numerous academic accounts pointed to the emergence of a substantial gap between southern and northern England in terms of employment opportunities, unemployment rates, average incomes, dependence on welfare support, and various other measures of socio-economic well-being (see, for example, Champion and Green 1988, 1991; Green 1988; Martin 1988; Smith 1989; Lewis and Townsend 1989). Authors talked variously of a North–South jobs divide, wealth divide, class divide and political divide, and numerous indicators were mapped and charted to lend support to this claim (Johnston 1987; Bryson 1996). But the emergence of the North–South divide as an issue in the 1980s owed as much to more popularist accounts in the press and in journalistic writings as it did to academic analyses of this or that measure of social and economic disparities across regional Britain. Journalists found powerful phrases and used colourful language to evoke the idea of a geographical divide, as illustrated, for example, by Ian Jack's vivid description:

Money has always tended to move south in Britain, as though it were obeying some immaculate Newtonian law, but now it is not just the cream off the top, a case of Bradford profit being spent in Bond Street. The actual generation of wealth has moved south, as well as the spending of it . . . ninety-four percent of the jobs lost since 1979 were north of a line drawn between the Wash and the Bristol Channel. This is a new frontier, a successor to Hadrian's Wall and the Highland Line. Above it, wealth and population dwindle; beneath it, both expand. (Jack 1987: ix)

Nor were such characterisations merely the product of a left-wing press and media anxious to assign blame for the divide on Mrs Thatcher's new free-market conservatism. Even the *Financial Times*, usually circumspect about journalistic sensationalism, expressed concern at the 'widening gap' (Duffy 1987). And when *The Economist* turned to an American for an outsider's view of late-1980s Britain, it was striking just how stylised – even caricatured – the portrayal of the North–South divide had become:

Roughly, with pockets of prosperity and blight on both sides, Britain is split by the north–south divide running from Bristol to the Wash. The victims of decaying smokestack industry live in the north; the beneficiaries of new high-tech, finance, scientific and service industries, plus London's cultural and political elite, are in the south. Cross the divide, going north, and visibly the cars get fewer, the clothes shabbier, the people chattier. (Critchfield 1987: 4)

Such images were reinforced by a whole raft of TV films and programmes that compared families and living conditions in the North with families and living conditions in the South. Documentaries brought into stark contrast the acres of industrial wasteland and run-down housing estates of northern towns and cities, and the booming landscape of commerce, finance and rampant consumerism in London and the South East: the 'loads-a-money' image of the southern yuppies seemed a different country from the impoverished northern communities populated by large numbers of workless families surviving on meagre benefit handouts from the welfare state.

Others, however, challenged this binary 'North versus South' picture. According to Wilsher and Cassidy, for example, the image of the North–South divide was false:

This is not to deny that Britain, when it comes to prosperity, is an increasingly divided nation. But the main split is not geographical but social. There is no Severn–Wash line separating the haves and have-nots. The poor . . . are certainly concentrated in the old, one-industry towns and decaying inner cities of the North. But they represent an equally intractable and numerically even larger problem in the boroughs at the heart of London. Meanwhile, the relatively affluent, those enjoying jobs, cars, home ownership, videos and regular foreign holidays are to be found almost everywhere. (Wilsher and Cassidy 1987: 25)

This counter-claim, based on the argument that the North is far from being characterised by relentless poverty and dereliction, just as the South is far from being a land of uninterrupted prosperity, has been a common one. Indeed, for many, the whole notion of a North–South divide is a myth. Thus for Joe Rogaly, economics editor of the *Financial Times*:

There is certainly greater inequality of income and possibly even of wealth than there was in 1979. There are specific areas of need and hardship. There are disgruntled communities, some of them smouldering with potential violence . . . But it is important to set the context: Britain's principal division is in the mind. On the one side is a collection of minorities that cannot be expected to share the *Weltanschauung* of Thatcherism . . . On the other side are those who feel that it is just this [political programme] that is required if Britain is to survive, let alone prosper as a modern economy. It is this division in the mind that leads to so much confusion about the real division on the ground. One of the most confused notions is that of the 'north–south' divide. It implies that virtually all the wealth is in the south, or even the southeast, while the rest of the country is a zone of unrelieved devastation. The truth is that there is an archipelago of wealth in the north, just as there is an archipelago of poverty in the south. For example, parts of Brixton or some of the council estates around Kings Cross in London, are as depressing as their counterparts in, say, Manchester. (Rogaly 1987: 14)

The idea that Britain had become 'two geographical nations' was also strongly contested by the Thatcher governments. Three different rebuttals were mounted. One was that if the South of the UK was leading the nation's growth in employment and prosperity in the 1980s, then it was only 'economic justice', since in previous eras the North had been the richest part of the country ('it's now the South's turn' argument). For example, according to Lord Young (whilst Secretary of State for Trade and Industry):

There was more industrialisation in the North originally, therefore there now has to be more deindustrialisation. Until 70 years ago, the North was always the richest part of the country. The two present growth industries – the City and tourism – are concentrated in the South. I try to encourage people to go North: that is where all the great country houses are because that's where the wealth was. Now some of it is in the South. It's our turn, that's all. (Lord Young, quoted in *Business*, 1987: 48)

The work of scholars such as Hunt (1973), Rubenstein (1977a and b) and Lee (1986) indicates that this picture is highly erroneous and that, even during the nineteenth century, individual wealth and per capita incomes were far higher in the South-East than in the northern regions of England.

A second rebuttal was that if economic growth was indeed favouring the South rather than the North, this was because the South was spearheading the creation of a new 'enterprise society' – itself the major policy goal of the Thatcher administrations (the 'South as exemplar' argument). As the new enterprise culture spread northwards, it was argued, so the same prosperity would also come to the North (the supposed market-led geographical diffusion effect). The third response was the 'archipelago argument' referred to above, namely that intra-regional disparities or 'South–South' and 'North–North' divides are more significant than any broad-brush North–South gap, a view echoed by Mrs Thatcher herself with her statement that 'the difficulties in . . . London are as great as any in the north' (Thatcher, quoted in the *Financial Times*, 1987: 6).

As the 1980s turned into the 1990s, however, the debate suddenly subsided. Unlike the recession of a decade earlier, which severely hit the nation's manufacturing base in northern Britain, the sharp economic downturn in the early-1990s had a surprisingly adverse impact on the service economy of the south east (Martin 1993a, 1997). For a while, the unemployment rate in the south east region, traditionally one of the lowest unemployment areas in the country, was on a par with that in Wales and Scotland, two of the traditionally high unemployment regions. Not only did it seem that the North–South divide had narrowed, it was even claimed that it had been reversed, though whether this was a temporary or more permanent phenomenon was questioned by some (see Martin, 1993a, 1997). Certainly by the late-1990s, talk of a North–South divide had all but ceased. Indeed, according to some observers, the UK had at last solved its regional problem:

The traditional 'North–South' unemployment problem has all but disappeared in the 1990s. This may prove to be a permanent development since the manufacturing and production sectors, the main source of regional imbalance in the past, no longer dominates shifts in the employment structure to the same extent. Future shocks will have a more balanced regional incidence than has been the case in the past. (Jackman and Savouri 1999: 27)

The Labour government elected in 1997 was no less emphatic about the demise of the divide. Like the Conservative administrations preceding it, the Blair government argued that the idea of a North–South divide was misleading and misplaced. Instead, the official line has again been the 'archipelago' view. Thus according to the Cabinet Office's Report to the Prime Minister, *Sharing the Nation's Prosperity*, 'although regional disparities undoubtedly exist, some of which have persisted for many years, the picture is much more complex than it is often portrayed. In particular there are wide variations in conditions within all regions, and areas of deprivation are to be found in all parts of the country' (Cabinet Office 1999: 7).

This argument has been maintained even in the face of protest from certain quarters within the Labour Party that it has effectively abandoned its concern with the economic and social plight of its traditional electoral heartlands in the northern industrial regions of the country in order to win the support of wealthier southern voters. It has also been maintained even though a number of recent research reports and media and business commentaries point to a continuing socioeconomic gap between the North and South. These indicate that the economic boom of the late-1990s saw the economy of south-east England once more pulling well ahead of northern Britain (Morris 2000). At the same time, analyses of incomes and poverty have pointed to sharp disparities between southern and northern localities (Joseph Rowntree Foundation 1995; Martin 1995; Howarth *et al.* 1999; CACI 2001). And still others suggest a widening North–South gap in health and health care (Mohan 1995; Shaw *et al.* 1999; Mitchell, Dorling and Shaw 2000; Davey Smith *et al.* 2001). These studies thus seem to run counter to the claim by Jackman and Savouri (1999) that the divide has now disappeared.

How do we explain such divergent views and findings? One source of the disagreement over the North–South divide has derived from the different social and economic indicators used by different authors: while different social and economic characteristics are often correlated, it is unrealistic to expect every such indicator to have an identical geography across the country, and thus to map out a consistent regional divide. Second, partly for this reason, and partly because the very notion of the North–South divide is itself a metaphor, a discursive device for simplifying what in reality is necessarily a complex socioeconomic landscape, ambiguity exists as to where, precisely, such a divide should be drawn. The notion conjures up a sharp boundary between two broad, contrasting geographical areas of England (and Britain). But where does the 'South' end and the 'North' begin?

As we have seen above, a recurring theme in the debate over the North–South divide during the past quarter-century has been that it follows a line drawn from the Wash to the Severn. Somewhere here, supposedly, The North begins, although on the A1 or M1 motorways signposts keep declaring its imminent arrival as far north as the Scottish border. The Wash–Severn line effectively defines the South to include the East region as well as the South East and South West, and the North to include Yorkshire-Humberside and the two Midlands regions as well as the North West and North East. However, the midlands are disputed territory. Historically, the East Midlands has had a more balanced and less industrial economy than the West Midlands, and perhaps in this respect has more in common with the South, while the heavily industrial West Midlands may well have more in common with the North. Perhaps because of these issues, some (for example, Steed 1986) have preferred to think about the geography of the UK less in terms of a simple North–South divide and more in terms of a fourfold division composed of an 'inner core' (roughly that area within a 60-mile radius – or one hour's train commuting time – of London); an 'outer core' (within a radius of roughly 60 to 120 miles radius of London, and including the rest of the South East, the East, the easternmost part of the South West and the southern parts of the East and West Midlands); an 'inner periphery' (within a radius of roughly 120 to 300 miles of London, and including the rest of the South West and the two Midlands regions, Yorkshire-Humberside, and the North West and North East); and beyond that an 'outer periphery' (of Wales, Scotland and Northern Ireland).

As for the 'archipelago argument', few proponents of the North–South divide would deny that local inequalities exist in every region or that such local inequalities are more pronounced than inter-regional disparities. After all, broad regional data are but statistical averages of the local data of which they are composed, and hence inter-regional differences will tend to be smaller than local differences. Few would seriously suggest that the North is a land of uniform deprivation, or that the South is a land of uniform prosperity. One can point to success stories in the North, such as Leeds (a significant provincial financial services centre and with one of only two branches of Harvey Nicholls – the up-market London-based department store – outside of Knightsbridge, the other being in Manchester), and to cities in decline in the South, such as Portsmouth (once the historic home of the Royal Navy, and now devastated by successive government defence spending cuts). And within most towns and cities themselves there are rich and poor areas, often in close juxtaposition: contrast, for example, the material wealth and associated symbolic architecture of London's West End or Canary Warf with the relative poverty and run-down environment of the East End. In this sense, most of Britain's major cities including London can be said to have their own North–South divides

Table 2.1 *Divergent trends in GDP per head in the English regions, 1975–2000*

Region	GDP per head (1975 = 100)						GDP per head (£)
	1975	1980	1985	1990	1995	2000	2000
South East	100.0	109.3	121.1	149.8	160.2	190.9	16,859
London	100.0	107.4	118.0	143.9	149.0	176.4	15,098
East	100.0	108.0	121.6	141.2	148.1	175.7	15,094
South West	100.0	109.8	122.4	144.3	151.6	168.8	11,872
East Midlands	100.0	105.7	121.0	142.1	149.9	165.8	12,146
Yorkshire-Humberside	100.0	106.0	118.1	139.0	144.9	163.6	11,404
West Midlands	100.0	100.5	112.0	135.2	145.3	159.5	11,900
North West	100.0	104.3	114.8	131.6	141.4	155.5	11,273
North East	100.0	102.6	112.3	128.8	136.0	142.4	10,024
UK	100.0	105.8	117.6	139.5	148.9	169.9	13,213

Sources of data: Eurostat and Office of National Statistics
Notes: (a) GDP is measured here as Gross Value Added (GVA)
      (b) Shaded regions are those with levels of per capita GDP above UK average

(Coyle 1999). Nevertheless, at issue is the *relative concentration* of pockets of local prosperity and disadvantage in different parts of the country, and whether these relative geographical concentrations map out a broad North–South pattern.

It is not my intention to review the full range of socioeconomic evidence here (see Martin 1988, and Smith 1989, for earlier comprehensive discussions). Two key dimensions of the socioeconomic landscape – gross domestic product (GDP) per capita, and unemployment – have often been used in discussions of the divide. Since the mid-1970s, and especially since the late-1980s, there has been an increasing divergence in per capita GDP across the English regions (Table 2.1). It has been precisely the three south-eastern regions (South East, London and East) that have pulled away from the rest of England, and particularly from the two northern regions (North West and North East). By the end of the 1990s, GDP per capita varied by some 50 per cent across regional England, from barely £10,000 in the North East to over £15,000 in London, the South East and the East (following convention, Greater London is distinguished as a separate region from the rest of the South East). While the South West region has a lower per capita GDP than the two Midlands regions, there is certainly a discontinuity between the South East, London and Eastern regions on the one hand, and the rest of England on the other. Only these three southern regions have per capita GDP levels above the UK average. However, these broad regional patterns inevitably conceal considerable local inequality (Figure 2.1). The area south of the Wash–Severn axis is clearly not

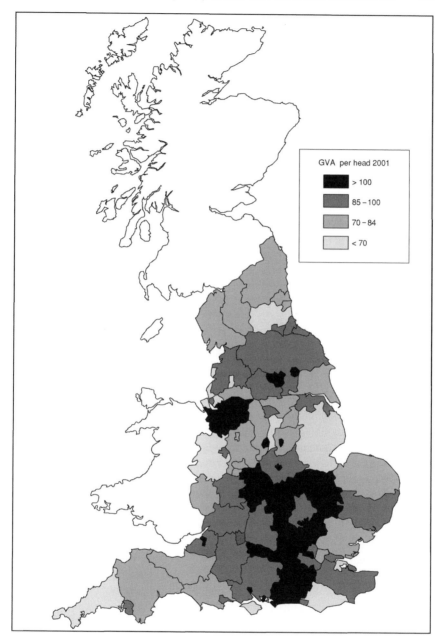

Figure 2.1 GDP per head for English NUTS3 areas, 2001 (Office of National Statistics data)

a land of unbroken relative prosperity: for example, sections of outer London, parts of Norfolk and Essex, the Medway towns and some areas of East Sussex have per capita GDP levels well below the UK average. Likewise, there are local pockets of relative prosperity in the northern regions, such as Chester, York and Leeds. Clearly the map is much more complex when we move down from a regional level to a more local scale.

During the 1980s, much of the debate surrounding the North–South divide focused on regional unemployment rates. There have long been unemployment disparities across regional Britain, with a persistent gap between the four southern low-unemployment regions (South East, East, South West and East Midlands) on the one hand, and the northern higher-unemployment regions (North West and North East, together with Scotland and Wales) on the other. This pattern goes back to the economic depressions of the 1920s and 1930s. Throughout the post-war boom of the 1950s and 1960s the scale of these disparities was relatively small – all regions enjoyed historically low unemployment. With the end of that boom in the early-1970s, regional unemployment disparities began to widen, and increased sharply in the 1980s, reaching a maximum in the middle of that decade (Martin 1997). Thereafter they declined, provoking the claim (as in the Jackman and Savouri quote) that by the end of the 1990s the 'North–South unemployment divide' had all but disappeared.

The problem with using standard claimant count unemployment rates, however, is that it has now been shown that from the early-1980s onwards official claimant rates became increasingly unreliable as an indicator of labour-market disadvantage, seriously understating the true extent of joblessness (see Beatty et al. 1997). To make matters worse, the extent of understatement appears to be most acute in the northern industrial regions of the country (where many unemployed have 'disappeared' into invalidity and sickness, or else into economic inactivity). The implication is that the apparent narrowing of the 'North–South unemployment divide' in the 1990s was greatly exaggerated (Grieve-Smith et al. 2000a and b). Although Labour Force Survey unemployment estimates – which use International Labour Office definitions and are usually regarded as more accurate – can be derived for regional and local areas, they are only available from the early-1990s onwards. For these reasons, employment rates provide a more reliable guide to trends in regional and local labour-market conditions.

Since the early-1970s, employment growth has been overwhelmingly concentrated in the South East, South West, East and, to a lesser extent, the East Midlands (Table 2.2). In contrast, in the North East and North West employment has actually declined over the period, and by the end of the 1990s had still not recovered from the sharp fall that occurred in the severe economic downturn of 1979–83. The remaining regions have all experienced negligible net job growth. Interestingly, whereas London has performed well in per capita GDP, in employment terms its experience has been more akin to the northern regions of the country: indeed London's employment rate (proportion of the population of working age in jobs) is the

Table 2.2 *Divergent employment trends in the English regions, 1975–2000*

Region	Total employment (1975 = 100)						Employment rate 2000
	1975	1980	1985	1990	1995	2000	2000
South East	100.0	107.4	112.5	129.7	121.1	137.4	80.6
South West	100.0	104.6	106.5	122.6	123.8	129.7	79.0
East	100.0	106.4	111.2	124.5	119.9	126.0	78.1
East Midlands	100.0	103.8	102.8	111.8	109.0	111.9	76.7
West Midlands	100.0	100.2	93.4	103.9	98.5	103.5	73.7
London	100.0	97.5	93.0	96.0	88.2	101.1	71.5
Yorkshire-Humberside	100.0	99.3	93.1	102.2	100.1	100.8	73.3
North West	100.0	99.4	90.0	96.4	90.9	96.2	72.4
North East	100.0	95.0	83.8	89.3	84.9	87.0	67.8
UK	100.0	101.4	97.7	107.1	102.3	109.1	74.6

Sources of data: Eurostat and Office of National Statistics
Notes: (a) Total employment includes self-employment; employment rate is measured as total numbers in employment as a proportion of the population of working age
(b) Shaded regions are those with employment rates above UK average

second lowest. Again, at the local level, parts of London, eastern Kent, Norfolk and areas in Cornwall and Devon, have below-average employment rates, while there are pockets of favourable labour-market conditions in the North West, Yorkshire-Humberside and the North East. Nevertheless, as in the case of per capita GDP, the majority of local areas in the South East and East have higher employment rates than those in other regions (Figure 2.2). Thus, while it would be too simplistic to use the Wash–Severn line as the defining boundary between North and South, there does appear to be a distinct and consistent gap between that south-eastern part of England bounded approximately by London-Cambridge-Oxford-Bristol-Southampton-Brighton-London, on the one hand, and the rest of England on the other.

Making sense of the divide: from industrial to post-industrial society

Why has the socioeconomic divide or gap between these two geographical areas of England widened progressively over the past thirty years? The temptation during the 1980s to blame Mrs Thatcher's policies was irresistible. The widening of regional and local disparities in economic fortune, wealth, employment, health, political allegiance and a whole range of related socioeconomic characteristics during the three Thatcher governments was surely not coincidental. Mrs Thatcher's avowed goal was to reverse Britain's long-run relative economic decline. The task,

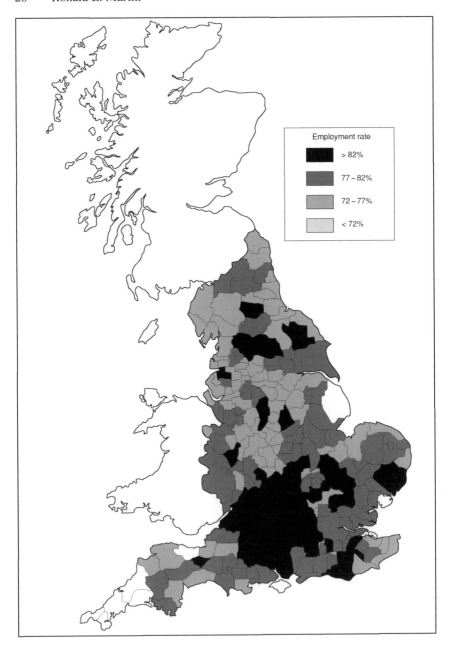

Figure 2.2 Employment rates for English Local Authority Districts, 2000 (Labour Force Survey data)

as she saw it, was twofold: to modernise the country by subjecting it to the full force of market competition and internationalisation, and to shift social interests and values away from the inherited culture of state support and subsidy towards a new ethos of enterprise, self-help, thrift, competition and individual initiative. This conversion of society from the old welfare-based social democracy to a new market-based economic democracy was intended to 'unite the nation' around a new 'popular capitalism'.

It is not possible – or necessary – to discuss the full details and impacts of this strategy here (see Martin 1992 for one such assessment). What does concern us is its effect on the regions. By the end of the 1980s, Mrs Thatcher and her supporters were claiming that their programme had wrought an 'economic miracle'. But it was an 'economic miracle' that had dramatically uneven results across the country. The refusal to pump-prime the economy during the recession of the early-1980s, combined with the pursuit of restrictive monetary policies, privatisation and the run-down of industrial subsidies, contributed to the acceleration of deindustrialisation during that decade. The brunt of this process was born by the older industrial areas and cities of northern Britain, together with London. At the same time, the enormous boost given to the financial sector by the deregulation of the City of London, the relaxation of exchange controls and capital movements, and the successive lowering of taxes, all helped to fuel a runaway boom in London, the South East and their immediate environs. Rather than being a 'single nation' project, in practice Thatcherism was more a divisive 'two-nation' one (Jessop *et al.* 1988), favouring the rich over the poor, services over manufacturing, and the commercial and financial economy of the South over the industrial economy of the North. It was also a 'two-nation' project in the sense that it was intended to 'rid the country of socialism', as Mrs Thatcher put it: the abolition in 1986 of the Labour-controlled metropolitan authorities (most of which were in the North) was part of that assault. There can be little doubt that Thatcherism must take some of the blame for the widening of spatial socio-economic inequalities and the emergence of a North–South problem in the 1980s and early 1990s. But Thatcherism itself has to be seen as part of a more fundamental and profound transformation at work in the British socio-economy during the last quarter of the twentieth century.

Geographers have long argued that regional differentiation plays a central role in capitalist development (see Massey 1979, 1985; Dunford and Perrons 1982; Harvey 1987; Hudson 2000). Three key aspects of this process are highlighted. The first contention is that capitalism – as an economic, social and cultural process – constantly uses and exploits spatial differences in the conditions and opportunities for profitable accumulation, and in so doing (re)creates a geographically uneven socioeconomic landscape. Second, once a particular geographical pattern of socioeconomic development is established, it can become cumulative and characterised by a high degree of persistence, or what economists call 'path dependence', over time. Success tends to breed success. There is a virtuous circle of growth as local economic expansion generates favourable conditions – such as a thriving market, rising incomes and skilled labour – which feed back to stimulate yet more growth, and so on. Depending on the type of local industries, labour processes and types of employment that develop in an area, particular patterns of social relations, class divisions and political allegiance may emerge that tend to give the area a distinctive social and cultural identity. So embedded can these local social, cultural and institutional traditions and structures become, that they survive long after the original economic activities and conditions around which they formed have ceased to be dominant.

But third, notwithstanding this path dependence and persistence, capitalist evolution is also episodic in nature, in that historically it is possible to identify periodic phases or rounds of particularly rapid change and development – what Joseph Schumpeter famously termed 'gales of creative destruction' – associated with the rise of new technologies, industries and methods of production, and with corresponding shifts in social regulation, class divisions and institutional arrangements. Further, these periodic phases of widespread upheaval and change, it is argued, involve the restructuring of the form and pattern of uneven regional development. During such times, the old social and economic landscapes are destroyed and superseded by new configurations. There are no guarantees that this process of 'creative destruction' is geographically neutral in its effects: indeed, it is almost certain to be spatially uneven, in that the regions that led the previous phase of development, and that are thus most dependent on and encumbered by old economic activities and social relations, are least likely to lead the new phase of development. As Jane Jacobs (1961) perceptively observed, during phases of pronounced change and restructuring the key tension is not so much the 'systemic' one between capital and labour – though conflict between workers and employers is undoubtedly heightened in such periods – but between those activities, interests and values associated with and committed to the old socioeconomic structures and those associated with and committed to the new. Because of the regionally uneven nature of capitalist development, this tension between the old and the new is almost certain to exhibit a distinct spatiality. In short, major regional disparities in wealth and welfare are likely to open up during these periodic gales of creative destruction, at least in the short to medium term, with real tensions between the rise of new social and cultural forms and those inherited from the past.

In Britain there have been two fundamental historical inflexions of this kind over the past century. The first was during the climacteric of the 1920s and 1930s. The economic crises and technological developments of those decades brought to an end the long phase of industrialisation, beginning with the Industrial Revolution and spanning the whole of the Victorian era, that had established northern regions and cities such as Liverpool, Manchester, Newcastle, Sheffield, Derby and Birmingham as the nation's primary centres of manufacturing production and exports. These growth areas suddenly became 'problem' or 'special' areas of industrial collapse, unprecedented high unemployment, widespread social distress and mass political unrest. While politicians, academics and local officials debated what to do about the 'old' industries, and the northern 'problem regions' in which they were located, a raft of 'new industries' – electricity, gas, chemicals, motor vehicles and mass-produced household consumer goods – emerged, located mainly in the West Midlands and South East. The geographical centre of economic gravity changed in fundamental ways in this period, turning what had been a successful nineteenth century North–South pattern of economic differentiation and specialisation into a problematic North–South divide of regional disparity.

For much of the post-war period, however, outwardly this divide remained largely obscured from view. Between 1945 and 1973, aided by a long boom in the world economy, and by the adoption of a Keynesian welfare-state model of socioeconomic regulation – itself a direct reaction to the crises of the interwar years – the British economy grew faster than at any previous time in its history (Maddison 1982). Not only did all parts of Britain, including the regions in the North, benefit from this growth, a new post-war regional policy, based on the experiments to assist the 'Special Areas' during the interwar years, diverted industrial growth and employment (an estimated 500,000 manufacturing jobs) from the South East and West Midlands to the (now renamed) 'Assisted Areas' of northern England, South Wales and central Scotland. As a result, although the northern areas of England continued to experience a higher rate of unemployment than the South East (and Midlands) throughout this period, the absolute size of the gap was negligible compared to that of the 1920s and 1930s.

Since the mid-1970s, Britain has been in the throes of another historical 'gale of creative destruction', far more profound in scale and implications than its interwar predecessor. Although most agree that a seismic shift in the structure and organisation of the economy, society and polity is underway, and that this shift started well before Mrs Thatcher's governments came on the scene, there have been different opinions as to its nature and direction. Some believe we are witnessing a transition from a twentieth-century 'Fordist' mode of economic and social organisation, based on mass production, mass consumption, social collectivism and extensive state regulation and intervention, to a new, twenty-first century 'post-Fordist' configuration based on flexible production, diversified and customised consumption, individualism and increasing privatisation of the state and public sphere. Both Thatcherism and New Labour's 'Third Way' have been interpreted as the search for a political model that best fits this new post-Fordist reality. Likewise, under this perspective, the widening of the North–South divide is interpreted as the unfolding of a new post-Fordist socioeconomic landscape to replace the outmoded post-Fordist one, in that the northern regions are alleged to have suffered most from the decline of Fordism while the South is claimed to be leading the emergence of the new socio-economy of flexible, post-Fordist capitalism.

An alternative, and in many ways more convincing, take on the upheavals of the past quarter of a century is that we have been experiencing an accelerating historic transition from 'industrial capitalism' to 'post-industrial capitalism'. Arguably, this transition had begun during the 1960s: certainly by the early-1970s, some scholars were talking of the advent of 'post-industrial society', of a service-dominated rather than industrially driven form of capitalism. Over the past few years, this notion has received renewed attention as several major forces have been gathering momentum. One development has been the extraordinary expansion of services, to the extent that they now account for more than 70 per cent of national GDP and employment. Another is what many claim to be a new technological revolution based on the production, processing, communication and consumption of information. A third element – itself promoted in large part by the new information and communication technologies – is a growing wave of globalisation. Numerous neologisms have been coined to describe the new post-industrial socioeconomic formation being forged by these three intersecting forces: the 'information society', the 'knowledge society', the 'e-economy', the 'i-Society', 'digital capitalism' and even 'dematerialised capitalism'. There is considerable overlap between these interpretations, to the point that the term 'new economy' has quickly become the popular, if contentious, shorthand to capture the new realities, especially amongst political and media pundits (see Leadbeater 1999). But whatever label is used, one thing is clear, namely that it is no longer appropriate to think about Britain as an industrial society. This is not to suggest that industry and manufacturing – what are now frequently, but misleadingly, referred to as the 'old' (or 'hard') economy – are no longer important. Patently that is not the case: manufacturing still creates a fifth of UK national output and produces the majority of its exports. However, it is to suggest that the main forces that now shape work, wealth, consumption, popular culture, identity and welfare are significantly different from what they were a quarter of a century ago, and that the economic, social and cultural features that had been forged by Britain's industrial past are in rapid retreat in the face of new configurations being created by the rapid advance of a 'post-industrial' or 'informational mode of development' (Castells 1996; Coyle and Quah 2002).

This accelerating shift to 'post-industrialism' has been a key factor behind the widening of social and regional inequalities in Britain over the last quarter of the twentieth century. Nationally, between 1975 and 2000, some 4 million jobs disappeared from traditional industry, while employment in services grew by more than 6 million (these data refer to the UK as a whole: traditional industry refers to manufacturing and energy production; services include private and public). The North–South divide is a direct expression of this transformation. The problem has been that the growth of the service economy has been slowest precisely in those regions that have experienced the most intense de-industrialisation (Figure 2.3). The South East, East, South West and East Midlands have led the shift to the new service-based society, while the dramatic slimming down of the industrial economy of the North has thus far not been compensated by an equally rapid growth of services. This pronounced geographical bias in the accelerating shift from industrial to post-industrial society explains the marked regional divergence in employment discussed earlier (Table 2.2). The West Midlands emerges as a sort of 'hinge region' dividing the service-based South and the de-industrialised North. London has been the major exception to this division: its experience has

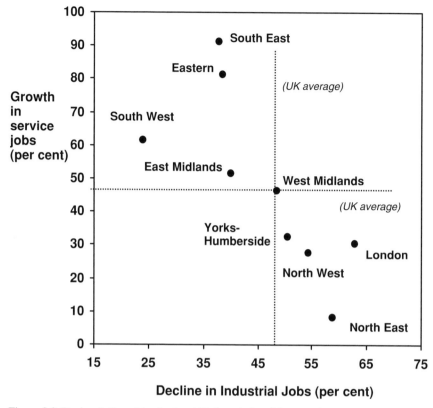

Figure 2.3 Regional disparities in the shift from industrial to service society, 1975–2000 (Office of National Statistics data)

been more akin to that of the North than that of the South. As a major centre of manufacturing industry, London has suffered de-industrialisation on a par with many large northern cities, and, similarly, has shown a low rate of service-sector growth. However, London has long been the nation's primary service centre, and, moreover, contains a disproportionate share of the nation's high-order business, producer, financial and government service functions. As such, it plays a formative role not only in the service economy of the 'South' (Table 2.3), but also in shaping the fortunes of the national economy as a whole.

But services are only one aspect of the new post-industrialism. What is also significant is that it has been the South or at least the South East and Eastern regions that have led the growth of the new 'information or knowledge society'. It is in these regions that innovative and high-technology activity and employment has thus far been concentrated. This part of England leads the nation in patenting, R&D expenditure, e-commerce and knowledge-based business (Table 2.3). Recent research indicates that it is in London and the South East that many of

Table 2.3 *A North–South divide in the 'new economy'?*

Region	Service activity as a proportion of GDP (2000)	Innovation: number of patents per million population (1999)	R and D expenditure as proportion of GDP (1999)	Proportion of businesses using e-commerce (1999)	Index of knowledge-based business (UK = 100)
London	84.0	74	1.5	12.2	146.7
South East	75.3	150	3.0	12.8	130.3
South West	66.9	99	2.0	6.7	124.4
East	72.2	184	3.2	3.1	107.6
North West	65.1	75	2.1	2.2	83.6
East Midlands	59.2	90	1.8	1.0	78.4
West Midlands	60.1	77	1.4	2.2	76.4
Yorkshire-Humberside	50.2	65	1.0	2.8	76.0
North East	60.1	72	0.9	0.8	72.6

Sources of data: Eurostat, Office of National Statistics, and Huggins (2000)
Note: Shaded regions are those with an index of knowledge-based business greater than UK average

the key industries and services supposedly spearheading the 'new economy' are concentrating, such as bio-technology, software design, Internet services, telecommunications and media activities (HM Government 2000; Miller *et al.* 2001). The main clusters are in the Cambridge and Oxford subregions, and to the west of London, especially in Bracknell, Wokingham and Reading. To be sure, certain locations in the North have also attracted new industries dependent on the information technologies, but the clusters involved are small by comparison with those in the South. And there is evidence of a distinct spatial division of labour emerging in some of these information-based service activities. The financial services sector is a case in point. In London, the new information and telecommunications technologies have enabled the financial City to take full advantage of electronic trading and banking (conducted by a well-paid, mainly male workforce) in order to retain its position in the global monetary system. For a number of northern cities, however, the new technologies have meant the rise of the 'call centre' phenomenon (of which Leeds is the capital). While call centres have certainly brought much-needed jobs to parts of the North (there are now reckoned to be more than 7,000 call centres in the UK employing over 250,000 workers), the working conditions, pay and career prospects in these 'service factories' of the post-industrial economy are a far cry from those of the City traders and bankers.

The southern bias in the emergence of the new service and 'knowledge-driven' economy has already had important implications. For one thing, it has been associated with considerable wealth creation amongst certain social groups in southern England. In the 1980s and early-1990s, those working in financial services in London and mostly living within one hour's commuting distance from the capital, saw their salaries rapidly outstrip the national average wage, with annual bonuses and reductions in the top rate of tax adding still further to the growth in their disposable incomes. In the mid- and late-1990s, it was the turn of those working in high-tech and the so-called 'creative industries' (software, Internet and a host of 'dotcom' companies), where high salaries were often combined with lucrative stock options and business sell-offs. Although the dotcom bubble burst after 2000, and many fortunes have since been lost – or at least much reduced – high-tech and the creative industries have become identified with the high returns associated with risky ventures and innovative entrepreneurialism. Without question, the shift to the service and high-technology-based post-industrial society helped to fuel the marked widening of the income distribution that occurred over the 1980s and 1990s. Income inequality (as measured, for example, by the Gini coefficient) had actually fallen slightly over the 1950s, 1960s and first half of the 1970s. But from the late-1970s onwards it increased sharply (the Gini coefficient of household incomes increased from 0.24 in 1977 to 0.37 by 1999). Not only has the income distribution widened, the extent of relative poverty has increased commensurately. Using the conventional definition of poverty as the proportion of households with incomes less than half the mean income, the extent of relative poverty in the UK more than doubled between 1979 and 1999, from just over 10 per cent to just over 25 per cent (Dickens and Ellwood 2001; Martin 2001). While the incomes of those in the high-technology, information and creative sectors of the new economy have pulled away, those working in unskilled service jobs have fallen progressively behind.

This 'new inequality' has been characterised by a high degree of spatial disparity. Much of the growth in higher incomes has been in the South, which has significantly increased its lead over the North in the personal wealth stakes. London and the South East have long had a higher proportion of top earners and incomes than other regions of the country, but during the 1980s and 1990s that lead increased substantially. For example, at the postcode area level, by 2000 mean gross household incomes ranged from just over £34,000 in West London and Kingston-upon-Thames to £17,000 in Sunderland in the North East (CACI 2001). All of the twenty postcode areas in England with the highest mean household incomes are in the South East; and fifteen of the twenty postcode areas with the lowest mean household incomes are north of the Wash–Severn line (Figure 2.4). At the more local level of postcode districts, spatial differences in incomes are even greater. At this scale, mean household incomes in 2000 ranged from £47,700 in South Kensington, London, to a mere £9,100 in Vauxhall, Liverpool, and no fewer than forty-one of the top fifty postcode districts in terms of mean household incomes were in the South East and Eastern regions. These contrasts are even sharper still if we compare London and northern cities (Table 2.4). All ten of the richest postcode districts (those in which 10 per cent or more of households with incomes

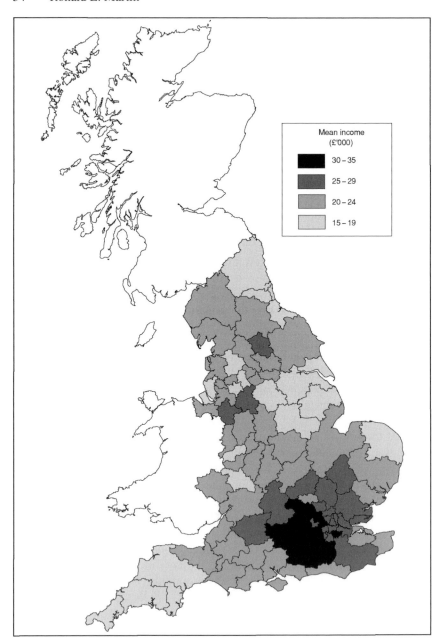

Figure 2.4 Average annual household gross incomes by English postcode areas, 2000 (CACI data)

exceeding £100,000) were in London. Conversely, the districts with the highest proportions of poor households (more than 60 per cent earning less than £10,000 per annum) were in Liverpool, Bradford, Blackburn, Middlesborough and Birmingham. No less than eight of the twenty poorest postal sectors in the UK are in Liverpool. Of course, low-income areas can be found right across Britain, with particular concentrations in the major cities and in the more remote rural areas and coastal towns. But it is clear that, overall, the incidence of low incomes and poverty is much lower in London and the South East than in the northern regions of the country (Martin 1995 and 2001).

Post-industrialism and the sociocultural divide

The wealth divide is only one expression of the uneven regional development of the new post-industrialism. Another issue concerns its impact on the country's social and cultural geography, on what has long been considered to be a North–South divide in social class, cultural identities and group politics.

Even in the nineteenth century stereotypical images of North–South differences in social class and cultural norms were rife amongst novelists and sociopolitical commentators. From the 1840s through to the 1930s, a succession of writers (Friedrich Engels, Elizabeth Gaskell, Charles Dickens, Thomas Hardy, Sidney and Beatrice Webb, Charles Booth, Richard Jeffries, Edward Thomas and D. H. Lawrence, to name but some) painted sharply contrasting social portraits of northern and southern England. In the highly industrialised North, the grim conditions of factory life and cramped urban dwelling were seen as having produced an exploited working class living in back-to-back tenements, possessing a strong sense of common identity, social community and political radicalism. At the same time, having invented an Industrial Revolution and an industrial working class, the English then invented a mental counter revolution: that of a southern rural idyll – 'the South Country' – a land dominated by agriculture and where work was shaped by the verities of the land and the seasons, rather than by the pace of factory machines, and social values were strongly rooted in the conservatism and individualism of the farming communities and the landed estates.

Such images were of course grossly overblown. Thus, as Paxman observes, socially and culturally there has never been a coherent 'north country': it exists only in contrast to southern England which is seen as fat, affected and above all 'soft'. The south country is based on counties, market towns and villages of great age, where any rivalries are long dead. The north of England contains a series of mainly nineteenth-century city-states. Manchester and Liverpool may be only thirty miles apart, but they are quite distinct in character: Manchester a Protestant seat of heavy industry, Liverpool a more Catholic dock city, the one an aggressive mill and trading town, the other a gentler, more wise-cracking port. Manchester has more in common with Leeds or Sheffield, its rivals across the Pennines, and Liverpool with Newcastle, than either has with the other (Paxman 1998: 157).

And within the North, there have also long been distinct geographically delimited dialects that have been integral to regional identities there – Yorkshire Tykes, Tyneside Geordies, Liverpudlian Scousers and West Midlands Brummies. As for the South, the notion of a pastoral idyll of rolling hills, village greens, hedgerows, and gentle farming folk was no less a myth than the idea of a socially and culturally homogeneous North. London always stood out from the surrounding southern shires. Its slums, sweatshops and pockets of poverty were as bad as anywhere, although they were offset by the city's status as the capital of the empire and the financial, cultural and political centre of the nation.

During the twentieth century, these two caricatures became transmuted into the idea of a predominantly working-class North versus a predominantly middle-class South. The archetypal northern working-class family was headed by a semi-skilled or unskilled manual worker, living in a council house, and who was both a staunch trade unionist and a fervent Labour voter. The archetypal southern middle-class household was headed by a blue-collar or white-collar worker, who was more likely to be an owner-occupier, less inclined to be a union member and much more disposed to vote Conservative. These stereotypes were of course precisely that. In reality, neither the working class nor the middle class were homogeneous sociocultural entities. And the North and the South were far from uniform geographical-social formations. Yet, as Massey (1985) and others have shown, these stereotypes did have some basis in fact.

It was in Britain's northern industrial cities that the trade union movement – one of the quintessential sociocultural products of industrialism – crystallised between the 1850s and 1870s. Born out of the various craft guilds, the movement was boosted by the spread of the factory system and the development of areas of specialised industry and manufacturing, especially in northern Britain. By the time the Webbs (1894) mapped the unions at the end of the nineteenth century, their northern heartlands were well established. And despite the spread of trade unionism into the new nationwide public services following the Second World War, the north of England still stood out as the main bastion of the union movement. At the height of British trade unionism in the late-1970s (when national membership reached more than 13 million, some 57 per cent of the labour force), union membership densities in the North were almost twice those in the South (Martin, Sunley and Wills 1996).

This north–south geography of labourism was itself closely associated with the regional distribution of the unskilled and semi-skilled manual working classes. In the 1970s these groups made up around twice the proportion of workers in the Northern and North West regions than in London and the South East (see Massey 1985). Likewise the proportion of households living in council-owned dwellings was also significantly higher in the North. And not surprisingly, the Labour Party drew the bulk of its electoral support from the same areas. In contrast, the South East contained around twice the national proportion of professional and managerial classes, had much higher rates of owner-occupation, the lowest rates of unionisation and was the Conservative Party's electoral stronghold. As the nation's major metropolis, London again stood out from the rest of south-eastern England in having a high proportion of council housing and a sizeable Labour voting population. Notwithstanding their internal diversity, in a broad sense it was indeed possible to point to regionally embedded differences in class structure between the North and the South.

However, since the early-1970s these regional differences have been undergoing profound change. The dramatic shift away from industry towards services and the information economy; the decline in male manual work; the growth in conceptual labour, in service jobs and in female employment; the general rise in incomes; and the impact of globalisation, are all promoting the rapid dissolution of the class structures and cultural identities that both sustained and were sustained by the traditions and institutions of industrial capitalism. British society, it is argued, has entered a new period of post-industrial modernisation in which 'de-traditionalisation' and the 'dis-embedding' of social life from its local contexts are rendering class and culture much more reflexive and fluid (Giddens 1994). Culture itself has become commodified, and consumption in turn a major sociocultural marker: we are what we consume rather than what we do for a living.

It is tempting to argue that the net result of the accelerating shift to a hyper-consumerist, post-industrial society has been to erase the historical class structure and class geographies of the country. Some talk about the end of the working class; others claim that we are all middle class now; others that Britain is now a classless society; still others that we now live in a multicultural Britain. One thing is certain, the meaning of 'class' is changing in historic ways. One of the most significant changes has been the rapid retreat – socially and spatially – of traditional labourism as a social and political culture. Trade union membership has collapsed to barely 7 million (35 per cent of employees), and some of the largest declines have been in the oldest and most traditional industrial sectors. The de-unionisation of British workers has taken place right across the country, including the historic northern union heartlands. Likewise, spurred on by incentives introduced by the Thatcher governments in the 1980s, tens of thousands of council-house tenants across the nation have bought their dwellings and joined the property-owning class. And perhaps most symbolically of all, Labour politics has moved distinctly away from its working-class values and orientation. From the mid-1970s through to the 1990s, the Labour vote progressively retreated back into its northern enclaves as the Conservatives increased their electoral support not only across large swathes of south-eastern England, but well into the Midlands and certain areas within the North itself (Martin 1988). The Conservative Party, it seemed, had successfully tapped – and exploited – what was a growing vein of individualism, consumerism and anti-unionism within society. To regain popular support and to be returned to power, the Labour Party was forced to jettison its 1920s socialist constitution, rooted in the class structure of industrial society in the late-nineteenth and early-twentieth centuries, and become – like the Conservatives – a party that appeals to the values and aspirations of a post-industrial electorate less interested in socioeconomic redistribution and more concerned with individual gain and material acquisition.

Even social consumption patterns have become less aligned with conventional class and income divisions. Rising affluence has reduced social inequalities in the ownership of household durables and related products. Napoleon once described England as a 'nation of shopkeepers'. We have become a nation of shoppers. The advent of mass consumption, and of those organs of mass consumption, the department store and chain store, dates back to the 1920s and 1930s. The bounty of the mature industrial economy, on show on the racks of chain stores such as Woolworths ('nothing over sixpence'), offered many people in interwar Britain the first glimpse of the Good Life. Over the past thirty years, supermarkets and multiples have all but killed the individual independent shop, and national and indeed international brands have come to dominate the goods available. Most accounts of life in modern Britain agree that the chain stores, the multiples, the multinational purveyors of fast food, clothing, leisure, entertainment and media goods are expunging diversity, not only from our High Streets, which have taken on a monotonous and depressing uniformity (with a consequential dilution of the distinctiveness of place), but also from pubs, chemist shops, the family butchers, bookstores and numerous other retailers. The enormous growth in the number of out-of-town superstores, and that cathedral to consumption, the 'shopping mall' (found in almost every region of England, from Gateshead's MetroCentre and Manchester's Trafford Centre in the North, to Thurrock's Lakeside and Dartford's Bluewater in the South East), reinforce this social and spatial convergence to a dominant lifestyle. Daily confrontations with brand-names retailers, out-of-town superstores and shopping centres, and proliferating fast-food outlets, make it hard to remember a time when shops, pubs, hotels and restaurants were not dominated by a handful of business corporations advertising their formulaic products in newspapers, on hoardings and the airwaves (Hobson 1999: 783).

Yet, notwithstanding this seemingly ineluctable trend towards formulaic mass consumption, incomes remain of central significance. If we are what we consume, what we consume depends on what we earn. The marked widening of the income distribution discussed earlier has sharpened social and spatial differences in access to consumption sites, and more especially in the brands of product consumed. Low-income households find it more difficult to get to the out-of-town superstores, and both the latter and the urban department stores target themselves and their products to different 'classes' of consumer. Income and wealth differences across the North–South divide thus translate into consumption and lifestyle differences (Table 2.4). For example, major North–South inequalities in diet and health have been highlighted by a number of recent studies (Department of Health 1999; Mitchell, Dorling and Shaw 2000; Davey Smith, Dorling and Shaw 2001): it comes as no surprise that the generally wealthier South maps into a generally healthier South.

Table 2.4 *Selected social differences across the North–South divide*

Region	Union density 2000 (percent of employees)	Consumption expenditure per head (household goods and services) 1997–2000 UK = 100	Standardised mortality rates 2000 UK = 100	Households in receipt of welfare benefits (family credits and income support) 2000 (percent)
South East	29	115.5	90	10
London	24	124.4	96	18
East Anglia	30	102.2	91	11
South West	33	97.3	88	14
East Midlands	40	91.3	99	14
West Midlands	43	93.9	102	17
Yorkshire-Humberside	45	90.3	101	16
North West	47	94.5	109	18
North	52	81.1	110	21

Sources: Office of National Statistics, Family Expenditure Survey
Note: The south-eastern 'core' regions are shaded

And while traditional class differences across regional Britain may have been eroded and made more kaleidoscopic, certain differences do remain. Thus despite its general decline, unionism continues to be noticeably higher in Northern regions. At the same time, new social and lifestyle differences may well be emerging across the country. For example, there has been much talk recently of a 'digital divide', between information-rich and information-poor households, and between their access to and use of new knowledge and information technologies and services. What evidence is available suggests that this new social divide also has a geographical dimension to it: thus far, household connection to the Internet has penetrated further in the London and South East regions, and even more striking are the differences between southern and northern towns in the frequency of e-shopping (Table 2.5), a pattern that is closely related to the wealth divide.

The policy challenge

Thus, over the final quarter of the twentieth century economic growth, employment and wealth all became increasingly concentrated in towns and communities in south-eastern England relative to towns and communities outside this area. As has been emphasised above, it would be misleading to imply that all parts of south-eastern England have shared in this success: indeed, London itself is in many ways a

Table 2.5 *The digital divide? The geography of Internet access and e-shopping,
2001*

Region	Percent of households with access to Internet	City	Percent of households that are frequent e-shoppers
London	32.8	Reading	17.9
South East	36.2	London West End	17.0
Eastern	25.7	Cambridge	16.4
South West	23.5	Bristol	12.0
West Midlands	24.5	Manchester	6.9
East Midlands	24.1	Hull	6.8
North West	23.9	Birmingham	6.3
Yorkshire-Humberside	20.3	Newcastle	6.0
North East	16.6	Liverpool	5.0

Source: Office of National Statistics, Family Expenditure Survey
Note: The south-eastern 'core' regions are shaded

microcosm of the North–South divide. Equally, it would be erroneous to suggest
that the rest of England outside this south-eastern 'core' is a post-industrial wasteland. As Coyle (1999) points out, there are a number of success stories in the North
(for example, she lists Leeds, York and Bradford as 'rising stars'). And it would
be wrong to belittle or decry the civic efforts being made in other northern cities to
achieve a new developmental momentum to offset their earlier industrial decline
(Manchester, Newcastle, Sheffield and Birmingham come to mind). But the fact
remains that, so far, the balance of growth and prosperity arising from the new,
post-industrial knowledge economy has been firmly tipped in favour of the South.

This disparity has in fact posed something of a dilemma for politicians. On the
one hand, as we noted above, Conservative and Labour governments have been
keen to deny or play down the notion of a North–South divide. Yet, at the same
time, they have viewed the success of the South as an exemplar of the sort of 'new
society' they have sought politically to represent and to promote. For precisely at
the same time that the North–South divide widened, so a particular image of the
South became used as part of the political discourse surrounding the social and
economic renewal of Britain as a whole.

Both for the Conservatives under Mrs Thatcher in the 1980s and for New Labour
under Mr Blair in the late-1990s, the South was seen as the dynamic locus of a
new culture of enterprise, innovation, individual initiative and self-help, a new
market-based economic democracy, that was counterposed to what was regarded
as the old and outmoded post-war culture of collectivism, welfare dependency
and state subsidy identified as persisting amongst the electorate in the North.

For the Conservative Party, for which the South had long been its heartland of electoral support, the task was to inculcate the same culture of enterprise and individualism – and hence political allegiance – in the northern, mainly Labour-voting electorate, using blatant policies of 'embourgeoisement' (via tax cuts, the promotion of property ownership by selling council houses to their tenants and encouraging popular share ownership) as part of its strategy. For its part, in order to get back into power 'New' Labour was forced to abandon its historical commitment to an extensive welfare-state, collectivist democratic political model in favour of a more modern, individualist and market-orientated project so as to appeal to the southern voter, even at the risk of alienating its traditional northern electoral supporters. Thus, notwithstanding the debates surrounding the very existence and definition of the North–South divide, the notion of a successful and modern South has nevertheless assumed key importance in the political discourse of a new, post-industrial Britain.

Whether the South is necessarily the best or only image or model of the new society that the rest of Britain should seek to emulate or is ineluctably destined to follow is, however, questionable. Several northern cities are determined to carve their own routes to regeneration and renewal (witness, for example, Manchester's successful bid to host the 2002 Commonwealth Games; and the bids of Liverpool, Bradford and Newcastle to be European City of Culture in 2008). A healthy reassertion of urban and regional identity, civic pride and cultural heritage is underway in several parts of the North. There is no one single model or path to regional prosperity, and each region needs to be able to shape its own priorities and prospects, though with support and assistance from the political centre.

In any case, the South is a questionable role model. The rapid development in the South is no less problematic than the slow growth in the North. For one thing, economic success in the South East, London and adjacent parts of the Eastern and South Western regions has led to considerable upward inflationary pressure, especially on housing and travel costs. For most categories of residential property, house prices in London are three times what they are in the North East. Average house prices in London have now risen above the threshold for inheritance tax (£263,000), so that even households with modest incomes and properties have now fallen within the taxman's net. On more than one occasion in the 1980s and 1990s, this compelled the Bank of England to raise interest rates to stem 'national' inflation, even though much of the North still had high unemployment. This elicited an understandable outcry from the northern business community that the Bank was conducting 'national' monetary policy to suit the South without regard to the adverse impact this was likely to cause in the North. The Governor of the Bank of England, Eddie George, was reported to have argued that 'if higher unemployment in the North is the price to be paid for keeping national inflation in check, it is a price worth paying'. In this way, the South distorts national economic policy-making, usually in its own favour. At the same time, the rising cost structure in the South together with mounting diseconomies of road congestion and pollution, mean that the standard of living and quality of life are not necessarily greater in the South than in the North. As *The Economist* observed back in the 1960s, 'What has the South of Britain got that the North really wants? Short answer: the economic and social stimulus of a London. What has the South got that it could well be rid of? Short answer: the inefficiency of a congested central London' (*The Economist* 1962: 989).

The North–South divide thus presents a complex challenge to policy-makers. On the one hand, policies are needed to help promote economic growth, jobs and prosperity throughout much of the North. On the other, the overheating and overdevelopment of the South also require policy action (Martin 1993b). Traditional post-war regional policy sought to solve these two issues simultaneously by diverting surplus growth and jobs from the South to the North by a combination of controls on development in the former and incentives to locate that development in the latter. During the course of the 1980s and 1990s this regional policy model was progressively abandoned: the idea of intervening directly to shift economic activity and jobs from South to North is now regarded as outmoded. Instead, Blair's Labour governments have pursued a new approach, a 'policy for all regions' (Balls 2000) aimed at increasing the rate of economic growth in every region, and which does not necessarily imply any convergence between regions at all. Amongst other things, this new approach is based on a view that every region should learn to help itself, and that it will be positively encouraged by central government to do so. The key institutional developments in this respect are the nine new Regional Development Agencies (RDAs) in England. Every English region, including London, now has an RDA to match those that have been in existence since the 1970s in Scotland, Wales and Northern Ireland. By being closer to the problems 'on the ground', the RDAs are supposed to be more sensitive to what is really required, and by working with local partnerships in the regions are supposed to deliver better results than if all the local players and actors had gone their own ways. To this end, the various other government schemes for promoting business, training and innovation are being channelled through these RDAs, which themselves are charged with drawing up regional development strategies. Where the RDAs do represent a major step forward is in giving new focus to the regeneration process in each region. For the first time, each English region has an agency of its own, with a clear brief to promote economic development and social inclusion. But how far these new Regional Development Agencies will succeed in closing the North–South divide will depend on the scale of resources made available to them from Whitehall, and on the extent of the powers they are given. At present both are limited. And in any case, while RDAs and their strategies are a much-needed ingredient of a new regional policy, they are far from being the full recipe. To assume that RDAs of themselves will close the North–South divide is to misunderstand the fundamental underlying causes of regional imbalance. As Anatole Kaletsky has forcefully argued:

Whether this economic gulf [the North–South divide] continues to widen or starts to narrow will depend crucially on decisions made by Mr Blair and his Cabinet. If he were seriously concerned about regional imbalances he would not be trying to bamboozle his northern constituents with public relations guff and meaningless statistics. Instead he should be thinking seriously about the causes of regional inequality and the regional implications of governmental economic decisions. (Kaletsky 1999: 31)

For at the same time that the northern RDAs are devising policies to improve the prosperity of their regions, the Labour government itself has prioritised the growth of the South. In an effort to ensure that the success of the South is not compromised, the Labour government has decided that the inflationary overheating and labour supply shortage problems in this part of England (and in the South East especially) are to be resolved not by encouraging and assisting business and jobs to go North, but by enabling yet more growth in the South. It has put pressure on local planning authorities to release land in the South East and Eastern regions for the construction of up to a million new homes over the next twenty-five years, a prospect that will no doubt swell many landowners', housebuilders', construction companies' and estate agents' profits but will also add to congestion and create additional pressures on public services that are already seriously overloaded. And such a policy, of itself, does little or nothing for the North, except further deplete the northern regions of their better-educated, enterprising and skilled people by attracting yet more of them to the South. Contrary to arguments about the spatially decentralising and regionally empowering nature of the 'new economy', the influence of economic, financial and political power in London and the South East continues to distort the policy agenda just as strongly as ever. Little is likely to change unless and until the regions are given much greater political autonomy – in the form of regional assemblies with powers to raise taxes and undertake public spending. Full regional federalism would indeed be a radical policy. New Labour's approach to this issue, however, is a cautious, incremental and *ad hoc* one: it envisages the possibility of different regional devolution models in different regions, with perhaps some regions not opting for this route at all. It is the northern regions – and especially the North West and North East – that are campaigning most enthusiastically for regional assemblies, whilst southern regions are much more ambivalent. This is, perhaps, just what the North–South divide would lead us to expect.

3

Distressed times and areas: poverty, polarisation and politics in England, 1918–1971

DANNY DORLING

Introduction

It is now commonly understood that for most of the first half of the twentieth century England (and Wales) was socially divided along simple geographical lines to a degree that has not quite recurred since and to a degree that had not occurred so starkly before. The truth of this statement lies in the meaning of the terms. By socially divided I mean the variation in people's life chances. These chances range from a person's chance of being ill and dying, to finding work, to the kind of work they do. It does not take a great leap of imagination to assume that if such fundamental chances as these were strongly polarised then much else that is much harder to measure was also starkly polarised during most of this period – ranging, for example, from the distribution of wealth, to opportunities for recreation and education. By 'along simple geographical lines' I mean very simple – in fact involving simply one line: the line that divided the North from the South. There have always been geographical divides – between streets within cities, between town and country and so forth – but I would argue that there has not been, at least since this period, such a simple line to be drawn across the map of England. The North–South divide is still very much apparent today, but it is now more an echo, and perhaps largely a product of the divide which grew so great in these years. In the first half of this chapter I try to demonstrate how great the divide was. Thus some of these points are substantiated and defended below, but they are not the most interesting aspect of the divide to me.

The most interesting aspect of the North–South divide of the 1920s, 1930s and 1940s is how little it was recognised at the time. This is a difficult argument to make – and the argument that is perhaps most suspect in this chapter (it is very hard to prove that something was not the case) – but if it is true the implications are important. How could it be that a country suffered such a schism and did not appear to recognise it? It is certainly true that you can find people and writings that did refer to the divide or aspects of it – but they are very much in the minority of contemporary writing on the social geography of England at that time. In the second half of this chapter I try to explain how it could be that this divide was so ignored, at least until wartime. There are two primary reasons to my mind. Firstly, not until the 1940s was there sufficient information to demonstrate the growth of the divide (work which required the lengthy compilation and subsequent analysis of the 1931 census). Secondly, there was a very strong incentive not to recognise such a national malaise in the aftermath of one Great War and the build up to another. The predominant rhetoric of the time was nationalistic. Much was written about how 'Great' Britain was, how its countryside and traditions needed to be preserved. At such a time of great nationalism, following the loss of most of Ireland, the nationalist rhetoric recognised local problems but found systematic geographical polarisation harder to stomach. The North–South divide of the 1920s and 1930s was very much recognised after the event. Not least because of the closure of part of that divide in the 1940s but also because recognising the divide served the interests of the dominant social-welfare agenda of the 1950s and 1960s that continued to underlie political discussion and academic writing through the 1970s, 1980s and 1990s. The period 1918–39 was cited as an example of 'what could happen' if progressive social and regional policies were not followed. How familiar Marwick's comment about the years 1918–39 seems today: 'now a new pattern established itself: a prosperous bustling South producing a tremendous range of new consumer goods; and a decaying North' (Robson 1990: 546, quoting Marwick 1968: 168). That said, it has to be acknowledged that relatively few geographical analyses have been produced of England during the interwar period. Twenty years ago, Alan Baker suggested that 'the inter-war years might be considered the real Dark Ages as far as historical geographers are concerned' (Baker and Gregory 1984: 187). That remark remains apposite, even though the period is gradually and increasingly being illuminated by new geographical research and reviews (Heffernan and Gruffudd 1988; Ward 1988; Robson 1990; Gilbert, Matless and Short 2003).

This chapter ends with what is the most interesting contemporary question that this story throws up. If the North–South divide was not recognised in the period under discussion until largely after the event, to what extent could current social trends in England be similarly misinterpreted? To what degree do we have more information now, or less of a dominant rhetoric? The first years of the twenty-first century have seen the release of statistics that suggest that the North–South social divide in Britain is again reducing. However, most of these statistics relate to changes between the late 1990s and today, ignoring polarisation that built up in the decades before. They also tend to concentrate on the slight improvement in the fortunes of those at the bottom of the social order, not at the still wide and sometimes still growing gap between those who have most and least. To what extent is the experience of 1918–71 a model for contemporary understanding of English society? Could a divide be growing now that we are loath and ill-equipped to recognise?

What is the North–South divide?

The North–South I have in my mind is a metaphorical cliff. It cuts the population currently living in England almost exactly in two, with only the slightest of variations from county borders. The divide begins where the river Severn meets the sea. Herefordshire, Worcestershire, Warwickshire, Leicestershire and Lincolnshire mark the northern borders of 'the South'. All of Wales, Shropshire, the West Midlands, Staffordshire, Derbyshire, Nottinghamshire and Yorkshire are in 'the North'. I have decided to include areas in Wales in the data and arguments made below, as the fortunes of people living in Wales have been so intricately connected to those of England that it does not make great sense to exclude it. Scotland could also be included in the North but some of the worst examples of social suffering in parts of Scotland have been so much worse than those south of the border that in terms of socio-geographical divides there is perhaps more to try to explain in Scotland than this chapter will attempt (see instead Mitchell and Dorling 2002). In this definition of the divide I do not envisage the dividing-line having moved over time. To me it was the divide that strengthened in the 1920s and 1930s that remains the divide we see today. The essays that follow in this book deal with the precursors of that initial growth in this divide – a single cliff that rose up at the start of the last century and continues to cast a shadow down across the south of England.

I first saw this cliff clearly when drawing a map of people's propensity to die of heart disease in the 1980s (Dorling 1995: 157). I painstakingly calculated a standardised mortality rate for over 9,000 local government wards in England and Wales and coloured each ward in one of five colours according to that rate. I need not have bothered. The map, instead of showing a detailed and complex geography of death, revealed the line described above, as a cliff on the map. North of that cliff rates were 10, 20 or 30 per cent higher than average, south of that cliff they were 10, 20 or 30 per cent lower than average. The sharpest change in the gradient of mortality occurred where the counties listed above met. There were some variations about this pattern, but what was staggering was just how strong this basic pattern was. Very little that I have seen or drawn subsequent to that map of heart disease has made me doubt the position of this line. Whether it is variations in tendency to vote, house price changes or unemployment trends – the line is there. It appears in numerous contemporary socioeconomic models as a 'dummy variable' (for an example, see Sloggett and Joshi 1994). Living in the North is put into regression equations to explain away variation in some social variable that cannot otherwise be explained. In many cases it is because the line separates the different histories of different areas that the 'dummy variable' remains significant, and that history is of the 1920s and 1930s.

When was the North–South divide?

People who died of heart disease in the 1980s tended to live to around seventy-five years of age. That is, they were born in the decades around 1910, grew up in the

1920s, some found work in the 1930s, had children in the 1940s, settled down in the 1950s, came to the end of their working lives in the 1960s and retired (if they had not already died) in the 1970s. Those living to the south of the cliff were much more likely to survive into the 1980s than those living to the north – and many times more likely to reach the 1990s. Geographical inequalities in death reached a peak in the 1980s and 1990s in Britain. A large part of the cause of that peak, many suspect, is that geographical inequalities in early life experiences reached a peak a lifetime earlier, in the period with which this chapter is concerned. The factors that affect, and are affected by, health are similar to those which affect people's life chances in general and their subsequent behaviours. The North–South divide had a direct effect upon the elderly living in England by the end of the last century and an indirect effect on their children's and grandchildren's life chances.

Pictures drawn of spatial divides in Britain before the 1920s tend to contrast urban and rural areas more and also divides within cities. This is a pattern to which we might well be returning, to some degree. Often the West Midlands is included in the South and Lincolnshire in the North, but in terms of each area's legacy of ill and good health it makes more sense to divide them as I have indicated. Similarly, in terms of legacies such as that on voting, it again makes sense to keep the line as I have described it. It is, in fact, intriguing that most of the discussion about alternative routes for the line varies so closely around where I have drawn it. For instance, when discussing the North–South divide in housing in 1931 a commentator writing in the 1980s stated: 'The west Midlands were an intermediate zone with towns like Stoke, West Bromwich and Dudley more "northern" and Coventry more "southern"' (Ward 1988: 29). Unsurprisingly the same author's other dilemmas in placing the line also fall along its boundary as described above: 'However on many indicators, notably unemployment, south Yorkshire was weaker than west Yorkshire' (Ward 1988: 13).

Even more intriguing is the fact that the strongest arguments against the imposition of such a simple divide were written by some commentators just at the time when the divide was becoming recognised. Geographers were involved in charting aspects of the divide at the time, but in general they did not recognise it as a divide. A geographer, Henry Daysh, argued that the divide which mattered in the 1940s was one between peripheral and urban Britain. To me, such a division harks back to earlier times, but also partly helps explain why the divide was not so clearly seen at the time in which, with hindsight, it appeared to have existed most strongly. Daysh expressed his view clearly:

It is obvious that the dominant circumstances of some parts of the country upon which my colleagues have written, and which include Development Areas, are in certain essentials markedly different from territories such as south-west England or the Highlands and Islands of Scotland. Nevertheless our readers will quickly realise that there are numerous common features of these otherwise geographically contrasting territories. The majority of them are peripheral to what has been called the 'urban axis' of England – a fact of considerable importance in the determination of policy in relation to national trends. In virtually all of them there are problems akin to those of the arbitrarily defined Development Areas. (Daysh 1949: xiii)

Geographers at this time were interested in geographical detail – as typified by Dudley Stamp's great land use mapping project – rather than in producing geographical generalities such as identifying a general North–South divide. Such interest in specifics was also encouraged at the time by governments, as Garside has pointed out:

In July 1929 the government's Chief Industrial Advisor sponsored the idea of establishing new enterprises in the depressed areas of Scotland, the North East and Wales and continued to monitor efforts made in this direction through to 1931. Official activity in the early thirties was, however, disappointing. It was limited to offering industrialists rebates on power, transport and rates expenditures and encouraging local development organisations to pursue whatever initiatives they felt were appropriate to their particular regions. This approach made it difficult to lay the blame for inadequate progress at the door of central government. (Garside 2000: 11)

Conventional explanations for the divide

Stephen Ward (1988) began his seminal history of interwar Britain by pinning much of the blame for economic polarisation in this period on the existing industrial structure in the North coupled with industrial innovation and control being concentrated in the South (or inner Britain as he termed it). Thus the decline in major export industries had a disproportionate effect on northern areas reliant on shipbuilding or cotton, coal, iron and steel. Simultaneously, new industrial growth in retail, motor vehicles and electrical goods tended to be concentrated in the South, as did banking and government which both grew greatly in this period, concentrating most money and power in the core. However, Ward argued against too simplistic a geographical description. In doing so he quoted one of the few contemporary observers of the divide:

In a classic 1933 description, which would bear extension to the whole of Britain, J. B. Priestley identified four different Englands; each representing different phases in the economic, social, political and cultural development of the country. Wisely, he did not seek to portray any clear-cut divisions between north or south, still less between inner and outer Britain, but saw clearly that the pattern was more varied than a simple regional divide. As he commented, the different Englands were 'variously and most fascinatingly mingled, in every part of the country I visited. It would be possible, though not easy, to make a coloured map of them. There is one already in my mind, bewilderingly coloured and crowded with living people. It made me feel dizzy.' (Ward 1988: 32)

Had either Ward or Priestley had the resources to draw such a map, however, they might have felt a little less dizzy. Albeit with hindsight and once various irregularities in the map are ironed out, the picture of the legacy of the North–South divide is much clearer than was either seen at the time, or interpreted a few decades after the event. One of the simplest reasons that people did not see the divide as starkly as I see it now is that the practice of collecting data for areas, sorting it and displaying it as a map or simply listing the extremes is a very modern preoccupation. Below, I take a few simple measures of the condition of areas in the 1930s and compare them to the 1970s. Neither Priestly nor Ward had the facility to do this easily whether writing in the 1930s or 1980s (although it was certainly easier by the 1980s). The tabulation and sorting of data was such an unusual and difficult practice in the past that more often than not information for a few selected areas are presented – where that selection has not been made in the light of all the available information.

Characterising the North–South divide

The North–South divide in health

Rates of infant mortality were published for 1928 for 229 county or metropolitan boroughs in England and Wales and for the rural remainder of the counties those boroughs fell in. Similar data was published for roughly the same areas in the 1970s – before the great reorganisation of administrative boundaries took place in 1974. Table 3.1 ranks these 229 areas of England and Wales by their infant mortality rates in 1928 and 1971. In 1928 all of the worst-off ten areas were in the North (including Wales). By 1971 all but one (Salford) of these areas were no longer amongst the worst ten and half of the worst areas were by then in the South – in inner London. In 1928 all of the best-off areas were in the South. Half of these remained in the best-off group over forty years later although one 'northern' area (the urban boroughs of Montgomeryshire) joined the best-off group by then.

Seeing the above areas listed together now, it is simple to see how clearly geographical the divide in 1928 was between South and North. It is very important to realise that it looks so stark only in hindsight and when the areas are arranged in this way. If you were not looking for a regional divide of this nature with these figures then you would not so clearly see one. If you were more concerned with local factors such as sanitation or hospital provisions for births then you would have no particular reason to look for such a divide. The ability to sort the data easily, the wish to do so and the contrast with the picture some forty years later are all needed to claim that there was a stark regional divide to health, as measured by infant mortality, in 1928.

The North–South divide in employment

The 1931 census provides the best measure of variations in employment during this period through its count of the unemployed. In terms of unemployment all the worst-off ten areas in 1931 were towns in the North (Table 3.2). Only two of these areas were still in the worst-off ten by 1971, although unemployment was still very much a northern (if more Celtic fringe) phenomenon by then. The lowest rates of unemployment in 1971 were all found in London boroughs. These

Table 3.1 *Infant mortality in 1928 and 1971 (by rank and per 100 live births)*

Area	rank 1928	rank 1971	rate 1928	rate 1971	change
Worst 10 areas in 1928					
Salford CB	1	5	10.3	2.3	−8
Bootle CB	3	16	9.4	2.1	−7.3
Liverpool CB	2	49	9.4	1.8	−7.6
Merthyr Tydfil CB	4	25	9.2	2	−7.2
South Shields CB	5	26	9.1	2	−7.1
Wigan CB	7	38	9	1.9	−7.1
Middlesborough CB	6	155	9	1.4	−7.6
Manchester CB	9	17	8.9	2.1	−6.8
St Helens CB	8	27	8.9	2	−6.9
Merionethshire rural	10	94	8.9	1.6	−7.3
Worst 10 areas in 1971					
Finsbury LB	21	1	8.1	2.5	−5.6
Oldham CB	25	2	8	2.5	−5.5
Chelsea LB	136	3	5.7	2.5	−3.2
St Pancras LB	28	4	7.9	2.4	−5.5
South Shields CB	5	26	9.1	2	−7.1
Bradford CB	64	6	7	2.3	−4.7
Birkenhead CB	70	7	6.8	2.3	−4.5
Hackney LB	73	8	6.7	2.3	−4.4
Bolton CB	84	9	6.6	2.3	−4.3
St Marylebone LB	26	10	8	2.2	−5.8
Best 10 areas in 1971					
Berkshire rural	226	220	3.9	1.2	−2.7
Gloucester CB	85	221	6.6	1.1	−5.5
Cambridgeshire urban	156	222	5.5	1.1	−4.4
Essex rural	211	223	4.5	1.1	−3.4
Berkshire urban	213	224	4.4	1.1	−3.3
Canterbury CB	228	225	3.6	1.1	−2.5
Buckinghamshire rural	184	226	5.1	1	−4.1
Rutland urban	229	227	3	1	−2
Montgomeryshire urban	128	228	5.9	0.9	−5
Montgomeryshire rural	153	229	5.5	0.9	−4.6
Best 10 areas in 1928					
Surrey rural	220	204	4.3	1.3	−3
Lincolnshire, Holland urban	221	68	4.2	1.8	−2.4
Sussex, West rural	222	219	4.2	1.2	−3
Rutland rural	223	153	4.1	1.5	−2.6
Oxfordshire rural	224	181	4	1.4	−2.6
Norwich CB	225	154	4	1.5	−2.5
Berkshire rural	226	220	3.9	1.2	−2.7
Oxford CB	227	93	3.6	1.7	−1.9
Canterbury CB	228	225	3.6	1.1	−2.5
Rutland urban	229	227	3	1	−2

CB = County Borough
LB = London Borough

Table 3.2 *Unemployment in 1931 and 1971 (by rank and per 100 people in workforce)*

Area	rank 1931	rank 1971	rate 1931	rate 1971	change
Worst 10 areas in 1931					
South Shields CB	1	34	33.3	11.1	−22.2
Blackburn CB	2	148	33.3	9.7	−23.6
West Hartlepool CB	3	2	30.6	13.1	−17.5
Sunderland CB	4	35	28.4	11.1	−17.3
Merthyr Tydfil CB	5	36	25.9	11.1	−14.8
Middlesborough CB	6	3	24.4	12.8	−11.6
Glamorganshire urban	7	37	22.9	11.1	−11.8
Durham urban	8	51	22.6	10.9	−11.7
Newcastle-upon-Tyne CB	9	138	21.8	9.8	−12
Tynemouth CB	10	20	21.6	11.5	−10.1
Worst 10 areas in 1971					
Pembrokeshire urban	76	1	12.3	13.4	+1.1
West Hartlepool CB	3	2	30.6	13.1	−17.5
Middlesborough CB	6	3	24.4	12.8	−11.6
Bootle CB	17	4	19.1	12.8	−6.3
Anglesey urban	69	5	12.5	12.7	+0.2
Rutland urban	161	6	7.9	12.4	+4.5
Flintshire urban	52	7	14.6	12.3	−2.3
Anglesey rural	68	8	12.5	12.3	−0.2
Grimsby CB	91	9	10.9	12	+1.1
Yorkshire, North Riding urban	32	10	16.3	11.9	−4.4
Best 10 areas in 1971					
Fulham LB	124	220	9.7	6.9	−2.8
Finsbury LB	72	221	12.3	6.7	−5.6
Paddington LB	132	222	9.4	6.6	−2.8
Kensington LB	162	223	7.8	6	−1.8
Hampstead LB	216	224	5.6	5.8	+0.2
Chelsea LB	150	225	8.3	5.5	−2.8
Westminster LB	175	226	7.2	4.4	−2.8
St Marylebone LB	182	227	7	4.4	−2.6
Holborn LB	99	228	10.7	3.5	−7.2
City of London	215	229	5.6	2.1	−3.5
Best ten areas in 1931					
Devon rural	220	65	5.3	10.7	+5.4
Sussex, West urban	221	193	5.3	9.1	+3.8
Sussex, West rural	222	129	5.1	10	+4.9
Surrey urban	223	202	5	8.7	+3.7
Hertfordshire rural	224	176	5	9.4	+4.4
Sussex, East rural	225	108	5	10.2	+5.2
Surrey rural	226	118	4.9	10.1	+5.2
Westmoreland urban	227	211	4.8	8.2	+3.4
Oxford CB	228	177	4.7	9.4	+4.7
Westmoreland rural	229	147	4.5	9.8	+5.3

CB = County Borough
LB = London Borough

contrasted completely with the areas with the lowest rates in 1931 which (other than in Westmorland) were all in the South in mainly rural boroughs.

Looking at the list of worst-off areas in 1931 it is perhaps possible to understand how contemporary commentators, not looking at a table sorted like this, could see unemployment being as much an urban phenomenon as a northern one. However four of the best-off ten areas in 1931 were urban. Again you need to be looking for the divide, to decide to sort all the data for all of England and Wales by the same rate (rather than to sort within regions) and to have something to contrast your numbers with (the 1970s) to see clearly the strength of the regional division. It is much easier in hindsight.

The North–South divide in work

The geographical distribution of people in work in the lowest social class again confirms how strong the North–South divide was by the 1930s (Table 3.3). All areas with the highest proportion in this class (greater than 20 per cent of those in work) were in the North. However some (often) more rural parts of Wales feature in the list of areas with the ten lowest proportions. By 1971 six of the ten areas with the highest rates were in London, but all the areas with the lowest rates were well and truly in the south of the country. Other than the very low rates in some rural parts of Wales in 1931, the divide in terms of unskilled work, for those in work, is again clearly apparent between the North and the South in the 1930s. In fact it is partly the rise of Inner London boroughs into the worst-off groups by the 1970s that shows how clear the divide in the 1930s was. Contemporary descriptions of the North–South divide in the 1980s have had the problem of where to place Inner London (which by the 1980s looked like part of the North). There was no such problem in the 1930s.

Contemporary perceptions of the North–South divide

Three pieces of writing are repeatedly cited as evidence of how the North–South divide was recognised at the time. J. B. Priestley is joined most often by George Orwell and less often by Walter Greenwood when the argument about contemporary understanding of the divide is made. This is emphasised by Helen Jewell in her study of the origins of northern consciousness in England:

in the sharp economic decline of the 1920s and 1930s, and again in the 1980s, the north was aware of its relatively greater suffering, and the sense of difference surged up into discussion and literature. Besides George Orwell's *Road to Wigan Pier*, first published in 1937, there was the haunting *Love on the Dole* of Walter Greenwood, published in 1933, and J. B. Priestley's *English Journey*, published in 1934. The second northern decline emerges from Beryl Bainbridge's new *English Journey* (1984), sub-titled *The Road to Milton Keynes*. (Jewell 1994: 4)

These writings are telling stories about places which are sorted, not by how good or bad living standards were, but by the ability of the writer to travel through the

Table 3.3 *Social class V in 1931 and 1971 (by rank and per 100 people working)*

Area	rank 1931	rank 1971	rate 1931	rate 1971	change
Highest 10 areas in 1931					
Kingston-upon-Hull CB	1	7	27.5	14.3	−13.2
Middlesborough CB	2	12	26.1	13	−13.1
Carlisle CB	3	52	25.3	9.4	−15.9
Swansea CB	4	53	21.8	9.4	−12.4
Yorkshire, East Riding urban	5	154	21.7	5.9	−15.8
Barrow-in-Furness CB	6	30	21.4	10.5	−10.9
Salford CB	7	8	21.2	13.8	−7.4
Bootle CB	9	5	21	14.6	−6.4
Liverpool CB	8	23	21	11.3	−9.7
Manchester CB	10	57	21	9.3	−11.7
Highest 10 Areas in 1971					
Bermondsey LB	43	1	17.6	17.8	0.2
Southwark LB	44	2	17.6	16.6	−1
Poplar LB	62	3	17.5	16	−1.5
Stepney LB	61	4	17.5	15.8	−1.7
Bootle CB	9	5	21	14.6	−6.4
Bethnal Green LB	58	6	17.5	14.6	−2.9
Kingston-upon-Hull CB	1	7	27.5	14.3	−13.2
Salford CB	7	8	21.2	13.8	−7.4
Warrington CB	24	9	19.4	13.8	−5.6
Finsbury LB	42	10	17.6	13.5	−4.1
Lowest 10 Areas in 1971					
Sussex, East urban	126	220	15.6	4.1	−11.5
Isle of Wight urban	113	221	15.8	4	−11.8
Surrey rural	123	222	15.7	4	−11.7
Eastbourne CB	150	223	15	4	−11
Sussex, West rural	127	224	15.6	3.8	−11.8
Surrey urban	86	225	16.8	3.7	−13.1
Bournemouth CB	143	226	15	3.7	−11.3
Isle of Wight rural	114	227	15.8	3.6	−12.2
Sussex, East rural	133	228	15.5	3.5	−12
Hampstead LB	72	229	17.5	3.3	−14.2
Lowest 10 areas in 1931					
Derbyshire urban	220	101	12.1	7.7	−4.4
Cardiganshire rural	221	178	12.1	5.4	−6.7
Rutland urban	222	188	12.1	5.1	−7
Nottinghamshire urban	223	161	11.9	5.8	−6.1
Leicestershire urban	225	166	11.8	5.7	−6.1
Nottinghamshire rural	224	215	11.8	4.3	−7.5
Leicestershire rural	226	207	11.7	4.6	−7.1
Carmarthenshire rural	227	130	11.4	6.7	−4.7
Carmarthenshire urban	228	87	11.3	8.1	−3.2
Brecknockshire urban	229	81	11.2	8.3	−2.9

CB = County Borough
LB = London Borough

areas they are describing. Jewell quotes only one such story from the 1980s. By the 1980s, reports on the North–South divide were dominated, not by travelogues, but by numbers. The kind of sorting process I have undertaken here for areas in the 1970s and 1980s was just beginning to become common in the 1980s as computers made the amalgamation and sorting of data relatively simple. Thus lists of 'booming' and 'failing' towns could be produced and maps simply drawn and redrawn until those with the clearest patterns were chosen for production. None of this was possible in the 1930s and 1940s. The 'Maps for the National Plan' drawn in the 1940s were unique creations (Association for Planning and Regional Reconstruction 1945). Once it was decided that a particular map was to be drawn, then a cartographer painstakingly drew it.

The map shown in Figure 3.1 is taken from the publication 'Maps for the National Plan', which was used to provide background information to the Barlow, Scott and Beveridge reports. It is just one of a series of maps, albeit one of the most detailed. I have included it here to illustrate how local conditions were still often presented as being 'local' rather than part of a national pattern even by the 1940s when the map was drawn. The map is based on information from the 1931 census and shows each administrative county and county borough drawn as a square in proportion to its employed population. Around the borders of each square the proportions of that population employed in various industries are shown (and a key is provided around the top left-hand corner of the map). The map allows the pattern of employment within a particular area to be studied, but breaks up the geographical patterns across the country. If areas have problems they are problems of those areas; viewing them as a problem of particular industries being concentrated across a region is not possible given this layout.

Contemporary observations of the North–South divide in this period are so skewed towards being either written or interpreted by the elite that it is extremely difficult to form a view of what most people at the time felt. I will explore this problem by looking at the extent to which the North–South divide was expressed through patterns of voting over the period. For contemporary verbal accounts, the best source of material is probably that produced by the mass observation movement and the archives held at the University of Surrey, but even that will be a very selective set of accounts. Peter Taylor has written widely on regional divides within Britain and sees the North–South divide as a largely elite southern construct. Arguing that 'as a regional label, the North (or North East or North West) has no meaning except with respect to the rest of England, it is a compass point not a people' (Taylor 2001). However, almost all regional constructions were and are elitist constructions. That the North–South divide was one such does not necessarily make its actual existence in terms of separating groups of people with differing life chances any less true. It is just that it was not defined on that basis. Taylor counts the number of pages given up to describing areas in H. V. Morton's (1942) *I Saw Two Englands* to illustrate the southern bias of the writer who describes the North as a 'queer country'.

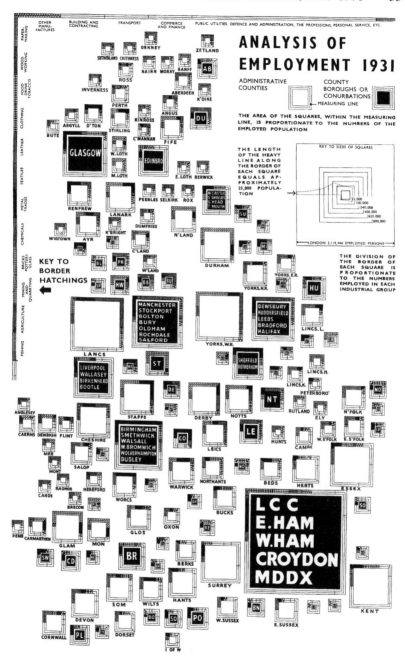

Figure 3.1 'Analysis of employment 1931' (Association for Planning and Regional Reconstruction, *Maps for the National Plan* (1945))

One final point to make on contemporary perceptions of the North–South divide was that they could well have been masked by the huge importance (and growing consciousness) of social class during these times. What mattered was where you were in the social rather than geographical order of things. Places were used by writers to epitomise being in a particular class. Given all this, I think it is very difficult to argue that there was a strong contemporary consciousness of the geographical divide which grew during these years and meant that being working class in one part of England was easier than being working class in another. The gap between being working class and middle class was so great that that was what people rightly concentrated on and where the battle for hearts and minds was fought. It was only later that the material geographical divide began to be realised more acutely. The North–South divide in the 1920s and 1930s was a fault line that cut across a social landscape so pitted with the local highs and lows of class divides that it could be ignored. Only later, when those local divides narrowed, did its underlying of that landscape become more clear.

Alternative measures of local perceptions: voting behaviour

Other than through the literature that is left, it is almost impossible to reconstruct a picture of how regional divisions in the 1920s, 1930s and 1940s were viewed by different groups of people at those times. The sources are heavily skewed towards those very few in society who put their opinions in print. An alternative although very indirect means of trying to measure the extent to which regional divides were apparent in the perceptions of people at these times is to look at how people behaved in an activity in which the majority (at least of men) were invited to partake: voting.

The 1918 general election was the first to allow all men in Britain (and Ireland) to vote. It resulted in an overwhelming victory for the coalition of parties headed by David Lloyd George. The major party in that coalition was the Conservative party. Party politics at this time were thus complex. However, for the purposes of assessing the size of regional disparities in voting I have simply reconstructed the present-day party labels of candidates at the general election. This has been done in Table 3.4 for each of the ten general elections of the period, showing the proportion voting for candidates of each party in England and Wales. In 1918 almost all of the Conservative candidates stood as coalition candidates. The Labour vote shown includes votes for the Independent Labour Party and some socialist candidates where they were not opposed by Labour candidates. The Liberal vote shown includes both coalition and non-coalition Liberals to allow comparisons with later years.

The period saw a strong Conservative vote weakening only in 1923, 1929 and 1945, a strengthening Labour vote and the decline of the Liberals. There was no significant nationalist vote in Wales in this period, which is telling when compared to the present day and when thinking about how regional divides are perceived. Most importantly, the table tabulates separately the votes counted in the North and

Table 3.4 *Voting patterns in England and Wales 1918–1951*

England and Wales	Con%	Lab%	Lib%	Nat%	Other%
1918	41	26	28	0	4
1922	41	30	28	0	2
1923	39	31	30	0	1
1924	48	33	18	0	0
1929	38	37	24	0	1
1931	59	31	10	0	0
1935	50	39	10	0	1
1945	39	49	10	0	2
1950	43	47	10	0	0
1951	48	49	3	0	0
North					
1918	33	31	32	0	4
1922	34	36	29	0	2
1923	34	36	29	0	1
1924	43	39	18	0	0
1929	33	43	23	0	1
1931	54	37	9	0	0
1935	45	43	10	0	1
1945	36	54	9	0	1
1950	39	52	8	0	0
1951	43	53	3	0	0
Divide					
1918	−8	5	4	0	0
1922	−7	6	1	0	0
1923	−4	5	−1	0	0
1924	−5	5	−1	0	0
1929	−4	6	−2	0	0
1931	−5	5	0	0	0
1935	−5	4	0	0	1
1945	−3	4	−1	0	−1
1950	−4	5	−1	0	0
1951	−4	4	0	0	0

in England and Wales, and expresses them as proportions of all votes counted at each election. These proportions are then subtracted from the national proportion to show to what extent the North voted differently from England and Wales as a whole.

What Table 3.4 shows is that, contrary to current popular perception of the period, support for the Conservatives strengthened in the North between 1918 and

1951. It was always lower than in England and Wales as a whole, starting at 8 per cent lower and ending at 4 per cent lower. However, this regional divide is small compared to what came later in the 1970s and 1980s. Secondly, the table shows that as the Labour Party grew in popularity its slightly higher level of support in the North had to fall slightly. For a party that began almost exclusively in the North of England and Wales to be receiving only 5 per cent more of the popular vote there in both 1918 and 1950 is quite at odds with the folk history of Labour told most often today. Thirdly, apart from in 1918 (when many Liberal candidates would not oppose Conservatives standing in the South for the coalition), there is no significant difference in Liberal voting North and South. Lastly the proportion of electors voting for other candidate groupings did not differ regionally over this period.

What, then, was the geographical pattern of voting at this time if it was not one of stark regional divides? To begin to answer this question I have taken one election from each decade of this period below and conducted the same simple sorting of areas as was done above for socioeconomic measures at the time. To save space I have not listed all the top and bottom-ranked seats, but simply comment on the extremes to show how there were strong pockets of voting for parties in places that we might not now imagine were such strongholds.

The general election of 1918

At the start of the period the Conservative's third safest seat was in Lancaster, and their fifth and eighth safest were in Cheshire. Issues such as Home Rule in Ireland influenced local voting (against Catholic minorities in the north of England) far more than any reflection of a North–South divide. The Liberals had two of their safest seats in the South. Labour at this time held all but one of their ten safest seats in the North. Seats which were unopposed have been excluded from this analysis – if these were included Labour would have held all their safest seats in the North. Note also that in places such as Durham, Consett (where Labour received their seventh highest vote), Labour polled fewer votes than did the Liberals. The party of 'the North' was still so weak in this period that not one of its top ten seats in terms of votes could fairly be called safe.

The general election of 1924

Four of the safest ten Conservative seats won at this election were situated in the north of England: Hyth, Staffordshire Burton and Westmorland, and a further seat on the northern side of the dividing line (Birmingham Mosely). Three of the safest Liberal seats – Bristol North, South and Devonshire Tiverton (following what was one of the worst-ever elections for them) – were held in the South. Again only Labour had all of its safest ten seats on one side of the divide: the North. However, looking in more detail at the votes it is apparent that two of the three highest

Labour opposition votes to the Liberals' best performances were in the south of the country. Similarly the share of the vote for Labour when it stood against the Conservatives in their strongest seats in 1924 was not that different between the southern and the northern constituencies.

The general election of 1935

Three of the top four safest Conservative seats were held in the north of England after the 1935 election was fought (Newcastle North, Yorkshire West Riding and Yorkshire North Riding – Ripon). Seven of the top ten Liberal seats were now in the South. And, again, Labour was the only party to hold it its safest seats on the north side of the line. The Labour vote opposing the Conservatives was higher in both Reigate and Richmond in Surrey than it was in all the seats in Yorkshire and Newcastle where the Conservatives did so well. However, where Labour was winning seats (almost all in the North) it was now doing so with increasingly huge majorities. The North–South divide was becoming apparent in voting – but only clearly in the voting for the party which represented those who were not to hold power for the subsequent ten years.

The general election of 1945

Half of the Conservative's safest ten seats following their huge defeat in 1945 were held in the north of England (admittedly not any of the safest five). Four of the Liberal's safest seats were held in the South, as they became a party of enclaves rather than areas. And still Labour's strongholds remained all in the North. However, at this election we also begin to see a regional divide in Labour's opposition. In three of the northern seats where the Conservatives still did well, Labour gained a third of the votes whereas they gained less than a quarter in the five southern Conservative strongholds. The North–South divide in voting could be seen to be settling in, but a decade and a half after the stark socioeconomic difference depicted in Tables 3.1 to 3.3, and the Labour vote in the North was only 4 per cent higher than that in England and Wales overall in 1945.

The general election of 1951

As the Conservatives regained power they still held half of their safest ten seats in the North (South Flyde, Knutsford, Sheffield Hallam, Ripon and Crosby). However, by 1951 only one of the Liberals' top ten seats was in the South (Dorset North). Labour completed their unbroken record of all their safest seats being north of the dividing line. It would be a few decades yet for the whole of the North to largely reject the Conservative Party. Locally, by 1951, it was still seen to be in the interest of people to vote by their area more than by their region.

Concluding comments

Analysis of the 1951 census provides the most compelling evidence that the North–South divide closed rapidly between the late 1930s and late 1940s. For example, unemployment fell dramatically and the distribution of people working in different occupations became a little more even. To me, however, the most compelling evidence is to be found in the stark reduction in inequalities in health when the late 1930s are compared to the early 1950s (Dorling 1995: 164). However none of these sources were used at the time to show the divide shrinking. Instead it was evidence from one heavily surveyed northern town, York, which provided the most striking contemporary account and was taken at that time, rightly it would seem in hindsight, to apply to the nation as a whole. York was surveyed by Seebohm Rowntree in the late 1930s at which time he identified three key factors causing poverty in that city:

> Our inquiry showed that 31.1 per cent of the working-class population were in receipt of insufficient income to enable them to live in accordance with the above standard [of living], and so are classified as living under the poverty line; . . . Three-quarters of poverty is due to three causes: 28.6 per cent is due to unemployment, 32.8 per cent to the fact that workers in regular work are not receiving wages sufficiently high to enable them to live above the poverty line, and 14.7 per cent are in poverty on account of old age. (Rowntree 1941: 456–7)

In simple terms the great reduction in unemployment and the establishment of wage boards and better old age pensions after 1945 contributed significantly to solving the three primary causes of poverty that Rowntree identified. It is interesting, however, to look back at what else he said would be needed when writing as the Second World War started and to think to what degree the war itself helped achieve the infinitely harder task he saw: 'To raise the material standard of those in poverty may prove difficult, but to raise the mental and spiritual life of the whole nation to a markedly higher level will be an infinitely harder task, yet on its accomplishment depends the lasting greatness of the State' (Rowntree 1941: 477).

Regional and local planning also, of course, grew in strength during the late 1930s and became a real possibility with the advent of war and the infrastructure for planning that it created. However the precursors for planning were laid well before 1939 and their impetus was as much concern about the unwanted effects of sustained growth in the South East. It was not simply altruism that led those in power in London to introduce measures that mainly benefited the North. They did not wish to see mass migration from North to South continue:

> The immediate effect of the financial crisis of 1931 was to bring about a reverse for housing and planning schemes, and at one time to threaten a real return to pre-war conditions. In the long run, however, it produced a new set of concerns which strengthened the economic aspects of housing and town planning. Strong disparities in regional growth connected the outward spread of London not to sloppy social thinking, but to the depressed regions of the North. (Yelling 2000: 489)

In 1950, Rowntree repeated his survey of York. The results, although contested since, were remarkable. A tenfold reduction in poverty was found in this northern town. It is hard to fault the reasons that Rowntree cited then as being pivotal. But it is telling that it was a study of one place that led to much of the acceptance of the fall of the North–South divide at this time:

That the number of persons in poverty has fallen between 1936 and 1950 from 17,185 to 1,746 is obviously in itself a cause of great satisfaction. But even these figures do not fully represent the improvement that has taken place, for a study of the examples given above shows that even when persons were in poverty in 1950 their suffering was less acute than that of persons in a corresponding position in 1936. This qualitative improvement is of course due primarily to the welfare measures that have alleviated poverty even when they have not been able to cure it. (Rowntree and Lavers 1951: 66)

Contemporary thinking during the 1930, 1940s and 1950s was based on local studies or on much-delayed national findings. The majority of influential national reports were produced during the war and the lag between their findings and the data they used was remarkable. For instance the Barlow Report of 1940 reported on a situation some twenty years after the beginnings of the polarisation. During the 1920s regional experiences tended to polarise in terms of wage rates and unemployment levels. This was revealed in the Barlow Report on the distribution of industrial population which highlighted a distinction between the declining outer regions of industrial Britain, affected by structural and cyclical unemployment in export-orientated staple industries, and the more prosperous regions (Reeder and Rodger 2000). The North–South divide narrowed rapidly. It was generally only after it had narrowed that the extent of the divide was well noted. In some ways it took the divide to open up again in the 1980s for its previous widening to be fully acknowledged. The story of the North–South divide in the 1920s and 1930s is as much, if not more, a story of what came to be fully realised some fifty years later. It was happening on the ground then – but not in the general consciousness. This is evident both in what was written at the time and in the politics of the time, which, save for the regional rise of the Labour Party, did not reflect well the regional socioeconomic polarisation of those times. The heyday of the North–South divide came long after the event itself.

What surprised me most in writing this essay was the apparently fruitless time I spent searching for contemporary commentaries on the divide. No doubt I would eventually have found useful extract after extract to point to contemporary observers noting aspects of the divide occurring at the time. The reports of medical officers for instance, or the speeches of particularly astute politicians. However, apart from this being a very partial picture, such a portrayal would have missed what most importantly was not generally being said and written about regional disparities in England at that time.

Instead, from work in libraries, I gained a very different picture of the 1920s and 1930s from that which I had expected of this period. I read numerous publications about the growing need to protect rural England and many books were published celebrating the different regional traditions of England but making no reference to geographical disparities. Much of what I read bordered on fascism. Eugenics was, of course, in vogue and where this reared its head in the writings of these times the concern was with immigration and/or the lower classes and their reproduction – but never with geographical differences. Because of the lack of comment on geographical divides I moved on to the next book or paper in my list, making no note of the last, in a search for people at the time who recognised what the statistics I had uncovered had in their turn revealed to me. Much that was written about England in the 1920s and 1930s simply did not show an awareness of regional disparities.

What this suggests to me is that, to a large extent, we both as individuals and as society at large tend to find what we are looking for and what we are used to seeing. I am used to seeing regional divides and so I find them when presented with data from the 1920s and 1930s. I find the divide to be staggering because it is greater and more clear-cut than divides that I am used to measuring. I am not too surprised to find it because much of what I have read was written in the 1980s and 1990s and talked about the divides of the 1920s and 1930s. It is only when I look back at some of what was written then, or at how people tended to express their political desires through their votes, that these divides are less apparent. In many ways it is the legacies of the sharp North–South divide that have led to its securing its place in history folklore. Its legacy is clearly seen in the political party that grew up in its wake and came to be the main contender for power against the Conservatives in the latter half of the twentieth century. Yet that political party's votes were most regionally polarised generations later. Its legacy is seen in the deaths of people from heart disease a lifetime after similar patterns were seen in the deaths of infants who never had the time to develop heart disease. Its legacy is seen in continued reliance on manufacturing two generations after its decimation. We would, perhaps, not be talking or writing about the North–South divide of the interwar years had its legacy not been so important.

At the start of this essay I said I would consider the implications of these observations for contemporary work on regional disparities in England. What is happening today that we are not commenting upon because other issues appear to be more important or because they do not fit into our traditional concerns? We are certainly talking about a North–South divide now, but we have been taught to spot that and almost to expect it. However, most current social research concerns the poor and how they are geographically located. When the numbers of people claiming various types of unemployment benefit decline in the North we think the divide may be falling. Other than in measuring trends in house prices we still do not tend to look at the changing fortunes of the rich. Were we to do that today I suspect we might find the North–South divide as strong as ever. We also tend to continue to rank areas at one point in time, rather than to look at trends over time between places – particularly over long time periods. If we were to project forward the changes seen in different places over the last thirty years, rather than be too concerned with the impacts of, say, the latest budget, I think we would again find a strengthening North–South divide.

Overall living standards would have to become a great deal worse in England if social divisions between places were to reach the levels they attained in the 1930s. Perhaps the most important lesson that can be learnt from this brief retrospective is that divisions deepened when they were not being watched. For regional divides to grow to unprecedented proportions required an indifference to the geographical divisions between the life chances of people living in different areas that is difficult to comprehend today. It can be found, but in the United States rather than in Britain. If you want to see one arguable legacy of the divide click on the Labour Party's website. Unless the site changes greatly in the next few years, or unless there is a major economic recession, you will find a button entitled 'what have Labour done in my area?' Click that button and you will be presented with at least three dozen statistics relating to life in your parliamentary constituency. An enduring legacy of the 1918–51 period (and its reversal 1951–71) may be that large parts of the country will not be abandoned so blindly again with the effects of that abandonment being recognised so late. But then again, it is easy to alter a website.

4

Industry and identity: the North–South divide and the geography of belonging, 1830–1918

PHILIP HOWELL

At the beginning of the twentieth century the world's first industrial nation had achieved an unprecedented level of economic development, its economy wealthier and more powerful than ever, its people more populous and prosperous. Britain's workshops, forges and factories still accounted for a quarter of the world's manufacturing output. The country retained its pre-eminent commercial position as the universal merchant to the world. And it had extended its role at the heart of the global financial system, becoming not only the world's biggest trading nation but also its biggest lender. More trade was invoiced in sterling than in any other currency, and, perhaps most remarkably of all, British citizens owned more overseas assets than their counterparts in all the other developed economies combined. On the eve of the Great War, the British people were three or four times more productive than they had been at Victoria's accession to the throne. They were living longer, living better – again, on average, three times better – and evidently made the most of their greatly augmented earnings in a fully developed mass consumer society (Floud 1997).

Generations of scholars have nevertheless come to view the central problem of modern British history as one of economic *failure* (Supple 1994; Tomlinson 1996). 'The principal question concerning the history of the British economy must . . . be why the rate of growth has always been so slow, performance so consistently mediocre' (Lee 1986: 271). Victorian and Edwardian contemporaries had already expressed their doubts, noting the inexorable rise of economic and political rivals. But their anxious assessments pale beside historical hindsight's identification of the late-Victorian period as one of signal and salutary decline (Levine 1967; Elbaum and Lazonick 1986; Pollard 1989, 2000a). It is the economic catastrophe and subsequent poor performance of the British economy between the two world wars which forms the necessary and immediate prompting for all such discussions, but the roots and significance of this economic decline have been extended often far back into the nineteenth century, so much so indeed as to qualify the achievements of the entire Victorian period.

Reconciling the seemingly incontrovertible fact of unprecedented prosperity with that of economic decline and endemic failure remains a vexing problem. The periodisation of success and failure is particularly contentious, lacking even the identification of a clear economic climacteric. It is worthwhile considering, as a complement rather than as an alternative to this concern with temporality, the role of geographical differentiation in British economic, social and political development as a force in its own right. Economic prosperity was always very unevenly shared, and it is a striking fact that the *range* of incomes hardly altered throughout the period 1830–1918: the rich and the poor remained, in Disraeli's famous phrase, 'two nations' (Disraeli 1845). But generations have followed Disraeli's lead in attaching particular significance to the divide between the industrial modernity of the 'North' and the rural tranquillity and tradition of the 'South', with Mrs Gaskell's classic treatment mapping the legacy of incomprehension between the 'two nations' quite decisively onto a symbolic geography of 'North and South' (Gaskell 1855). The 'North–South divide' thus became a central social postulate of the age, a convenient and conventional shorthand for representing the underlying tensions in Victorian England (Pocock 1978; Dellheim 1986, 1987; Goetsch 1996).

This essay examines the North–South divide in the 'long' Victorian period, after the achievements of the first 'industrial revolution', but before the acknowledged era of British industrial crisis after the Great War. The regional encapsulation of the ambiguities of the modern British experience seems entirely appropriate, of course: nothing represents better the legacy of early industrialisation than the northern manufacturing districts and the great factory towns, whilst the era of British economic decline is best memorialised in the twentieth-century fortunes of the 'Depressed Areas'. Emphasis on the rise and fall of the industrial North runs counter, however, to reassessments of the nature and significance of industrialisation and the 'industrial revolution'. Identifying the North–South divide with an industrially conferred regional prosperity, and its subsequent reversal in the twentieth century, is both easy and wrong. Another difficulty, though, readily in evidence in the revisionist historiography, is the danger of reading present-day patterns and concerns back into the Victorian age. Taking the modern contours of the North–South divide as more or less permanent features is no less damaging and misleading than overemphasising the industrial regions, and this chapter cautions against any ahistorical emphasis on the continuity of regional patterns and relations. Questions of culture and representation, finally, are hardly exhausted by reference to the novelists' imagined geographies of North and South. The complexity of regional cultural formations and their relationship to national identities is acknowledged in the concluding section of this chapter. Given the general movement here from a discussion of economic and material issues to one that ultimately deals with representations as social facts, I hope that the decision to take my cue from Victorian rhetorical conventions and concentrate exclusively on the condition of *England* will appear less arbitrary as this chapter progresses.

The 'Industrial North' in history and historiography

Any discussion of the Victorian North–South divide must be positioned in relation to two neighbouring debates that are situated at the beginning and end of our period, one defined by a distinct economic climacteric, the other more ambiguous in its temporal markers. On the one hand is the discussion of Britain's industrial and economic decline *after* 1914, a discussion that characteristically emphasises the over-commitment to the export trade and the failures of the so-called staple industries that were disproportionately located in the north of England. Their 'obsoleteness as an industrial system' (Barnett 1986: 259–60) exemplifies the problems of the British economy as a whole, bearing responsibility for the mass unemployment and social deprivation that would be passed on to posterity as the 'regional problem'. This view of industrial decline underpinning wholesale economic failure necessarily depends on a portrayal of British industrial success and prosperity up to, in convention, at least the 1870s. It is a view that underscores the contribution of the 'industrial revolution', understood as essentially complete *before* 1830, to the economic prosperity of the early Victorian years. On the other hand, we can take stock of the various strands of econometric research that have downplayed the discontinuity represented by early industrialisation in favour of a longer-drawn-out transformation whose rates of economic growth are substantially below contemporary experiences and expectations (Crafts 1985, 1994). This emphasis on gradualism – the relatively slow progress of development as measured by macro-economic indicators – has laid the foundations for a full-blown historical revisionism which has tended to stress continuity over discontinuity, and also, rather more tendentiously, a traditionalism and conservatism that has all but removed revolutionary energies from the social, political and cultural history of modern Britain (Mayer 1981; Clark 1985).

Though the substance and ramifications of these debates need not detain us unduly, it should be noted that a central element of this revisionist approach is the argument that the contribution of industrial manufacturing, and the leading sectors like cotton, has been systematically overestimated. It is not just the 'revolution' that has been questioned, therefore, but also the 'industrial'. As Clive Lee has commented: 'the low rate of growth of the British economy before 1914 and the modest and faltering contribution of manufacturing to that growth is witness to the weakness and fragility of industrialization in the first industrial nation' (Lee 1986: 106). From a purely economic perspective, services, finance and overseas investments have been rightly recognised as key contributors to Britain's economic performance. But if we downplay industrialism, of course, the relative significance of the northern manufacturing districts must also be reassessed; and the temptation must be to trace the North's seeming marginality *after* 1914 ever backwards in time. Just as some have been led, in a common rhetorical flourish, to deny the reality of any 'industrial revolution', so too has the once-assumed centrality of the industrial North to national life been replaced by a focus on London and the City, on the service-based South-East, and on the commercial and financial networks of the British Empire, all of which have been systematically reasserted in significance (Rubinstein 1977a, 1977b; Lee 1981; Cain and Hopkins 1993).

These two broad historiographical positions, however crudely I have sketched them here, are plainly irreconcilable. It is not possible to assert that the 'industrial revolution' never happened whilst maintaining that the prosperity it conferred has been betrayed by the subsequent decades of industrial decline. Any attempt to have one's cake and eat it, by asserting a waning of industrial self-confidence and the rise, from the mid-Victorian era, of a markedly anti-industrial culture that fed the subsequent British economic malaise, is notably unconvincing both in method and substance (Weiner 1981; Raven 1989). As W. D. Rubinstein (1993: 24) has put it, there is no need for a specific 'cultural' explanation of industrial and therefore economic failure if Britain was *never* fundamentally an industrial and manufacturing economy in the first place. For a commentator like Rubinstein, indeed, there is no need to invoke British economic 'decline' at all, in so far as developments in the late-nineteenth and early-twentieth centuries mark merely the working out of a process by which Britain's long-term comparative advantage in commerce and finance reached a decisive settlement. However extreme this view – and it does not command general assent – the importance of industrial manufacturing to the British economy clearly needs to be put in its proper perspective. Until about 1860, manufacturing was certainly rising in importance at a disproportionate rate, but there was, over the period under consideration here, remarkably little change in its contribution to the economy as a whole; the main difference in working life lay rather in the rapid decline in the agricultural sector and a corresponding rise in the proportion of labourers in retailing, banking, transport and the other service industries (Tables 4.1 and 4.2). In aggregate terms, the service sector was clearly the greatest beneficiary, accounting for three-quarters of the total increase in employment in the century after 1851; the average employee in services was, moreover, more productive than his or her counterpart in manufacturing, by a factor of two or even three (Lee 1994: 122). Such figures suggest a real continuity between the mid-nineteenth and early twenty-first centuries, and the early emergence of Britain's role as a post-industrial nation.

It might seem, at first glance, as if the very basis of our conventional understanding of a North–South divide is comprehensively challenged by these revisions, dependent as it has been upon the asserted impact of 'industrial revolution' in the North. We cannot, certainly, uncritically accept assumptions about northern industrial prosperity before the First World War, and its replacement by the endemic problems of the 1920s and 1930s and later. Some have unwisely inferred that there was no identifiable 'regional problem' before the symptoms of industrial decline became apparent in the early-twentieth century and that the North was in this era more prosperous than the South, with the economic climacteric of the Edwardian era marking therefore a complete reversal of fortunes between a previously advanced and prosperous North and a backward South. According to Eric Jones,

Table 4.1 *Regional employment structure, 1841–1911*

	Percentage of the total employed population							
	1841	1851	1861	1871	1881	1891	1901	1911
South-East								
Agriculture	21.7	19.8	16.3	13.7	10.8	9.6	6.7	6.3
Mining, manufacturing, construction	32.9	35.9	36.5	35.8	36.4	35.4	38.2	36.6
Services, transport, government	45.4	44.4	47.2	50.6	52.8	55.0	55.2	57.1
East Anglia								
Agriculture	43.4	44.3	42.2	38.0	35.2	33.4	28.7	28.6
Mining, manufacturing, construction	24.6	27.4	27.3	27.6	27.9	27.0	30.4	28.1
Services, transport, government	31.9	28.2	30.5	34.4	36.8	39.6	41.0	43.3
South-West								
Agriculture	31.0	32.4	27.7	24.3	22.6	19.8	16.7	16.0
Mining, manufacturing, construction	34.9	37.6	37.9	36.7	36.0	35.3	37.6	35.6
Services, transport, government	34.1	30.0	34.4	39.1	41.4	44.9	45.7	48.4
West Midlands								
Agriculture	23.9	20.6	18.0	14.6	12.6	10.9	8.3	7.8
Mining, manufacturing, construction	48.1	53.1	54.5	55.1	54.9	54.9	58.2	58.3
Services, transport, government	28.0	26.3	27.5	30.3	32.5	34.2	33.5	33.9
East Midlands								
Agriculture	31.9	29.3	28.0	23.4	19.5	16.6	13.0	12.0
Mining, manufacturing, construction	39.4	46.7	46.2	47.5	49.8	51.0	54.6	55.2
Services, transport, government	28.8	24.0	25.9	29.1	30.8	32.4	32.4	32.9
North-West								
Agriculture	10.1	9.5	8.3	6.4	5.0	4.6	3.6	3.2
Mining, manufacturing, construction	64.6	63.8	65.1	63.0	63.0	62.0	61.9	61.7
Services, transport, government	25.3	26.7	26.6	30.6	32.0	33.5	34.5	35.1
Lancashire and Humberside								
Agriculture	16.2	14.1	12.7	9.5	8.2	6.7	5.4	4.8
Mining, manufacturing construction	60.3	64.8	64.2	64.8	64.3	64.1	63.4	63.2
Services, transport, government	23.6	21.1	23.3	25.7	27.6	29.3	31.2	32.0
North								
Agriculture	25.4	25.9	21.0	15.6	13.1	10.9	8.6	7.8
Mining, manufacturing, construction	43.2	45.9	48.3	52.4	52.8	53.3	57.0	57.3
Services, transport, government	31.4	28.2	30.7	31.9	34.1	35.8	34.4	34.9

Source: Lee (1979)

Table 4.2 *Regional employment structure, 1841–1911*

	Per 10,000 people							
Agriculture	*1841*	*1851*	*1861*	*1871*	*1881*	*1891*	*1901*	*1911*
South-East	714	828	695	531	416	371	266	261
East Anglia	1349	1781	1772	1525	1381	1337	1146	1188
South-West	1002	1379	1204	995	889	782	664	666
West Midlands	817	892	439	598	482	427	340	328
East Midlands	1095	1304	1258	1001	778	682	544	516
North-West	376	440	391	291	213	197	156	145
Yorkshire and Humberside	549	641	566	418	333	284	228	211
North	830	1028	827	594	461	394	319	292
Mining, manufacturing, construction								
	1841	*1851*	*1861*	*1871*	*1881*	*1891*	*1901*	*1911*
South-East	1084	1500	1562	1392	1407	1372	1526	1514
East Anglia	765	1102	1147	1106	1095	1080	1214	1164
South-West	1129	1596	1647	1501	1416	1393	1497	1481
West Midlands	1641	2301	2349	2252	2105	2159	2384	2463
East Midlands	1352	2080	2076	2029	1989	2099	2286	2374
North-West	2398	2957	3076	2857	2661	2664	2702	2792
Yorkshire and Humberside	2041	2958	2895	2864	2620	2723	2695	2175
North	1414	1821	1900	1990	1861	1924	2121	2157
Services, transport, government								
	1841	*1851*	*1861*	*1871*	*1881*	*1891*	*1901*	*1911*
South-East	1498	1861	2018	1967	2042	2133	2204	2365
East Anglia	992	1134	1280	1382	1442	1581	1639	1797
South-West	1104	1276	1494	1600	1631	1774	1817	2011
West Midlands	955	1137	1187	1239	1247	1346	1372	1430
East Midlands	988	1066	1163	1245	1231	1334	1359	1414
North-West	940	1237	1259	1389	1351	1438	1506	1589
Yorkshire and Humberside	798	965	1049	1135	1124	1243	1326	1404
North	1027	1116	1205	1212	1200	1290	1280	1314

Source: Lee (1979)

for example, the 'North–South problem' emerged as a result of the divergence of regional fortunes attendant upon the shift of the centres of industrial activity from the south and east of England to the north and north-west (quoted in Lee 1986: 126). Evidence for wages, employment and standards of living are, however, no better than suggestive in this regard. As far as wages are concerned, virtually all the evidence, broadly consistent with growth pole theory, does indeed indicate a clear advantage for the northern, manufacturing districts and their employees in the staple industries, whilst the South-East outside London and its immediate environs was marked by distinctly low, predominantly agricultural, wages (Hunt 1973, 1986a, 1986b; Snell 1981; Botham and Hunt 1987). There is evidence, too, that after 1914 unemployment was substantially higher in the north and west than in the south and east, at a time when wages were somewhat lower in the former areas (Hatton 1994: 364). The wages map of pre-industrial Britain, as Hunt (1986b: 937) notes, thus had a great deal in common with the pattern that prevailed after the 1920s, with the South relatively prosperous, the North relatively poor. This would all seem to confirm the contrast before 1914 between the backward rural counties of the South and the prosperous manufacturing North which Macaulay, writing in 1830, installed as a seemingly well-established theme in the national story, an assessment remarkable both for its prescience and for its delineation of received wisdom on the eve of Victoria's reign:

If we were to prophesy that in the year 1930 a population of fifty million, better fed, clad, and lodged than the English of our time, will cover these islands, that Sussex and Huntingdonshire will be wealthier than the wealthiest parts of the West Riding of Yorkshire now are, . . . that machines constructed on principles yet undiscovered will be in every house, . . . many people would think us insane. (Macaulay 1830, quoted in McCloskey 1994: 243)

Building up a pattern of general northern prosperity and southern retardation, subsequently reversed at or around 1914, cannot be justified quite so easily, however. High wages in the industrial North are simply no guide to the robustness of the provincial economies. The ephemeral nature of working-class prosperity, and the continuation of deprivation in the North, is easily attested, for instance (Rowe 1990; Walton 1990). The North and the Midlands were demonstrably more prone to the trade cycle and therefore to unemployment, so that '[I]f stability of employment is taken into account, it can be argued that the most important contrast emerging before the end of the nineteenth century was that between the industrial North . . . and a broadly defined southern region, especially outside London, whose superiority in terms of higher levels of employment was structural in nature' (Reeder and Rodger 2000: 563). The most intensive regional investigation of unemployment records confirms this judgement, demonstrating markedly high unemployment in the northern industrial areas well before the Great War: Humphrey Southall has shown that mass unemployment was not an invention of the post-1918 period, at least for certain key unionised sectors, and cautions against associating mass unemployment with a decaying industrial base (Southall 1986, 1988a; Gilbert and Southall 2000). More importantly still, work on regional *incomes* clearly confirms the relative affluence of the South-East throughout this period, with an enormous gap existing between the Home Counties and the rest of Britain: London and Middlesex alone accounted for nearly 40 per cent of national income in 1812 and close to 50 per cent a century later (Lee 1986: 130–1). For England alone, Rubinstein's well-known work on probate inventories and taxable incomes uses a geographical shorthand – London and the Home Counties for the commercial and financial middle classes of the South, Lancashire and Yorkshire for their industrial and manufacturing counterparts in the North – to establish this marked division in the Victorian geography of wealth (Rubinstein 1977a, 1977b, 1981, 1993). He determines that the northern middle classes at no time established a lead over the former, and actually declined from the 1850s until they accounted for, immediately before the Great War, not even 20 per cent of the national total. Though by no means incontestable, these findings clearly indicate that the industrial districts fared very poorly in their share of incomes, whilst the South-East's relative and continuing affluence owed little to industrial manufacturing. The role of industrialisation in establishing northern prosperity, at the expense of the backward South, must be severely qualified by a recognition of the very limited and partial advantage conferred upon the North by industrialisation, and at the same time the continuing power and significance of London and the South-East. We should recognise not just the structural weakness in the northern economy – its dependence on a narrow range of industries and the seeming inability to convert the temporary prosperity it granted into a broad and diverse economic structure – but also such plain facts as that even in the heyday of the staple industries and the regions, a third of all new employment was created in Greater London, which was growing *faster*, in this period, than Lancashire.

There is much in these arguments to discredit the geographical implications of the conventional historiography of late-Victorian and Edwardian industrial decline. Any argument that ties the North–South divide to the 'industrial revolution', to the emergence of industrial prosperity in the North, and its subsequent reversal after 1914, is vulnerable to such revisions. In one of the most explicit statements, the economic geographer Ron Martin argues that the climacteric of 1914 makes little sense in terms of the geography of inequality, the 1920s and 1930s witnessing not a reversal of the geography of poverty and prosperity but the intensification of a long-established imbalance between the northern 'industrial periphery' and southern and south-eastern England. As Martin goes on to argue, 'The relatively advantageous position of the South East economy and the inherent weakness and instability of the industrial "north" were . . . established features of the British space economy well before the inter-war period' (Martin 1988: 393–4).

We should not jump too quickly, however, to consider the notion of a Victorian North–South divide as moribund. There are three issues here. For one thing, the case for gradualism that underpins the various strands of revisionism has been based on aggregate statistics and macroeconomic trends that may be fundamentally inappropriate to an economy that was largely regionally rather than nationally integrated (Hoppit 1990; Berg and Hudson 1992). A 'regional perspective' (Hudson 1989, 1992) on the age of industrialisation certainly qualifies the revisionist case and allows us to reinstate the experience of industrial transformation on a local and regional scale. The appearance of internally integrated and sectorally specialised regions was a clear departure from preceding regional formations, and there is abundant evidence to indicate that there was no fundamental realignment in this pattern until the end of the nineteenth century (Langton 1984). Though there were important countervailing developments, the regional scale remained crucial for, *inter alia*, the labour process, labour markets, wage bargaining and wage differentials, unemployment, migration, employer organisations, capital markets and industrial credit. Greater consideration of geographical differentiation than cliometricians have usually been willing to grant leads us at least to qualify the most extreme emphases on gradualism, continuity and the survival of a British *ancien régime*. The 'industrial revolution' may remain contentious but the dynamism of the early industrial economy should not be too quickly dismissed. Indeed, the original econometric revisions affirmed that there had been a major transformation in the structure of the economy: British industrialisation simply combined rapid and sustained structural change with slow growth (Daunton 1995: 125–45). There certainly should be no real difficulty in tracing the emergence of a distinctive and dynamic 'industrial' society in the manufacturing districts of the North, even if its aggregate contribution is debated.

Secondly, the category 'industrial' is more of a hindrance than a help in understanding the nature of the Victorian economy. It is more advisable to speak of a regionalised 'economy of manufactures' than of an *industrial* economy we would now recognise (Price 1999: 17–51). This is quite impossible to characterise as a modern and homogenous industrial system, allowing as it did for a series of different *paths* to industrialisation whose full implications were not realised for many decades. Rather than insisting on industrialisation as a radical and singular discontinuity, only in order to downplay its significance, an emphasis on the differentiated regional, sectoral and chronological patterns allows us better to balance the claims of continuity and discontinuity. There is space here for perhaps just one example, but we can see in the history and geography of the gender division of labour, elements of regional differentiation that contributed to the broader socio-spatial patterns in this way. Importantly, too, there is some worth in tracing a persistent differentiation between northern and southern 'industrial' patterns. We can trace, in the gendered process of proletarianisation, a particularly important contrast within the 'industrial' sector, between the manufacturing districts of the North and the artisanal cultures of London. Whereas the formation of gender cultures in the northern districts tended towards a culture of collaboration between the sexes, those of the southern artisans typically pitted men against women in the struggle for jobs, wages, status and working conditions (Clark 1995). In Lancashire, a patriarchal, family-based economy, with female and child labour an indispensable part of the productive unit, generally muted gender antagonism, its members knitted together by neighbourhood and community-based networks of mutuality and solidarity. Urban artisans in London, by contrast, sought to keep their families out of their trades, by enforcing strict apprenticeship and journeymen distinctions, and by policing a fraternal, and often thoroughly misogynistic, bachelor culture centred around the workshop and the alehouse. These broad distinctions were formed in the early-nineteenth century, but there is abundant evidence to suggest that these strategies in the gendered division of labour continued to shape the patterns of provincial and metropolitan industrialisation down to the end of the nineteenth century and the decisive separation between provincial factories and metropolitan sweatshops (Berg 1985). One recent example of this divide comes from the co-operative movement, where northern traditions of mutuality between the sexes were translated into an emphasis on women's subordinate domesticity, in marked contrast to southern patterns (Blaszac 2000). The reworking and renegotiation of gender and class was thus critically dependent on regionalised experiences and cultural formations that are at least broadly equitable to a divide between North and South, none of which is captured by the category of 'industrial'.

Finally, and most importantly, the existence of complex alignments between these spatially disaggregated regional economies and their priorities tends to reinforce rather than reduce the perception of a divide between North and South. As the evidence for wealth, incomes and inequality suggests, it is the continuing economic strength of London and the South-East and the region's persistent advantage over the North which is most apparent. This version of a North–South divide, uncoupled from a misleading emphasis on industrial hegemony, is established as arguably the critical feature of the Victorian economy and society. Effectively, the North–South divide is removed in terms of a later *discontinuity* established by industrial failure and the reversal of fortunes that had prevailed since the 'industrial revolution', only to be reinstalled as a more or less *continuous* separation between economic sectors, social constituencies and structures of authority. Reinstating the importance of service occupations, for instance, positions the South and East in a position of unassailable importance, a pre-eminence which increased after the Great War but which was clearly prefigured in the dominance the region exerted throughout the preceding century (Tables 4.1 and 4.2). The massive growth in demand for services fundamentally advantaged London and the towns within its orbit (Lee 1981, 1984, 1994; Garside 1990), and more than compensated for the precipitate decline in agricultural employment. A historian of the service industries notes quite conclusively: 'we should interpret Victorian Britain in terms of the South East being the most advanced region in the British economy, and making a commensurate contribution to the development of that national economy' (Lee 1981: 452).

These strands of the revisionist argument thus develop the thesis of a North–South divide to an extreme hitherto unimagined by those who posited merely a reversal of fortunes either side of 1914. The result is a North–South divide installed as a more or less permanent feature of the national story, with industry and the North subordinate, throughout the period, to the financial and commercial sectors dominated by the South. Rubinstein (1993: 37) is characteristically emphatic: 'What is perhaps most striking about the continuing and chronic gap between the prosperous South and the impoverished North is that, *despite* the best efforts of most modern British governments, the geographical divide continues to appear and reappear with the regularity of clockwork.' In theoretical terms, too, capitalism and its constituencies are understood as both structurally and geographically divided, the interests of a commercial and financial class fraction, centred in the South, pitted against that of the industrial and manufacturing heartlands (Ingham 1984). In this tale of two capitalisms, a 'gentlemanly capitalism' (Daunton 1989; Cain and Hopkins 1993; Dummett 1999) kept the industrial sector demonstrably subordinate up to and beyond the latter's formal eclipse immediately after the Great War.

Whilst there is much to commend in this thesis of a geographically differentiated British capitalism, the premise of a continuous, more or less permanent, perhaps even *essential* North–South divide remains dangerously ahistorical and ill-suited to tracing changes in the *relationality* of North and South, centre and margins, core and periphery. Discarding the thesis of a reversal of regional fortunes and accepting the long-term continuity of southern affluence and prosperity does not mean that the relations between North and South have remained unchanged, nor indeed that they were always antagonistic and dysfunctional in the way that many commentators charge. The temptation to equate geographical differentiation, economic dualism and capitalist dysfunctionality is a strong one, but it ought to be subjected to a degree of scepticism. Most importantly, perhaps, the portrayal of a necessary and entrenched competition between the claims of (northern) industry and those of (southern) commerce or finance barely holds up to either theoretical or substantive scrutiny. It is perfectly possible to understand these capitalist sectors, and their geographical locations, as separated, but the question of dysfunctionality is left begging, as Richard Price (1999: 51) observes in his argument for the continuities of English development over the period 1688–1880:

It is undeniably true that each of these sectors historically tended to have differing visions of the ideal political economy for Britain. Manufacturers favoured protectionism and the domestic market. Commercial merchants and financiers gradually came to favour free trade and the foreign market. Yet it is neither helpful nor necessary to designate either of these options of industry or commerce as the dominating hub of the British economy in this period.

In a wide-ranging critique of the revisionist arguments, Simon Gunn (1988) has likewise pertinently observed that the distinction between 'industrial' and 'commercial' Britain is profoundly unsatisfactory, particularly the supposedly categorical difference between the 'industrial' North and the 'commercial' South – which is of course a crude caricature difficult to reconcile with the cosmopolitan reality of, say, mid-Victorian Manchester or Leeds. In his survey of the available evidence Gunn foregrounds the integrative rather than the divisive trends within the nineteenth-century middle class. Northern 'industrial' and Southern 'commercial' interests could, in the 'economy of manufactures', coincide and harmonise, with little sign of antagonism. There is no need to separate commerce or industry as mutually incompatible forces, and to treat the segregation between finance and industrial capital as 'an endemic reflex of British capitalism' (Price 1999: 54).

What evidence there is suggests that the separation of interests between commerce and industry was a construction of the *late*-nineteenth century, no earlier, and belonging to the age of urbanised, heavy industry, rather than to the age of manufactures. In this sense, the North–South divide is a product of the later period, if by this phrase we mean the systematic marginalisation of the industrial districts and their relative and absolute *decline* when compared with the South. Through much of the period under review here the economy of manufactures was little more than a collection of regional economies, a pattern inherited from the seventeenth century and in crucial ways little altered; by the end of the nineteenth century, however, the new spatial arrangement of the economy signalled the transition to a modern industrial economy. Defined in terms of the application of heavy machinery and scientific techniques, the large-scale factory as the necessary location of work, and the development of bureaucratic, hierarchical management, the industrial economy for the first time truly integrated specialised regions at a national scale (Price 1999: 46). This might be thought of as the beginning, so to speak, of a regional *system* rather than a regional pattern – and it is arguably only at this time that something like a systematic North–South divide was installed, one that would work to further the interests of the South over the North.

It is worth cementing this point by considering the question of banking and the role of finance in the funding of manufacturing enterprise, one of the cornerstones of the argument for economic mismanagement and industrial decline, and typically also cited, albeit inconsistently, in the divided capitalism thesis (Cottrell 1980; Kennedy 1987; Collins 1991). The City of London, notoriously, played only the smallest part in industrial finance, which was left instead largely to the regions and localities, and to the system of country banks that had been established in the eighteenth century. The extension in 1826 of note-issuing rights beyond the Bank of England stimulated the creation of branch networks and the geographical coordination of savings and investment through the discounting of local bills in the metropolitan market, though banking remained fragmented and essentially regionally autonomous. There is much to suggest, however, that this was an era of largely functional integration, not competition, between finance and industry, with few difficulties faced by industrial entrepreneurs and a relatively successful channelling of investment to available opportunities by the system of discounting which coordinated domestic financial arrangements: Iain Black (1989) has demonstrated the early emergence of this 'national distributive mechanism for credit' (Cottrell 1980: 16). The system of provincial banking meant that the City was free to assume its position as financial market to the world, promoting capital export and coordinating the flows of investment income, but there was no reason for this to be necessarily detrimental to the home market. What counts therefore is not the existence of two fractions of capital nor their geographical separation, but the degree of complementarity between them. In the earlier period, the needs of financial and industrial interests seem to have been more or less ably met in this relatively autonomous arrangement (e.g. Hudson 1986). From the 1870s, though, and the bank failures of that decade, provincial autonomy was rapidly dismantled, local banks (still numbering nearly 400 in 1870) consolidated into national chains headquartered in the capital. The capital and credit markets moved from particular regions or industries to a national capital market at the end of the century – and it was only then that the tie between industry and finance at the local level was broken. Increasingly centralised and bureaucratic, at exactly the time that the 'second industrial revolution' required a steady supply of investment capital, the financial system arguably failed to deliver. The whole question remains inconclusive, for sure, but in so far as it failed to provide such capital, and to allow financial and industrial interests to develop separately, this pivotal shift towards finance and the metropolitan economy appears to have decisively widened the persistent divide between the North and the South.

The North and South in political space

The national economy is, however, also a 'political space', subject to the discipline of state-sponsored forces of national 'integration' (Gregory 1987: 150). And since arguments about the proper role of the Victorian state were debated primarily in terms of centre and locality (Hoppen 1998: 105), regional economic experiences were inescapably conjoined with questions of authority and autonomy, integration and differentiation (Robbins 1988). The emphasis on the discontinuity represented by industrialisation has been, for instance, closely associated with the argument for regional *differentiation* and the rise of a distinctive and powerful industrial society in the North, in a period of relative political autonomy before the forces of national integration asserted themselves later in the nineteenth century. The most purposeful of these arguments have pointed to the role of the resource-based endowments of the industrial regions, and the multiplier effects generated by these incipient growth poles in differentiating the industrial provinces, generating regional identities and securing a powerful political presence as a counterweight to the metropolitan core (Langton 1984; Turnbull 1987; Wrigley 1988; Lawton and Pooley 1992).

It is probably the provincial urban transformations that are the most clearly outlined and the least contentious. The comprehensive overturning of the urban hierarchy of 'pre-industrial' England had been accomplished by 1830, the early decades of the nineteenth century being the period of most rapid growth (Corfield 1982). At the beginning of our period half of the provincial centres of population, with over 10,000 inhabitants each, were already to be found in the English North-West and in Yorkshire. With the signal exception of London, though, the largest cities and conurbations continued to be disproportionately located in the industrial North and Midlands; by way of contrast, it was only after 1900 that the South-East developed a corresponding array of medium-sized towns surrounding the capital. Urban growth rates in the established industrial regions may have peaked in the 1840s, but population growth was sustained by natural increase and immigration until at least the 1880s, and the industrial cities absorbed over 90 per cent of the country's natural growth in the period 1841–1911 (Lawton 1986, Reeder and Rodger 2000: 559). The agricultural counties lying to the south-east of a line between the Severn and the Wash (excluding London, Surrey and Middlesex) correspondingly declined from a proportion of 44 per cent of the population in 1801 to just 29 per cent in 1881, an imbalance that would be sustained well beyond the period under consideration here (Anderson 1990: 2). This pattern opened up *despite* the marked North–South divide in the geography of death, which was dreadfully emphatic in urban infant and maternal mortality, and which would not be closed until the 1870s or 1880s (Woods and Shelton 1997; Szreter and Mooney 1998; Szreter and Hardy 2000; Woods 2000).

There should be no doubting the scale of what had taken place in the nineteenth century. By 1918, the English had become incontrovertibly urban, even metropolitan, with over half of the population living in large towns and cities of over 100,000 people, the majority in the provinces and the North. The great factory towns, with their unprecedented specialisation in industrial structure, represented a particularly astonishing transformation that was no less remarkable for attracting the overheated attention of contemporary observers. Bradford may well be the best exemplar of the rapid growth and transformation engendered by such large-scale industrialisation, its population rising from a few thousand at the beginning of the nineteenth century to over 100,000 in 1850 and nearly 300,000 by 1911 (Elliott 1982; Firth 1990; Koditschek 1990). The experience of towns like Bradford, where industrial capitalism's triumph was more or less unconditional, is, as Koditschek has claimed, of epochal significance, however much revisionist historians may wish to play down industrialism at the national, aggregate scale. In the urban-industrial crucible, a distinctive culture was fomented and fostered, encompassing and embracing both working people and their social superiors in a collective project of stabilisation, improvement and political representation. The development of networks of mutuality and solidarity, the backbone of a vibrant proletarian culture, is evident, of course, but the Marxist model of class conflict has obscured the promotion of cross-class identities and identifications (Joyce 1980; Morris 2000: 406). Municipal improvement, civic pride, the culture of voluntarism and association, church and chapel: all allowed for the promotion of an urban order that was distinctively bourgeois but also inclusive, collective and corporate.

The provincial middle classes, so long portrayed as a 'failure' at a national scale, thus fared rather better at the level of the municipality and region (Gunn 1988; Nenadic 1991). It makes little sense, once again, to portray the provincial and northern bourgeoisie as somehow 'industrial' rather than 'commercial' in character; and Richard Trainor (2000: 677–91) has in any case indicated that the differential between the middle classes of London and the provincial towns was not so great as is sometimes alleged. But in the northern provinces, at least, the industrial bourgeoisie was fully able to express itself, as much in the civic gospel of urban improvement as in the rituals of cultural patronage. The provincial municipal elites promoted, for instance, albeit tardily, a public health crusade that by the early-twentieth century had brought the notoriously unhealthy industrial cities up to par with the relatively salubrious capital. At the same time they presided over the flourishing of a civil society and municipal culture that fully deserves the title of public sphere and which was self-consciously celebrated – for instance in the appropriation of the past and their commitment to the nineteenth century's various architectural revivals (Webb 1976; Dellheim 1982; Hardman 1986; Hartnell 1995; Macleod 1996). Ruskin's old charge of provincial middle-class philistinism – levelled at the announcement of the competition for the Bradford Wool Exchange in 1864 – simply failed to appreciate 'the claim to provincial identity and to national significance' (Daunton 2000: 43) that was embodied in stone in places like Bradford, the visible embodiments of an 'urban-industrial, bourgeois, civilization' (Green 1992: 231) whose power and significance would survive well into the twentieth century.

One of the great hallmarks of this northern, provincial civilization was its commitment to urban and regional political autonomy, to 'localism', broadly understood. The characteristic institutional forms of middle-class life 'ensured that nineteenth-century bourgeois civilization was never a purely local culture. But in their concrete, local, existence, they also ensured that it was never a merely national, homogeneous, undifferentiated, culture either' (Green 1992: 246). At least at the local level, provincial middle-class social, cultural and political authority was all but hegemonic. This localism, however, was not something that caused friction with central authority, for a belief in local responsibility for local needs was repeatedly sanctioned and almost sanctified by central government (Hennock 1982; Thane 1990; Davis 2000). The one false dawn of centralising reform, in the 1830s, quickly petered out in the face of trenchant criticism, its well-known proponents ideologically matched by the less celebrated likes of Joshua Toulmin Smith, who had a prominent influence in northern towns in the 1850s (Greenleaf 1975, 1987: 32–5). This provincial anti-centralisation was a recognisable programme and philosophy of government, and an effective stimulus to local initiative (Fraser 1982: 9). So much so that no serious attempts were made to challenge the accommodation reached between localism and centralism until at least the 1860s or 1870s, with the majority of social policy initiatives remarkable for the reassertion and reinvigoration of local authority. 'Centralisation' was not absent, to be sure, but in this context it amounted to little more than permissive legislation (which was no great departure from past practice), the theory and practice of government inspection (whose reach was notably limited and ineffective), and (rather more important for the future) the award of grants-in-aid. To take just one of these, we can note with John Prest (1990) the importance of permissive legislation in sustaining localism and the 'autonomous interest', and as an effective engine of improvement in northern towns like Huddersfield.

Disaggregation of North from South could thus develop with relatively little hindrance even from the first abortive wave of centralisation in the 1830s, precisely because of the robustness of the philosophy and practice of localism. The continuing endorsement of the structures of local authority and the promotion of municipal and regional autonomy authorised the political strength of the provincial towns: the age of manufactures was also an 'age of localism' (Price 1999: 183). It would be a mistake therefore to allow aggregate national critiques and their dismissal of industrial discontinuity to overshadow the strength of provincial England and its elites within the sphere of their local and regional hinterlands (Read 1964). To appreciate fully the nature of the North–South divide in Victorian England we need to acknowledge the integrity of this provincial culture, its rootedness in the urban and industrial experience and its relatively comfortable accommodation with central state authority (Gunn 1988: 38). The industrial North was as a result probably freer of London's influence than it had been at any time in the previous two centuries (Hudson 1992: 105).

It is not proposed here to do more than dip into the development of social policy, but it is worth taking the Poor Law as a critical index of the strength of localism, and, indeed, of the clear divide between North and South that necessitated and informed it. Given its ideological background in utilitarianism, its dismissal of traditional structures of authority and its installation of central control, the 1834 Poor Law ought logically to have been at the forefront of governmental centralism, as the first nationally uniform and nationwide system of elected local government in Britain (Thane 1990: 17). In reality, the reforms neither truly promised nor produced any such 'national' system (Harling 1992; Driver 1993: 41). More importantly in this context, it was the divide between the industrial North and the agricultural South – the real target for the reformers' zeal (Mandler 1987) – that scotched any hope of establishing a uniform national system. The geography of pauperism shows that recourse to the poor laws was more frequent in some parts of the country than in others, with the industrialised and heavily urbanised counties having far lower proportions of their population on relief than the agricultural areas of the country (Lees 1998: 182). But rather than use this as an index of southern agricultural backwardness, it must be straightaway conceded that the geography of poor relief was 'primarily determined by administrative and social factors, and only indirectly linked to the economic forces which created unemployment' (Southall, 1988a: 240–1). There was a clear difference between rural and urban pauperism: in the countryside, poor relief remained tied to rural labour markets, with out-door relief continuing at a high level, whilst in the northern boroughs the inadequacy of the system to cope with economic distress and industrial unemployment made the workhouse test wholly impractical. Accordingly, the New Poor Law met with entrenched resistance in the North, local authorities both unwilling and unable to impose the stringent conditions on out-door relief. The resulting acceptance of local discretion is clearly demonstrated in the maps of pauper regulation drawn up by Felix Driver (1993), where the North–South divide is strikingly in evidence. This remained the situation up to at least the 1870s, and it is arguably only after this point, in the era of rationalisation, modernisation and specialisation of service provision, that the spirit of 1834 came close to being realised.

These developments in social policy and the role of the state clearly impacted upon working people most directly, as the anti-poor law movement in the industrial North indicates, and the latter's continuities with early Chartism and labourism prompts a brief recognition of the role of North and South in structuring working-class social and political movements. For all the attempts at combination, union and association, the discursive, sectoral, social and geographical limits to coordination of popular political action remained insistent in this period, disproving E. P. Thompson's (1968) thesis of an *English* working class formed by the 1830s. This is not to argue, however, that these various movements were always local and regional in character at the expense of the national. We ought rather to recognise that the political presence of the working classes was national *and* local, which is to say, locally organised and concentrated, but nationally connected and coordinated. Like the provincial urban middle class, the North would play the strongest role in proletarian associative life, but the horizon of the national was ever-present in discourse and organisation. The Owenite movement, for instance, remained solidly centred in the northern industrial heartlands, and yet elaborated an impressive and innovative culture of association at the local, regional and national scales (Cross 2002). Much the same could be said of their Chartist counterparts, with whom they often in fact overlapped. Chartism had a significant metropolitan presence but was heavily over-represented in the industrial North; and yet, in their attempts to transcend its limitations as a movement, Chartists pioneered initiatives that tied the regions together within a national system of organisation and practice, making the national scale a reality without ever challenging the dominance of their northern constituency (Goodway 1982; Thompson 1984; Howell 1995). As a final example, the geography of unionisation may be particularly important, given the unions', by contrast, continuous legacy. The strength of the trade unions remained throughout our period concentrated in the skilled occupations, with the result that union power and influence were much greater in Lancashire, Yorkshire and other parts of the north of England, with rural areas remaining infertile soil. The gulf between London and the provinces was beginning to be bridged only from 1851 with the formation of amalgamated unions (Southall 1988b). And yet, as with Owenism and Chartism, whilst we must confirm the existence and persistence of North/South divisions the emergence of a national presence can be generously affirmed. Localism remained strong and endorsed, but the traditions of mutuality and mobility ensured that the national scale was of real significance for large numbers of ordinary workers (Southall 1991). As far as social and political organisation is concerned, then, the North–South divide is both characteristic and misleading. Overwhelmingly, popular mobilisation (if not necessarily class conflict – see Musgrove 1990: 276–84) was strongest in the North, and its localism is evident, but the regional differentiation that resulted did not preclude significant attempts at national integration.

This *interdependence* of integration and differentiation (Gregory 1988) may be extended somewhat further, though. It is arguable for instance that it is only through the forces of national economic integration that the regional economies emerged as specialised dynamic systems in the first place. This spatial dialectic maintained the structure of core-periphery relations even as it conceded vitality and relative autonomy to the regions: 'The dynamism and variety of the parts increased at the same time that they were being moulded into a wider core-periphery system' (Langton and Morris 1986: xxx). Regional differentiation, and the prominence of the North in both middle-class and working-class organisation, went hand in hand with the unchallenged dominance of London, the progress of national integration and the continuing elaboration of core-periphery relations (Garside 1990: 490). It is a mistake to see the growth and vitality of the provinces, and the significance accorded to the industrial regions, as being bought at the expense of London and the nation. In the same way that we must be wary of reading a dysfunctional division between commercial and industrial capitalism back into the past, so too should we resist thinking of the political relations between centre and locality as a kind of zero-sum game that remained essentially unchanged throughout our period.

Once again, we need to look to the changing relations between North and South within our period, and to the impact of a late-nineteenth-century caesura in prompting a movement towards a more intensified core-periphery structure. We can argue that the relationship between state and society was fundamentally realigned in the decades leading up to 1914 (Colls 1986; Harris 1993), challenging the culture and philosophy of localism, foregrounding the claims of the nation, reasserting the importance of London and transforming the relation between North and South from one that was more or less symbiotic to one that was more or less oppositional. Indicative of the changes at hand was the fact that the word 'state', hardly heard in the 1830s, was becoming widely canvassed in the later-nineteenth century. Changing political philosophies were also increasingly in vogue – emphasising the unity of state and society, positing the state as the embodiment rather than the antithesis of communal responsibility and justifying interventionist government (Thane 1990: 60; Hoppen 1998: 124). Later-nineteenth-century legislation – preceded by the likes of the Sanitary Act of 1866, the Education Act of 1870 and the Health Act of 1872 – was characterised by a greater willingness for central authority to assert itself, with permissive legislation giving ground to compulsion, and central subsidies increasing the directing power of the central state. The most important elements here, as Price sees it, were 'a greater legislative direction from London, a much more extensive local administration that performed more sophisticated and professionalized functions, and an increasingly entangled fiscal relationship between the centre and the localities that necessarily expanded the role of national government' (Price 1999: 191; see also Millward and Sheard 1995). Much had been prefigured in earlier legislation but it is only at the end of the century that these particular chickens came home to roost. By the 1880s the voluntary principle was by no means dead, but the move towards social legislation was more and more incompatible with its precepts. All of this signalled the beginning of another, harsher, era in North–South relations, the 'increasingly metropolitan, national, and even international orientation of British social life' (Harris 1993: 30) bringing to a close a distinctive era in the relations between state and society, centre and margins, metropolis and provinces, core and periphery, North and South.

North, South and the geography of belonging in Victorian England

The previous sections have discussed, respectively, the history and historiography of the 'industrial north', its economic significance and its fluctuating fortunes, and the matrix of social and political relations which bound together North and South whilst preserving the characteristic, persistent but historically ambivalent tension between them. The aim has been to insist on, firstly, the complexities of the process of uneven geographical development which differentiated the regions, and secondly the historical, dialectical, development of the relations between them. What was at stake, ultimately, were questions of inclusion and exclusion, centrality and marginality, questions essentially of *representativeness*. When George Orwell, among many others in the period between the wars (Priestley 1934, Morton 1927: see Giles and Middleton 1995), self-consciously set out to explore the 'strange country' of the industrial North, he was testifying to its exclusion from the national story, its marginal status, its alienation and abjection (Orwell 1962 [1937]: 98). Commenting on the northerner's self-deluding insistence on industrial employment as the only 'real' work, Orwell's famous pilgrimage prefigures the recent critiques of the centrality of industrialism to England's history. He questioned the extent to which the experiences of the *industrial* North could stand in for the economic fortunes of the nation as a whole. We can conclude this chapter by asking, in much the same way: at what point did the North's very industrialness (real or imagined) become uncoupled from the train of national progress?

Orwell was quick to argue that the 'strangeness' of the North was due to 'certain real differences which do exist', but still more so 'because of the North–South antithesis which has been rubbed into us for such a long time past' (Orwell 1962 [1937]: 98). Recognising not merely the material economic differences that divided the nation, he directed attention to a legacy of cultural alienation and mutual incomprehension that strictly separated the experiences of 'northerners' and 'southerners'. The North–South divide was not so much an economic, or even a social and political, but rather a *cultural* formation (in the broadest definition of the word). Representativeness is here understood in terms of *representation*, and the role of journalists, novelists and social commentators in the imagined geography of North and South can be easily attested. It has been persuasively argued, for instance, that it was the literature of the mid-nineteenth century that played the key role in establishing 'the North' in the popular imagination (Pocock 1978). Robert Gray (1996: 238) has examined the ways in which a variety of modes of representation were engaged in establishing industrial England as an imagined place and a 'strategic space' (see also Gallagher 1985; Thomas 1985). Paul Goetsch (1996), too, insists that the contrast between the industrial North and the rural, tradition-bound South was never more rhetorically salient than in the Victorian years, only overwhelmed at the end of the nineteenth century by a mythic (southern) England of timeless rural tradition. Others have pointed to the role of these various cultural imaginaries – 'the space-myth of Northern Britain' as Shields (1991: 208–9) puts it – in *continuing* to position the 'industrial North' on the nation's cultural periphery.

Useful as such work is, however, the role of representations as social facts can be expanded very considerably to encompass the variety of ways in which representations contributed to the formation of social identities and social and political constituencies (see Kirk 2000). We cannot avoid examining the Victorian North–South divide in terms of what has been called the 'geography of belonging' – the constant human attempt to abjure the demands of distinction and difference and to secure relatively stable group identities, to bind individuals into a shared collectivity and social narrative. That the primary mechanism by which this was attempted and achieved was *cultural* – rather than being organically or mechanistically derived, as in, respectively, the assumptions of nationalism or orthodox Marxist theories of class – is an assertion which cannot be justified in full here. It may be enough to emphasise that changes in the realm of imagination mattered, not somehow at the expense of alternative ways of ordering the real, but in a complementary and constitutive fashion. It should not require too much effort to insist on the discursive formation of both 'region' and 'nation', but, as the protracted debates over the post-modernisation of social history indicate, other social identities like 'class' can be revealed as discursively constructed (see Poster 1997). No longer required to fulfil its foundational role, 'class' has become one amongst a series of *overlapping* cultural imaginations and discourses, whose historical interrelation becomes the very stuff of social history (Joyce 1994).

Arguably the most important protagonist in these debates has been Patrick Joyce, and it is his work, most notably *Visions of the People* (1991), which clearly offers the most insightful analysis of the development of 'North' and 'South' as moral, political, cultural and imaginative identities. In his account, we note, the importance of industrialism and the great industrial staples is fully affirmed. Against the tide of historical revisionism intent on downgrading the role and significance of industrialism, Joyce makes the case that industrialism and the industrial landscapes of the North remained throughout the era central to the cultural discourse of the nation and the very landscape of Englishness. There are of course difficulties with Joyce's use of Lancashire as representative of the 'industrial North', and by proxy England itself, but he is able to make the case for a kind of industrial revolution in consciousness and social identity. Industrial culture, he suggests, was so pervasive that it not only bound people together at the urban and regional scale but constituted a 'class culture' that was inseparable from a claim to a national solidarity affirmed in the name of 'the people'. Industrialism, then, in culture if not in macroeconomic accounting, could lay a claim to England and the soul of the English people.

The most important element of this argument is the claim made on behalf of *populism* as a way of ordering social reality. For all that Joyce is ambivalent about the term, the collective imagination of 'the people' becomes in his account, and in those that have followed, the only historically appropriate and acceptable discursive identity in the nineteenth century. With its inclusive appeal to 'the people', to a kinship and solidarity with other human beings who are linked through a common, vernacular, national identity, populism would seem, at one level, to override regional affiliations and to be at odds with a regionally differentiated social order. Yet, as Joyce (1991: 292) ably demonstrates: 'People . . . saw little contradiction between these different elements, say of class, nation, people or region. They seem to have made up a coherent popular outlook, with the regional as a very strong element, often framing the other aspects.' Indeed, precisely because populism offered the possibility of an imagined community, an imaginary notion that national identity could be distilled into particular qualities and particular places, it opened up a cultural space in which these regional identities were promoted rather than prevented. The dynamic and flexible nature of populism as a vision of the social order ensured that working experiences, the consciousness of class, regional identities and identifications could be constitutive of the national community, not in opposition to it. This potential was realised in the industrial North through custom, language and the intricacies of popular culture. In the flourishing of dialect literature, for instance, a powerful unitary vision of the nineteenth-century labouring poor was promoted, in which the working, industrial North could lay a claim to true Englishness, contrasting this with London and its people, and aligning in this way both region and nation against the capital. This mythologising of the northern, industrial working man (the male bias is deliberate), and his conscription in an anti-metropolitan world-view, was the poetic counterpart to a political radicalism that gave to constitutional and democratic struggles a distinctively northern accent.

Rather than simply a 'space-myth' created by a literary elite, the elision of populism with provincial and industrial experiences constituted a demotic 'northern mythology' with both radical and reformist connotations (Joyce 1991: 318). This is clearly related to the robust provincialism discussed above, particularly in so far as provincial pride was a cross-class affair, shared by working people as well as masters and magistrates. Provincial – 'to live in or near an industrial town to which the industrial revolution gave its significant modern form' (Horne 1970: 38) – was of course closely connected to the impact of the industrial revolution, but it had not yet been tarred with the modern denigration of industrial ugliness so memorably instanced by Orwell and Priestley and Morton. Quite to the contrary, provincial industrialism could be a matter of pride, 'the provinces (especially in the industrial north) being not at all abashed by their provincialism, and indeed using it as a badge of their superiority over the centres of power and high culture' (Joyce 1991: 210). Read as a northern, or labourist, form of populism, provincialism here pitted itself directly against the South, and asserted a claim to the truth of the 'nation' itself:

The emphasis upon the integrity of the provincial might be the way in which a sense of Englishness or Britishness was achieved that united the country as a whole. But this emphasis could be a source of tension as well as agreement with the national centres of power and authority, the assertion of regional and local pride against the metropolis and the south. In turn, this implied the idea that the heart of the true nation beat in the north. This sense of the industrial north as the seat of productive activity and the obverse of southern privilege took many forms. (Joyce 1991: 315)

The longevity and vigour of this northern, labourist populism is demonstrable and still fitfully powerful (Shields 1991), though in the twentieth century it was but one among many variations on Englishness (Matless 1998: 17–18). Even in the rarefied circles of the art world between the wars, as Michael Saler (1998) has recently reported, a 'myth of the North' could be conscripted in opposition to an effete, cosmopolitan, and 'anti-English' London establishment. Yet, just as in our day 'Coronation Street' struggles to match the ratings of 'Eastenders', so too was this northern mythology to be effectively challenged by an upstart southern and metropolitan rival. In a popular but nonetheless stimulating treatment, Donald Horne (1970) introduced the notion of northern and southern 'metaphors' for Englishness – the northern being a familiar amalgam of supposed regional characteristics, and the southern its contrast and counterpart. The 'North' is characterised, for instance, by Puritanism, Protestantism, pragmatism and a calculating empiricism, the 'South' by an Anglican and romantic vision of traditional social order. Whatever the value of these particular assertions, however, the notion of a competitive, regionally inflected nationalism has proved worth pursuing. Horne's 'metaphors' are better understood though as synecdoches, discursive operations where a (regional) part might stand in for the (national) whole: so that Orwell was more prescient than he knew in calling regional snobberies 'nationalism in miniature' (1962 [1937]: 102).

It is clear from Joyce's account and others' that a powerful 'southern mythology' promoted a shift towards London in the 1880s and 1890s (Joyce 1991: 19–20). By contrast to the work of Wiener, this southern mythology was more metropolitan than rural, and should be regarded as a popular vision of the social, rather than being confined to the established cultural elite. In this metropolitan vision of the people, a southern populism emerged as a rival to the northern glamour of the industrial districts. The place of the metropolis in defining Englishness was newly affirmed and elaborated, for instance, in the figure of the 'cockney'. The history of the cockney, as Gareth Stedman Jones makes clear, was universalising in its inclusive appeal, and 'suggests how representations emanating from London might have coloured representations of the nation as a whole' (Stedman Jones 1989: 279). Whilst dialect literature had previously rejected the South and its speech, the reinvention of the 'cockney' towards the end of the nineteenth century shows how a metropolitan working-class identity could come to rival that of the industrial North and the provinces. It is the late arrival of the 'cockney', in both linguistic and social terms, that is the most notable aspect here. Linguistically (Phillipps 1984;

Doyle 1986), the emphasis must be on the effects of cultural standardisation and the Education Acts of the late-Victorian years, and the consequent identification and abjection of the South's incorrect other (McCrum *et al.* 1986: 275). Only then does 'cockney' become understood as the dialect of the working classes of East London, rather than the language of all Londoners. Socially, though, as Stedman Jones demonstrates, the historic transformations of the 'cockney' also point towards his late-Victorian emergence. The music halls, emblematically, sponsored the new 'cockney' archetype, with Albert Chevalier's first performance of the East-End costermonger as a 'supreme type of Englishman' occurring in 1891.

Stedman Jones has read this emergence in terms of the taming of the metropolitan working man, and the coupling of this figural identity to a reassuring and patriotic Englishness: 'The prevailing tone of this new depiction and exploration of the cockney was conservative rather than reformist, and populist and celebratory rather than elitist and moralistic. Cockneys were not shams, usurpers, or outcasts, they were part of the nation' (Stedman Jones 1989: 300). Like Joyce, then, Stedman Jones points to the populism inherent in this metropolitan vision of social order. But the radical and reformist potential of northern populism has been effectively displaced or replaced by a southern cultural formation as reassuring and unthreatening as the Pearly Kings and Queens or the Lambeth Walk of early-twentieth-century fame. As a way of incorporating the working class into the national community, the history of the 'cockney' is thus about the safe extension and integration of the political nation, and it is closely related to the revaluation of patriotism and the monarchy in the late-Victorian and Edwardian era. Just as the invention of 'cockney' reclaimed the metropolitan poor, so the remaking of the monarchy decisively reclaimed patriotism in the service of authority. David Cannadine links, for example, the successful rebranding of Victoria to the drive for national integration and the makeover of the capital: 'Once more, London re-asserted its national dominance, as provincial identity and loyalties markedly weakened. It was at the end, rather than at the beginning of the nineteenth century that Britain became a preponderantly urban, industrial, mass society, with class loyalties and class conflicts set in a genuinely national framework for the first time' (Cannadine 1983: 122; see also Kuhn 1987; Samuel 1987; Richards 1990: 73–188; Harris 1993: 17; Evans 1995). This quite deliberate manipulation and deployment of the monarchy parallels the impact of the 'culture industry', and provides an instructive contrast with the more genuinely democratic 'northern mythology'. It forms indeed one element in a late-nineteenth-century 'nationalization of culture' (Harris 1993: 17–23). 'This did not mean that regionalism disappeared', Price points out, but '[It] did mean that the relationship of the regional to the whole changed' (Price 1999: 334).

The newly institutionalised 'southern' populism, fostered too by new concerns for race and empire, was, we may surmise, ultimately more powerful than its 'northern' counterpart. The notion of 'the people' could always be a principle of social exclusion as well as of social inclusion. Yet its co-option by the culture industry and by the forces of political conservatism, represented the most debilitating development as far as a radical or even a reforming populism was concerned. This would be an inclusiveness built on exclusiveness, to the extent that it was nearly impossible to tell where one started and the other ended:

Englishness was appropriated by and became the responsibility of certain narrowly defined groups and their institutions, and yet meaning and function were (con)ceded to the subordinated groups and institutions. . . . Everyone had a place in the national culture, and had contributed to the past which had become a settled present. The people of these islands with their diverse cultural identities were invited to take their place and become spectators of a culture already complete and represented for them by its trustees. (Dodd 1986: 21–2)

If these suggestions are right – and their speculativeness is readily conceded – we can consider the power of representation as being perhaps *principally* responsible for cementing a North–South divide which would systematically affirm the interests of London and the South-East, at the expense of the now decisively marginal North. In this cartography of identity, a kind of triangulation between populism, provincialism and patriotism, the southern metaphor emerged – at the end of the nineteenth century and into the twentieth – as the dominant vision of the people (Dellheim 1986: 230). This process, though only fully worked out after 1918, systematically denigrated the provinces and the industrial North, and established a more or less stable hierarchy of regional identities and cultures, with the South-East clearly identifiable as a cultural-political synecdoche of Englishness, an 'upper England' or 'Crown heartland' constituting the nation's permanent core (Taylor 1991). At the same time, the industrial North was well on the way to becoming a foreign country for the cultural elite, a 'Deep North' constructed as separate from 'Deep England' (Rawnsley 2000). Industrialism, whatever objections contemporary historians muster, remained symbolically important in these years, but its legacies left the northern metaphor of Englishness significantly weaker, vulnerable to those for whom industrialism was objectionable, alien and distasteful – the real, frightful and arresting ugliness of industrialism that Orwell understood as beginning immediately north of Birmingham. There were exceptions – like Arnold Bennett (see Hudson 1982) – who could find beauty as well as power in the industrial landscape, but the North was well on the way to becoming an estranged landscape, where, as Gissing (1903, quoted by Dellheim 1986: 226) said of Lancashire: 'something of the power of England might be revealed, but of England's worth little enough'.

5

Divided by a common language: North and South, 1750–1830

MARK BILLINGE

Chalk and cheese

In 1755, two years before Clive finally secured Bengal for the Crown and four years before Sir Edmund Halley perceived pattern in a comet, Dr Johnson published the 'first' English dictionary. It was a defining moment in every sense: not, of course, that it was simply a matter of words. The *Dictionary of the English Language* also contained an *English Grammar* together with a rudimentary *History of the English Language* and, taken together, they surely spoke of a wider intent. Johnson's project – which enjoyed significant patronage – was no less than an attempt to moderate a language and, through it, to establish a culture: a terminological pretext for a national biography (Winchester 1998). So, as soldiery and science reached out to place England in its widest context, lexicography reached in: to regulate Englishness and to calibrate its nature. Yet, even as Dr Johnson searched for this common key to a common history, obvious questions arose: by whom was this language spoken and (precisely) whose history did it express? Words and their pronunciation: standard, received, dialect, colloquial, foreign or archaic are indicative not of commonality, but of difference; of the specific not the generic; and once defined in their difference, different they remain: chalk is not cheese, just as sense is not sensibility [the latter is, of course, the title of Jane Austen's novel (1811). I use it precisely because linguistic sport of this kind was much enjoyed in the late-eighteenth century].

So, at the heart of the *Dictionary* lay a paradox, and that same paradox was central to the experience of the English Enlightenment more generally. Difference calibrated is difference squared; the beam that illuminates at its centre intensifies the darkness that it cannot reach: as knowledge exposes ignorance and centre defines periphery, so England known implies England unknown; us positions them; and – closer to home – south presumes north. Shoehorned into the Procrustean bed of a defined vocabulary, feelings, suspicions, even instincts become fixities and the inarticulate is made absolute. To a certain mind, to divine an impression of difference is as good as to establish it. As Thomas Gradgrind would remind his daughter almost a century later in *Hard Times* (1854), the only work by Charles Dickens set in the north of England: 'Louisa never wonder . . . by means of addition, subtraction, multiplication and division, settle everything somehow and *never* wonder.' Though often an object of curiosity and, perhaps more often, a simple – sometimes ironic – device, the juxtaposition of opposites was a characteristic genre of the later-eighteenth century. North and south were, of course, cardinal examples: maybe because they struck a chord, or, equally plausibly, because they answered to a pre-textual agenda. Whatever the reason, 'north' and 'south' appear to have come to mean *something* at this time and the idea itself certainly seems to have stuck.

It was also paradoxical – though not perhaps coincidental – that at the very moment that Dr Johnson sought fixity, the world immediately around him was in greatest flux. The period between 1750 and 1830 has legitimate claim to be considered the most transformational in Britain's written history. Conventionally marked (at home) by the triumph of machino-facture, the end of the old organic dependencies and the explosion of urbanism, it was characterised (abroad) by the consolidation of trade and – as a geographical expression at least – the apogee of empire. (The 1763 Treaty of Paris would mark its height, the American War of Independence thirteen years later the beginning of its demise.) For many commentators the period witnessed nothing less than the metamorphosis of a mildly significant offshore island into the greatest terrestrial power the world had hitherto seen: a power whose tentacles stretched to the farthest shores of the newly discovered Australia (1770) and whose authority would survive not only significant reverberation from across the Channel (the French again), but would defeat the greatest continental force (and perhaps the greatest European ideal) yet assembled, first in 1805 at Trafalgar and then in 1815 at Waterloo (Lane 1981). Meanwhile, as though in mundane counterpoint, the engines and devices of the 'workshop of the world' cranked away, getting ever more steadily into gear – that description, if not coined by Benjamin Disraeli (1804–81), was certainly popularised by him in the House of Commons in 1838. An era which began with barely an agricultural machine of any sophistication or reliability ended on the eve of the Railway Age, with the invention of the difference engine, the Cambridge mathematician Charles Babbage's precursor to the modern computer.

Responsibility for these developments (as well as for their collateral effects) was not, of course, evenly distributed amongst the English regions, for this was also an era in which relations between a resource-rich, industrialising north and a still largely agricultural south were in the process of crucial – material as well as intellectual – renegotiation. As Britain industrialised and its perspectives internationalised, north and south made far from equal contributions and experienced, as a result, a far from uniform benefaction. But, like the division of labour and the division of spoils upon which they significantly depended, the divisions of geography were neither self-evident nor unambiguous, neither static nor agreed. This was a messy world which as often defied logic as it defied Dr Johnson's attempts to incarcerate it.

What would become popularised as the *North and South* of Mrs Gaskell (1855) and the 'two nations' of Disraeli (1845) were, in truth, as much two sensibilities, two attitudes to life as two wholly independent fiefdoms. *North and South* was far from being a straightforward exposition of geographical difference, while Disraeli's two nations were even less geographically the 'Privileged and the People'. Invoking 'common sense' – to which we shall return – *feelings* were often at the heart of differentiation and, significant as material transformation was (not least in its reconfiguration of the landscape and renegotiation of the very currency of north and south), it was radical change in the realm of ideas that contributed most to the *impression* of North and South as discrete entities. In what follows this is paramount: distinctions *can* be, and sometimes *were*, made between a progressive, industrialising, North and a preternatural perhaps supine, South, but their expression (however often repeated) did not, and does not, establish an unambiguous *geographical* truth, let alone a historical reference point from which the fortunes of Britain after the Industrial Revolution can be chartered and explained. The remarkable thing about the drawing of oppositional north–south distinctions is often not their veracity but their persuasiveness.

In that realm of ideas, geography was, of course, important, not least as an increasingly familiar tool of analysis (Livingstone and Withers 1999). Much of the technology of the period was designed purposively to conquer distance and to assert greater human control over it. Yet the period's character derived as much from its determination to rethink the status of people and their relationship with God and with nature (as well as to consider the purpose of civil society and the expectations of a modernising state) as from any of its more practical space-defying accomplishments. In England, what began as a general intellectual premise, closely aligned to the European Enlightenment, was harnessed to a secularising programme of scientific improvement which, by the end of the period, would unconsciously permeate much that might be thought of as plain English 'common sense'. But again, characteristically, 'common sense' was not everywhere the same (it could not always survive the Pennines let alone traverse the Trent): indeed it was the rich elaboration (as well as the uneven acceptance) of these essentially humanist critiques which lay at the heart of the process of regional differentiation as, simultaneously, metropolitan political dominance gave way to provincial regeneration and the economies of the 'nether' regions were progressively freed from the iron control of the London-based merchant companies. These same de-centralising forces, abetted as they were by the new technologies of the turnpike and canal, were also responsible for the burgeoning growth of the northern and midland cities and for a pattern of demographic redistribution which would create, in the minds of many contemporaries, a clear sense of town and country overlying and, as often, displacing a vague impression of northern vitality and southern stagnation.

Of course, as such progressive ideas (and their practical effects) spread, they were subject to opposition (and caricature) along lines defined both by geography and by social position. As a result the advance of a 'northern' (essentially bourgeois) prospectus (and its slow but steady incorporation into the mainstream politics of the South) did much to entrench a 'southern' mentality grounded in tradition, propriety and natural superiority. But was such 'difference' a necessary invention and its articulation a device rather than a sustainable divination?

It is easy to say from the perspective of today that the citizens of 1750 and those of 1830 inhabited very different worlds. Whether North and South inhabited the same at any time is more difficult to assert. We might, for example, note that in 1750 the deaths of Sir Christopher Wren, of William Hogarth and of Alexander Pope were within living memory, as was the South Sea Bubble and the beginning of the Hanoverian line. Come the new century, steam power was common, agricultural reform an accepted necessity (even a fact), and the slave trade was heading for abolition; whilst, by 1830, the eclipse of Anglicanism was an uncomfortable certainty and the triumph of Daltonian chemistry – *pace* Thomas Kuhn (1970) – a harbinger of the Victorian future. In all of this, it is tempting to see an inevitable drift from a comfortable, settled – even patronizing – metropolitan purview towards a more practical, instrumental – even aggressive – provincial aspiration. But from soft South to gritty North? From ancient right to modern responsibility? Macro-questions of this sort require consideration: but then so do others on a different scale; not least questions of perspective. From whose point of view were such changes noticeable and to whom did they matter? Intellectual or labourer? Merchant or farmer? Clergyman or parishioner? Traveller or drudge? And from a different angle still, along what line of cleavage did attitudes divide: town or country, land or industry, traditionalist or reformer, native or immigrant, northerner or southerner? These too are at the heart of perception and at the heart of difference; and they are, almost invariably, objects of definition, not matters of fact.

Domenico Caracciolo (1715–89) may have been right when he concluded that there was something altogether peculiar about a nation in which 'there are sixty religions and only one sauce'. He might have noted, however, that this same nation produced one undisputed sovereign, an unchallenged parliament and several hundred distinctive cheeses. In Dr Johnson's world, chalk might be chalk but cheese was not cheese: it was another, and, in its indicative complexity, wholly different matter.

Muck and brass

Some sort of a pattern?

Between 1700 and 1851 the population of England and Wales slightly more than tripled from an estimated 5.5 to just over 18 million. In 1801 it stood at approximately 8.9 million. Though there is now almost universal agreement that this increase was fuelled by a significant rise in fertility (rather than a decline in mortality) and reasonable indication that the balance of the swelling population was ever more urban (with a decline in the rural population after 1820) relatively little can be said about the exact regional balance of population at any given date before 1801. However, since the major cause of urban growth in the later eighteenth century was industrialisation, it is not unreasonable to suggest that it was towards the north and midlands (as well as towards London) that the majority of rural migration was directed and there that the greatest population expansion was experienced.

In quasi-demographic terms, then, the picture of a growing North and a stagnant (later even a declining) South – pretty much taken for granted by a number of commentators in the late-eighteenth century – appears to be broadly sustainable (Wrigley and Schofield 1981). Inspired by the dynamic economies towards which migrants were generally drawn, this shift was encouraged and, to a degree, fashioned by the progressive integration of the economy which the turnpikes and canals promoted. True, the rapid and cheap transport of people would become epidemic only once the railways were commonplace, but these other, less spectacularly integrative, features worked their own peculiar magic; not least in greatly facilitating the movement of goods – the backbone of Georgian commercial and industrial expansion. Transport integration brought other significant factors into play as well, for with integration came differentiation and, with that, the imposition of a new regional character upon the English landscape. There are those who argue that it was only with differentiation of this kind that the broad and relatively uniform landscape of local self-sufficiency (rooted in a medievalism the sixteenth and seventeenth centuries had done little to disturb) was characteristically unmade; for integration's corollary was local specialisation within a greater functioning whole, something contemporaries certainly noted in the ever-widening difference between urban and rural places. Though it was as often held an object of manners as of topography, the more analytical noted too the emergence of a 'commercial' (sometimes 'manufacturing') North in contrast to an agricultural South: perhaps, where identified, the single most arresting line of cleavage. The issue of the impact of development – and more specifically industrialisation – on regional identity has been much debated (see, for example, Langton 1984 and Gregory 1988). I incline to the view that industrialisation allowed for far greater regional diversity (through specialisation and a kind of internal comparative advantage), albeit within the framework of a broadly homogenising national culture. Whether the extent of differentiation *within* the North (or South) was greater than that which existed *between* them remains a significant issue, but like so many such issues it is a matter of perspective as well as of demonstrable economic reality.

Some idea of the contradictory ebbs and flows in regional fortunes can be gleaned from the pattern of agricultural wages. These, in turn, comment on both the health of the rural economy and the competing demands for labour in any region at any given time. In the late 1760s, wages were highest in East Anglia and the southeast, average in the Midlands and lowest in the north and north-east. By the middle 1790s, the pattern had almost entirely reversed with wages lowest in the southwest and parts of the Midlands, average in East Anglia and highest in the Home

Counties and the north (Hunt 1986a). Though by no means a clear north–south split, the general pattern none the less leans towards a sense of northern economic buoyancy. The fragmentary evidence for non-agricultural wages tends to confirm this pattern. After about 1780, northern wages (particularly in Lancashire) began to match those of London rather than of Exeter, the city whose economic fortunes it had most closely shadowed for the previous century and a half. One author has suggested that it was between the 1760s and the 1790s that definitive north–south wage transformations came about: a neat elision, if sustainable, of sectoral change, economic development and regional geographical response (Hunt 1986b).

Outright wealth alone is more difficult to track before the early-nineteenth century, though after 1806 the pattern of income tax yields shows, outside of London, a significantly higher than average northern (most strikingly north-western) take. Such taxation is a poor measure of landed wealth, but it is not unreasonable to assume that the majority of the landed rich were to be found in the south, even if their estates were scattered more broadly and their sources of income more diverse – both geographically and sectorally – than was at one time allowed (Rubinstein 1981 and 1986). Turning to the obverse – it being held that a measure of a nation's worth is the manner in which it treats its poor – it should be noted that the pattern of pauperism between 1750 and 1830, hard as it is to establish with any consistency, also admitted to an increasingly convincing North–South divide. As employment opportunities in the north expanded and wages increased, pauperism – at least as officially noted – declined. The obverse was true of the south. Under the Speenhamland system, during certain periods of distress in the mid- to late-eighteenth century, the south as a whole reported over 20 per cent of its population subject to parish relief whilst, by 1837, the southern Poor Law Unions were engaged in an almost equally brisk trade. Their northern associates, in contrast, appear to have been in virtual clover from the 1750s onwards with only occasional departures from the relatively healthy norm at any intervening stage (Marshall 1978; Crowther 1981).

Any net benefit which the North derived from these developments was reinforced after 1730 by the progressive dismantling of the London trade monopolies: the London merchant guilds had controlled English overseas trade since medieval times and the marketing of major commodities (not least textiles) through London had been a vital source of the capital's wealth and a major barrier to independent provincial expansion. This relaxation of trade (alongside the exploitation of the dominion territories) quickly led to the growth of provincial markets, the expansion of northern manufacture and the revival of regional ports nationwide. As foreign seaborne trade blossomed, the fruits spread progressively to the north and north-west as never before. In the south, the south-western ports as well as East Anglia also grew, though much of this was (with the exception of Bristol) the result of coastal rather than overseas trade. Throughout the period, London continued to be the major beneficiary of imperial (as opposed to transatlantic) trade and continued to grow (albeit more slowly in the second half of the eighteenth century) as a direct result (Jackson 1983).

What the pattern of trade makes clear is that the expansion of opportunity in the north did not always spell absolute decline or even relative disaster for the south. The same was true of many manufactures. Textiles for example – perhaps the single defining commodity of the English Industrial Revolution – were increasingly manufactured in Lancashire and Yorkshire alone. By the later-nineteenth century this would mark out the two counties so distinctively as to create a 'north within a north' (and a proud Lancastrian knows that the Industrial Revolution was a creation not of the North or even of the north-west but of an area of a few dozen square miles based around Manchester). Yet, during the late-eighteenth and early-nineteenth centuries Lancashire and Yorkshire grew at the expense of Scotland, Ireland and neighbouring Cheshire rather than the other English counties. Indeed it was not often the case that economic activity shifted uniformly and inevitably from south to north, but rather that explosive growth in manufacturing in the north (often *de novo*) left areas of the south struggling to maintain a shaky *status quo*, although in the south the service sector remained buoyant, both in the countryside and in the towns (Lee 1979). That there was a general shift in the balance of wealth generation in the later-Georgian period speaks, of course, of the degree to which even a revived and commercialising southern agriculture (another example of the specialisation which integration allowed) could grow only at comparatively stately rates compared to northern industry where investment capital secured more significant, if not always steady, returns. Over the longer span, as local and temporal uncertainty eased, this became a virtuous circle as far as northern industry and commerce was concerned. By the early-nineteenth century, banking (particularly of the provincial private variety) was a broadly urban activity, whilst financial intelligence spread more rapidly and more widely along the urban-centric arterial networks than it did amongst the old networks of the (generally southern) country associations. These developments continued to serve London well, but they also offered opportunities elsewhere: opportunities that, once recognised, the northern towns and cities were quick to exploit. In investment terms alone (and again outside London) the balance now favoured the north decisively, though this is not, of course, to say that it was not southern as well as northern capital which primed the pumps nor that it was not to southern investors and southern investment opportunities that some of the profits returned (Pressnell 1956; Cottrell 1986; Black 1995 and 1996). Finally, we should note the other crucial yet invisible networks on which much – particularly northern – progress depended: that of science, technical knowledge and the dissemination of effective management practice. In both scientific and technical terms, the balance of innovation greatly favoured the industrial north where broadly cultural issues also showed their hand (Musson and Robinson 1969a, 1969b).

It would be tedious and to a degree impossible to track the pattern of north–south development in every sector of economic activity, so that the general impression of a buoyant north and a readjusting south indicated in the foregoing vignettes must do for the present. They are sufficient at least to establish that the later-eighteenth century was beginning to witness a reversal of the 'traditional' fortunes of north and south on a scale hitherto unknown. The old adage 'the further from London, the further from prosperity' did not now hold as it once had, and though still 'provincial' in the modern sense, the northern provinces were developing: enough at any rate to unsettle the sleep of a few of the more traditional 'southern' interests.

Important as they were, these visible transformations were underpinned by decisive shifts in the social realm. If the old society of the south had been based upon a moral economy of master and men (pockets of which survived even the commercialisation of agriculture and, later, the impact of parliamentary land reform); the newer settlements of the industrial north were based on, and systematically exploited, the new political economy of the capitalist workplace. Not by coincidence did the period witness the birth of economic and moral philosophies designed to rationalise, justify and extend this new relationship, be they Benthamite, Utilitarian, or more loosely derived from the stirrings of Smiles's self-help (Harrison 1983). At the local level this often meant a fundamental renegotiation of the nature of community. For if, on the whole, the pre-industrial world (and to a considerable extent the rural heartlands of the south) had been dominated by hierarchical prescriptions of descending rank and degree held together by a complex system of patronage, then the industrial world brought a powerful solvent in the form of a professionalising middle class whose social role was increasingly defined in terms that were oppositional to the aristocracy it sought to supplant and incorporative of the working class it determined to employ. Whilst it was commonplace in the nineteenth century (and indeed in the twentieth) to characterise northerners as communitarian, co-operative and even gregarious, albeit in a rough and ready manner, it should be remembered that such neighbourliness was often forged in adversity and was based on a pattern of self-recognition broadly respected by those trapped in similar circumstance. It did not easily transcend class. The so-called southern reserve owed much to a sense of place, an awareness of rank and a clear recognition of the status which even the lowest position in a strictly hierarchical society conferred. Neither system, incidentally, guaranteed gentility on a continental scale. As the Earl of Chesterfield (1694–1773) reflected on 15 November 1748 in his *Advice to his Son*: 'It must be owned that the graces do not appear to be natives of Great Britain; and I doubt, the best of us here have more of rough than of polished diamond.'

In the wider public sphere, parliamentary reform in 1832 and the municipal Corporations Act of 1835 (which granted self-government to most of the burgeoning English towns though not significantly to London) reflected the degree to which the northern middle class had, on the back of their new social contract, brokered institutional political success and gained a toehold in government. The contrast with the 1790s could hardly be clearer. At that time, the landed aristocracy dominated government and continued in exclusive occupancy of executive office. Even within this cosy arrangement, the centre itself was thought to be strengthening. John Dunning, Baron Ashburton (1731–83) proposed a motion in the House of Commons in 1780 that: 'The influence of the Crown has increased, is increasing and ought to be diminished.' At the time of the American War of Independence (which we should remember was fought, ostensibly, over the principle of 'no taxation without representation') only one in twenty citizens in Britain had the right to vote, and cities as substantial as Manchester and Liverpool had no directly elected Member of Parliament. The degree to which this excluded and 'made different' even the denizens of the northern 'political' establishment should not be underestimated. From a local base and a number of not very remarkable precepts, the northern middle class had forged an identity, established a programme and propelled the North into the politics of the nation. The later nineteenth century would both consolidate and advance this position, as though born to do little else; yet in 1830, even at its most precocious, it remained only a fledgling achievement. Still, industrial capitalism had inevitably promoted northern interests at a national level and to a hitherto unimaginably successful degree, so that it is little wonder that a number of southern, as well as specifically metropolitan, interests felt threatened as never before by this, for them, vexatious progress.

Where then do these rather crude generalisations leave us? On the face of it, at least, with a broad impression of a loose North–South divide and of a pattern of diverging fortunes either side of it. Further, there is a suggestion that, for the first time in modern history, it was the North that was the scene of the most dynamic development and that (alongside those who 'directed' its fortunes) it was the North that was beginning to gain the upper hand on the nation's economic tiller. Politically, change was in train, though the North was not yet a fully cohesive element, let alone an equal partner, in the determination of state affairs; whilst an alternative 'northern' model of social relations (which would prove highly adaptable outside its native environment) was now properly established and gaining ground apace. In plain matters of geography, the North was 'prosperous', whilst the South, outside London and one or two urban islands, was becoming relatively less so. Just where these norths and souths began and ended is, of course, a significant point at issue: for if battle lines were being drawn, where exactly were they being configured and who precisely was determining their limits?

Dissonant identities

'A servant of two masters: the problem of London'[1]

In any account of North and South, the issue of London looms large. Naturally, the capital remained the nation's focus and foursquare its metropolis: always centre, never periphery. It survived every crisis (including destruction by plague and fire), defied every prediction and remained linked to all of the regions, yet fully characteristic of none of them (George 1951; Porter 1982 and 1994; Ackroyd 2000). It remained, too, part of the burgeoning phenomenon of urbanisation, even though its growth slowed in the second half of the eighteenth century as it lost ground to the maelstrom which was the rise of the northern cities. Contemporary fears about London and its influence wavered between a fear for its health and a concern for vigour, either being held detrimental in their potential impact on other places. George Coleman the Younger (1762–1836) inclined to the latter in coining in his *The Heir at Law* (1797, London) his famous lines:

> Oh, London is a fine town,
> A very famous city
> Where all the streets are paved with gold,
> And all the maidens pretty.

Tobias Smollett (1721–71), friend of Dr Johnson and famed for his picaresque novels, inclined to the former: 'The capital is become an overgrown monster; which, like a dropsical head, will in time leave the body and extremities without nourishment and support' (Smollett 1771). William Cobbett (1762–1835), a popular journalist who championed traditional rural England against changes being wrought by industrialisation, doubtless spoke for many when he remained resolutely unsure: 'But what is to be the fate of the great wen of all . . .? The monster, called "the metropolis of empire"' (Cobbett 1821).

Though for much of the period London and its influence (political, economic and social) was the object of scorn and even derision in some northern intellectual circles – many of the provincial Literary and Philosophical Societies prided themselves on their apparent usurpation of its intellectual position (Billinge 1984) – this hardly (except by rather parochial cultural exclusion) placed it firmly in the 'South' as those same interests might have conceived such an entity. As the seat of national government, London (more strictly Westminster) was clearly the target of opposition to government policy of whatever stripe, and it is hard not to conclude that much of the antagonism between North and South – as well as much of the foolishness in seeing it in these terms – was really a reflection of the provinces' characterisation of London as the natural enemy. This was indeed ironic, for much of London's natural ecology – like many of its needs – aligned it more closely with the commercial forces of the northern periphery than with its own immediate rural hinterland with which it shared location but little else. For this reason, much of the South (outside the Home Counties) had equal reason to fear and suspect the power of London and to divine that the capital's interests were not always coincident with their own.

Even so, if London was part of the complex web of capital that transcended geography, its personality remained stubbornly distinctive. Never subject to the factory-based, large-scale industrialisation characteristic of the North, London's economic structure together with its idiosyncratic – broadly courtly – social relations continued to function in a manner more recognisably medieval than modern and, in this sense, it was tied to a tradition no longer healthily extant in any other region. Yet, in other ways, London was the most modern and progressive of all of the nation's cities: the arbiter of taste, the centre of consumer culture and the nerve centre of government, finance, information and power. As such it was sufficiently

influential in the conduct of the affairs of the North (and in turn sufficiently dependent on the North's commercial success) to be inalienable to it, so that despite
what one suspects was a mutual suspicion and (imitation being the highest form
of flattery) a sneaking admiration, London could be characterised as outwith the
North only in the strictest topographical or, alternatively, most perversely senti-
mental terms. If northern magnates were often found complaining about London
(or boasting about Leeds), it was usually because it disappointed them in the profits
it returned to their London-based and other portfolios, or frustrated their purpose
by failing to promote with sufficient alacrity policies designed to advance still
further the radical 'northern' cause. It was not, in other words, because northern
interests understood the city to be an entity whose fortunes lay always in natural
and direct conflict with their own. Since almost every technical innovation benefited the capital by increasing the range of its intelligence and power, its central
position in the nation's fortunes neither declined nor was significantly deflected
between 1750 and 1830. Thus, whilst it is possible to argue that socially and politically its instincts were of the 'South', economically London moved to a rhythm
dictated as much by northern industry as by southern commerce and in this sense,
it was a law unto itself: neither of the North nor the South; in fact, neither one
thing nor the other.

Neither fish nor foul: the status of the Midlands

If, in specific terms, London's problem in the North–South issue is less one of
location than of nature, then the Midlands represents a quite different case. The
industrial status of the Midlands (albeit quirky in its structural form) was hardly in
doubt by the late-eighteenth century. Indeed it could be argued (depending, naturally on where certain lines are drawn) that at its inception, the Industrial Revolution
was a broadly Midland phenomenon and that it spread northwards as opportunity
arose and comparative advantage dictated. Almost all of the iconography (as well
as the hagiography) of early industrialisation is firmly tied to a Midland anchor –
from the forging exploits of the Darbys in Coalbrookdale, the potting achievements
of the Wedgwoods in Burslem and later Etruria, the textile innovations of the Needs
and the Strutts in Belper and the engineering innovations of the Boulton and Watt
Company in Soho, Birmingham. Birmingham itself had even been home to the
Lunar Society – a coterie of scientists and manufacturers – which almost certainly
provided the model for the broader Literary and Philosophical Society Movement
which would later feature so distinctively in the progressive bourgeois-intellectual
landscape of the industrial north. Even later, when large-scale textile manufacture
moved north, the Midlands remained a buoyant and significant partner in the engineering of that success (Fitton and Wadsworth 1958; Musson and Robinson 1969a
and 1969b; McKendrick *et al.* 1982; Reilly 1992). However, emphasis on cotton in
particular (which was after all the single largest export earner by the mid-nineteenth
century) and the retrospective homage paid to its early Derbyshire/Lancashire

masters (Arkwright, Crompton, Hargreaves, etc.) shifted decisively north the focus of the Industrial Revolution (both for contemporary commentators and for subsequent historians) and in so doing problematised the Midlands in the general balance of affairs. Too far south to be northern, the Midlands were too far north to be southern: a push-me/pull-you, truly betwixt and between.

The Midlands remained stigmatised for other reasons too. In Jane Austen's *Emma* (1815), Mrs Elton made a characteristic point: 'One has no great hopes from Birmingham. I always say there is something dreadful in the sound.' Names and accents apart, there are other more plainly geographical issues at stake. Wedged between north and south, and different from both, the Midlands has no natural home in so simple a dichotomy as them and us. In the 1750s, Wolverhampton was a long way south to any northerner (about a day and half by stagecoach) and as good as abroad to anyone travelling from the south (about two days from London). Even by 1821, when journey times had tumbled, it took twelve hours to reach Dudley from Manchester by road and about sixteen from London. Any friends one might have there were hardly neighbours, whilst, conversely, any feelings of contempt were unlikely to be bred by familiarity (Pawson 1977; Freeman 1980 and 1986).

Matters of distance, of contact and of commerce are obviously important in aligning the Midlands to either a northern or a southern pole, but so too are matters of character: that is, what the Midlands represented and what its nature might be taken to be. It is a particularly tricky problem, for there is a strong argument that the personality of the Midlands was strongly redefined at precisely this time. Money (1977), in his fascinating study of the relations between urban Birmingham and rural Warwickshire, has persuasively argued that the industrialisation and economic rise of the city challenged and later eclipsed both the rural economy and the rural political interests of the county as a whole. Further, it might be suggested, the ensuing renegotiation of status between city and county is a microcosm of a wider process that transformed the Midlands from a broadly northern offshoot of a southern rural interest to a substantially southern partner in an increasingly northern enterprise.

This history argues that prior to the 1720s the largely rural Midlands (which would wait until the early- to mid-nineteenth century before experiencing commercially significant agricultural reform) was bound into a nexus of economic and social values which connected it to the prevailing county interests of the south (Overton 1996). Anglican, Tory, protectionist, this 'estate' culture was inimical even to the pre-industrial values of the less heavily 'countified' north. Thus, from a northern perspective and prior to the 1750s, the Midlands could be fitted more easily into a pattern of southern otherness than of contingent similarity. Later, the eclipse of the Warwickshire interest and the rise of industry in the Midland towns appears to re-centre the region in the general scheme of things, bringing its character (if not its exact structure) more into line with the north and causing some renegotiation of its currency. But it remains arguable whether, coming rather late, this renegotiation was ever wholly successful in the general scheme of things and perhaps, like London, but for wholly different reasons, the Midlands remained – as it does to this day – an area easily identified but in a straightforwardly appositional sense, contextually, more difficult to locate.

To add to the ambiguity, it is worth noting that, even more than was the case in the north, the market for many of Birmingham's products remained southern – often London specific, and that its commercial and social ties to the capital were both important and strong. Thus, what was true of territories was reflected in the lives and allegiances of individuals – particularly those whose commercial inclinations or social pretensions straddled the geographical and social divide. Typical was Josiah Wedgwood. Wedgwood, who patented his pottery in 1763, was a man of scientific pretension (as a member of the Lunar Society) and of classical aspiration. His factory at Etruria was a model of enlightened industrial practice and industrial relations and yet he relied for its wellbeing on aristocratic patronage. A rational, quasi-scientific manufacturer with broadly radical views, he managed to subordinate himself and his enterprise to a fashionable metropolitan taste. Later in life he was as likely to be found in Bath as in Burslem, threading a seamless link between commercial sense and polite sensibility. By the end he had the aristocracy eating off his plates, if not exactly out of his hand (Schofield 1963; Reilly 1992). Equally, it should be noted, the distinction implied here is as much about a bourgeois/landed and a rural/urban theorem as it is about a specifically north/south divide.

Neither here nor there: the country and the city

It is at once clear that the general pattern of migration, together with the reconfiguration of the networks of capital and the growth of urban manufactures, created a dichotomy of country and city at least as persuasive and at least as insistent as any between North and South. Any argument which seeks to paint this urban revolution as an exclusively northern affair (to which the south was somehow less subject) is confronted not only with London, Birmingham and the like, but also with the obvious experience of towns in every other part of England. With the notable exception of those areas where either local agriculture or local industry was failing, all urban places were undergoing similar, albeit variedly spectacular, differentiation and growth. By the 1750s, the era in which the local urban dynamic was fuelled almost wholly by local economic circumstance was coming to an end, and though hierarchical stability in the urban network was yet to be established (Robson 1973), the effect of transport and other communications improvements was beginning to make the urban network function as a discrete whole rather than as the series of fragmented arrangements it had once been. The corollary of this – the divorce of towns from their local countryside and the breakdown of the old œcumene of mutual dependency – was not yet everywhere manifest, but the fortunes of town and country were clearly diverging: two separate entities the very terms for which were becoming metaphors for difference itself.

As Raymond Williams (1973) has reminded us, throughout the late-eighteenth and early-nineteenth centuries country and city were two worlds of almost wholly juxtaposed values. Blake reflected them in *The Songs of Innocence and Experience*, just as the Romantic poets and painters confirmed them in their Arcadian visions of the country and their almost total disregard for the city. But it was ordinary people who witnessed this disjuncture in the real: in unequal opportunities, divergent incomes, disparate fortunes and disappearing trades, as well as in the wholly synthetic institutions of the towns to which they were increasingly subject.

That the countryside (both northern and southern) fell into relative economic decline after 1750 is a truism, though a less cursory account might note the differences between those areas where urban growth and transport innovation transfused agriculture for the better and those where it bled it for the worse. Again there was a micro-topography to such fortunes, in which trends were neither exclusively northern nor southern in their character. Only a mindset obsessed with such a distinction could shoehorn the pattern into a preferred north–south model, and of all the objections thus far raised to a regional dichotomy based on a hermetic north/south division, the most powerful and persuasive is surely that, in the experience of ordinary people, it was location in either town or country which determined most decisively the significant parameters of their lives.

Heroes and villains: a question of attribution

For its widest sustenance, the articulation of a North–South divide might be held to rely, in part, on a largely unconscious thesis which links urbanism, the Industrial Revolution and the economic philosophy which underpinned them both to a northern ethic which was itself the exclusive invention of an emerging middle class. This whole family of concepts is often, unthinkingly, bundled together as part of a broad assumption. Like many of the concepts in this whole debate, it is only through such gross stereotyping that mutual exclusivities can be sustained. By extending the assumption it might be claimed that, since all eighteenth-century industrial enterprise was an offshoot of this 'northern' mentality, any southern manifestation of it was merely a physical dislocation: an ultramontane north seeping gravitationally into an open and less-developed world: a sort of 'northernising' by stealth.

Leaving aside, for the moment, the obvious fact that not every member of the middle class was a product of the northern counties (nor a recent product at that), it is worth considering the extent to which increases in commodity production, as well as a good deal of early industrialisation, came about as a result of initiatives launched by landed (often southern) interest rather than the middle class (whether drawn from its northern or southern 'family' branches).

A great deal of eighteenth-century enterprise developed from a natural extension of the commercial instincts which the great landowners had already applied to the exploitation of their estates, and it is clear that innumerable noble families, either through inclination or necessity, found themselves heavily committed to the progressive exploitation of their properties north and south of the midland divide. David Spring and others have charted the extent of this and, in the process, established the debt which the Industrial Revolution owed to the English aristocracy as well as the minor peerage (Spring 1963; Thompson 1963; Word and Wilson 1971; Cannadine 1980; Mingay 1990 and 1994). The Dukes of Northumberland, Devonshire and Westminster (active in mining, land-development and urban estate building); the Dukes of Bridgewater (in transport), the Earls of Dudley and the Dukes of Chandos (in industrial enterprise more generally) were all the – admittedly highly elevated – tips of an extensive iceberg which subtended deep within the fabric of the establishment in general (Porteous 1977; Freeman 1986). Cobbett ruefully characterised the aristocracy of the early-nineteenth century less as a dynasty of landlords than a coterie of 'fundlords' noting their extensive investments in real estate, lease agreements, commodity production, enterprise and the financial institutions. More recently, Roy Porter (1982) has noted that the aristocracy in general 'made money with enthusiasm and without shame'.

What was true of production was also true of the places in which production flourished, so that much of the townscape of the eighteenth and early-nineteenth centuries (in the provinces as well as London) relied for its character and growth either on aristocratic capital or, even more commonly, on the release of the landed interest's circum-urban property under a revitalised leasehold system. Such projects (often impelled by the landed interest's need to increase revenues in order to service debts) required a good deal in the way of start-up capital and it was not unusual for them to be undertaken in partnership. Partnership commonly straddled the social divide and brought the capital-rich bourgeoisie and the property-rich peerage into immediate as well as symbolic proximity. In a real sense, North and South (or at least northern and southern interests) were coming into congress and in such circumstances it is hard to sustain a thesis of financial and business separation between the two, let alone contemplate a landscape divided into areas of discrete, non-overlapping control.

Taken as a whole, then, evidence of the aristocracy's involvement in finance, commerce and industry, together with evidence of its close financial relations with elements of the middle class challenges the over-prescriptive categorisations of an agricultural aristocracy in competition with an industrial bourgeoisie and, by extension, challenges too the absurd formulation of a clear commercial and productive separation between North and South. If, in the eighteenth century, the progressive incorporation of the regions into the national space economy suggests an early example of combined and uneven development, then the distinctiveness which such a process brought to the landscape was certainly not reflected straightforwardly in patterns of ownership or allegiance, let alone in the substructure of venture capital or financial control.

In broadly social terms, there was, of course, another side to this coin and arguably one with a more systematic geographical implication. The aristocracy's involvement in industry and enterprise was mirrored by the bourgeoisie's drift into domains traditionally considered the preserve of the aristocracy alone. The opening of pathways which would eventually lead to a flurry of new peerages spoke of an ambition amongst significant elements in the middle class, not to challenge the edifice of landed power, but to join up and to underpin it. A wholly common practice was for well-established industrial magnates from the north – such as the Peels, Gregs, Kennedys – to launder their image, purchase estates in the south, and establish their successors as the traditionally educated Anglican gentlemen they would never themselves become. Even pending such generational translation, it was not wholly uncommon in the late-eighteenth century for the sons of the northern wealthy to be seen heading for London (on a temporary or permanent basis) whilst their fathers (and mothers) toiled at home. Such journeys took time and cost money, but were evidently thought well worth it. Social mixing of this kind, together with the intermarriage which sometimes followed, contradicts further the easy characterisation of the middle class and the aristocracy as separate and competing elements each living within their own exclusive domains. Such arrangements may, however, have contributed to a contemporary impression that the natural home for a 'gentleman' was in the South and that, whilst the North was the place in which to earn money, the South was the place in which to spend it.

Movers and shakers: a matter of class

Finally, the clearest objection to almost all that has gone before must be the homogenising perspective it advances. Whilst there are obvious problems in defining the North and South as geographical entities, there are even greater problems in identifying a single voice which can be held to speak for the 'common' experience of either. Differences in class, education, opportunity and mobility surely dictated the lens through which North and South were viewed: what the essential nature of each might be held to be and what, if any, difference existed between them. Whilst some (the travelled? the entrepreneur with distance-dependent costs?) may have been hyper-sensitive to geography, others led lives the immediately insistent demands of which surely afforded little time for speculation about matters as abstract as those of place and personality let alone location and context. In such circumstances home and work were likely to provide more immediately concrete geographical reference points than anything so arcane as cardinal orientation.

The scope for thoughtful individual perception was clearly greater for some than for others. The views of northern farmers, for example – estate owner, tenant or labourer – were hardly likely to conform with each other, let alone with a mill-owner, a banker, a lawyer, a shopkeeper or a doctor. Indeed there may even have been greater uniformity of view amongst similarly (pre)occupied individuals (free-traders, Unitarians, physicians or Tories) either side of any notional divide than there was within a given northern or southern community the most likely characteristic of which was diversity not conformity. That the issue of North and South naturally arose amongst, and was openly debated by, the general populace seems unlikely. Even amongst the opinion-makers, systematic debate would most likely arise in the face of specific issues the geographical component of which may have been incidental or but one, amongst several, concerns. From time to time, of course, politics did throw up issues which had *potentially* different implications for the north and south (the repeal of the Corn Laws was one such) but it is by no means clear that other lines of battle (rich: poor, capital: labour, industrial: agricultural) were not also drawn, or indeed that geographical allegiance did not prove fragile when sectoral interests were at stake. Certainly, the history of protest in the late-eighteenth and early-nineteenth centuries, for example (whether single issue or generically reformist), does not suggest that solidarity of attitude was uniform over space, easily achieved over long distances, constant over time, or even when accomplished, necessarily respectful of pre-existing social or geographical divides (Jones 1975; Dinwiddy 1979; Gregory 1982; Charlesworth 1983 and 1986).

We must remember too that even by 1830, information was not a ubiquitous or reliable commodity. Information did not percolate quickly, evenly or accurately down the social hierarchy, so that opinion formation in the modern sense was often non-existent, ill conceived or, perhaps more often, straightforwardly manipulated. In such circumstances, ritualised argument is a poor substitute for common sense and it is hard not to conclude that any conscious perception of, or systematic thought about, a North–South divide was the preserve only of those with a strong vested interest, or the leisure to intellectualise their perceived misfortunes.

Ways and means

Many of the arguments set out so far may be taken either to establish the 'reality' or to challenge the status of a North–South divide between 1750 and 1830 in a broadly material sense. Many measure difference (and authority between differences) in the straightforward language of accounting: where the balance of population, income, productivity or disposition lay. Yet it was not until later in the nineteenth century that accounting alone was seen – at least in terms of public rhetoric – as the true measure of the national estate. It was not until the 1840s that the prevailing view was that 'the transactions of society should be expected to yield their balance books like those of industry' (Hobsbawm 1977: 51). It follows that it may be more appropriate to establish the everyday reality of a North–South divide in the public consciousness before 1830 through other means: which is to say, through the cultures of places.

It has been argued elsewhere that an understanding of the culture in which material life is located often provides a better understanding of the manner in which life is ordinarily sustained and commonly experienced. Raymond Williams, for example, has reminded us that culture is both 'ordinary' and powerfully insistent; that far from answering only to some human need for perfectibility and its expression,

it lies deep within our consciousness as the framework through which we interpret, and often learn to deal with, the exigencies of everyday life. An issue which
necessarily arises from such a perspective is that of whose culture this everyday
culture is. Which social group (or class) is most responsible for its manufacture
and which other groups fall most naturally into its embrace? In short, in whose
image and to whose advantage is culture made and how does it relate to the places
from which it arises?

Clearly arguments of this kind, based as they are on a concept of hegemony
(which is as universalising as it is intangible), admit to no easy congruence with
a straightforward geographical divide, though the idea of separate 'northern' and
'southern' *cultures* is often advanced (even presently) not least to explain the inex-
plicable or to justify the unjustifiable. Certainly rural–urban cleavages in attitude
can be identified (or devised), but did a division between north and south exist in
this same sense? Did the citizens of each live different lives imbued with different
values? Alternatively, in attempting to understand consciousness (from the bottom
up as it were) how did the far from mutually exclusive allegiances borne out of
parochialism, localism, regionalism and even Englishness fall out in the general
scheme of things? At what level was cultural experience meaningfully engaged or
identity sensibly established?

In seeking to articulate a clear north–south schism, a typical formulation might
imply, for example, a southern culture dominated by the needs of an estate-owning
landed interest (the world of natural deference and dependency), and a northern
culture forged in the image of a capitalist middle class (a world of class consciousness and of wage-bargains). It might go further in linking these values to
a sense of evolution: for surely, if these prescriptions can be made to stick, then
they speak not only of geography but of history; of the passing of Georgian society
and the coming of Victorian economy; the rise of the North and the fall of the
South. Were there then two cultures in Georgian England in the late-eighteenth
and early-nineteenth centuries?

At the level of caricature, it is not difficult to sketch such a division. The rural
Anglican parish, for example, could hardly be more different from the isolated
Methodist mill-town; Lord Leicester's estate at Holkam more contrasted with
Arkwright's Cromford or Darby's Coalbrookdale; or, in more general terms still,
the affairs of the southern country house less coincident with those of the northern
counting-house. Surely, then, in matters of philosophy, religion, politics, aspiration,
lifestyle and outlook, these were two separate and non-contingent worlds. As Jane
Austen noted, in her novel *Emma* (1816): 'One half of the world cannot understand
the pleasures of the other.' An expansion of this characterisation is provided in
Table 5.1. It needs little further comment, though I offer two.

Firstly, in matters of science and religion (critical in that they defined attitude
and awareness in and of themselves as well as in restive arguments between them)
there are few easy theorems to be advanced. It is not untypical to see eighteenth-
century science portrayed as altogether inimical both to the aristocracy and to

Table 5.1 *Stranger than fiction? North–South stereotypes in Georgian England*

CHARACTERISTIC		NORTH	SOUTH
GEOGRAPHY		PROVINCIAL	METROPOLITAN
		URBAN [THE CITY]	RURAL [THE COUNTRY]
		COUNTING-HOUSE	COUNTRY HOUSE
		LOCALITY	STATE
CLASS		BOURGEOISIE	ARISTOCRACY
POLITICS	PARTY	LIBERAL/WHIG/REFORM	TORY [THE ESTABLISHMENT]
	IDEOLOGY	MERITOCRACY, FITNESS, AMBITION, QUALIFICATION, REPRESENTATION, CERTIFIED ACHIEVEMENT	PRIVILEGE, PATERNALISM, PATRONAGE, DIVINE RIGHT, AUTOCRACY, OLIGARCHY, INHERITANCE
	INSTINCT	REFORM	DEFENCE OF TRADITION
ECONOMICS	THEORY	FREE-TRADE, LAISSEZ-FAIRE, COMPETITION [PARTICULARLY IN TRADE AND INDUSTRY]	PROTECTION/REGULATION [PARTICULARLY OF AGRICULTURE AND TRADE]
	PRACTICE	PRODUCTION OF CAPITAL FOR INVESTMENT [THROUGH MANUFACTURE AND TRADE] TO EXPAND WEALTH AND PROFIT. POLITICAL ECONOMY OF CAPITAL AND LABOUR	PRODUCTION OF COMMODITIES FOR CONSUMPTION AND EXCHANGE TO MAINTAIN SOCIAL POSITION AND POLITICAL INTEGRITY. MORAL ECONOMY OF MASTERS AND MEN
RELIGION	DENOMINATION	NON-CONFORMITY, CHARISMATIC EVANGELISM, CALVINIST, LATER METHODIST [WESLEYAN]	ANGLO-CATHOLICISM LATITUDINARIANISM
	STANCE	MORAL INJUNCTION, PRACTICE [SCRUPLE] THE MORAL CONDITION OF THE PEOPLE INDIVIDUAL BEHAVIOUR	ETHICAL IDEAL, RITUAL [THE LITURGY], THE WELLBEING OF THE COMMUNITY, COLLECTIVE OBSERVANCE
SECULAR PHILOSOPHY		HUMANISM, INSTRUMENTALISM, TRANSFORMATIONISM, ANTHROPOCENTRISM, EMPIRICISM, INDIVIDUALISM	TRUSTEESHIP, PARTNERSHIP, COSMOLOGY, COLLECTIVISM
EDUCATION	STRUCTURE	BOARD SCHOOL, DISSENTING ACADEMY, APPRENTICESHIP	PRIVATE TUTOR, PUBLIC SCHOOL, OXBRIDGE, GRAND TOUR
	PURPOSE	ACQUISITION OF KNOWLEDGE, SKILL, TRAINING, VOCATION, EXPERIENCE SHAPED BY KNOWLEDGE, A MERITOCRACY OF CERTIFIED ACHIEVERS	'LEARNING', MANNERS, TASTE, EDUCATION KNOWLEDGE REFLECTS EXPERIENCE, PRIVILEGE AND NATURAL SUCCESSION
CULTURE	ICON	SCIENCE	ARTS
	PURPOSE	RATIONAL UNDERSTANDING, PRACTICAL ACCOMPLISHMENT, REASON, STUDY/APPLICATION/ENLIGHTENMENT	AESTHETIC APPRECIATION, LEISURE, RELAXATION, DIVERSION

Anglicanism and the two thrown together as a straightforwardly middle-class vade-mecum. Equally, it is commonplace to find non-conformity (particularly of the Unitarian, Quaker and Congregationalist kind) marshalled alongside enterprise and imprisoned in a northern landscape. But such formulations are matters of gravity not exclusivity, of identifying a purity and generating a 'typicality', of finding a point and inventing a pattern. Denomination was no more tied to landscape than it was confined to context. Anglicanism remained (though almost certainly in decline) an Establishment and was present almost everywhere. It even had a toehold in the city. Wesley's mission (perhaps – because the most openly evangelical – the most indicative of all) was neither northern nor southern in its prescription, and neither urban nor rural in its intent. Nor (in the late-eighteenth century at least) was it notably more successful in one rather than the other.

As for science, suffice it to say that the great behemoth was not the exclusive middle-class utilitarian preserve it has sometimes been held to be. Whilst the 'northern' middle class certainly annexed it to their culture and even marched behind its 'republican' flag, it was never theirs alone. The aristocracy had cultivated science from its inception and, though they may have found themselves occasionally estranged in the face of an insistent middle-class suitor, theirs was never a divorce. In practice, a mind which could contemplate systematic scientific farming was not wholly at odds with one intent on applying the same broad precept to industry or even to nature in the round. Where the landed interest and the bourgeoisie divided was more over science's moral purpose: a justification for the *status quo* or a transformation of the world as hitherto known. The hardening as well as the juxtaposition of such attitudes was firmly evident in debates about trusteeship and transformation, issues which themselves connected to a wider family of concerns. In practice this separated those who felt at home with nature and just a little inclined to improve it, from those bent upon fashioning it anew and manufacturing from it things that even God had neglected to create. Such divisions were not wholly social in origin, neither were they geographically distributed in any meaningful sense. The relations between science and religion, and between the two and society, were rehearsed on the national stage and no proscenium arch divided audience from actor or even laboratory from pulpit at some convenient spot near the outskirts of Wolverhampton. Moreover, debates about science, religion and other such matters were confined to a relatively small and articulate portion of the population. This is not to state that the consequences of such discussion did not touch ordinary people, for as they found their way more steadily into political thinking, policy was increasingly derived from them.

Secondly, the association of the rural South with leisure and the industrial North with work, whilst patently absurd, gained some currency in the iconography of the period and may have reflected a more general attitude (Cosgrove 1984; Strong 2000). It may be pure artistic convention that scenes of relaxation, sport and plain conviviality register these activities in a broadly rural (southern?) frame, whilst those of toil take a distinctly northern flavour; but there was a political agenda here too, not least in the tendency amongst northern intellectuals to try to establish a moral high-ground by insisting on the virtue of their endeavours in contrast to the idleness held typical of the southern landed interest. It was not simply a matter of 'muck and brass' (though the muck that made brass in the North was certainly different from the muck that made manure in the South). Rather it was the articulation of a defiantly northern work ethic.

The fact that the rural South continued to vibrate more nearly to the natural rhythm of the seasons and of the daylight hours almost certainly contributed to a northern suspicion that the lifestyle of the South was intrinsically more relaxed (even privileged) than its own. The synthetic discipline of the clock together with the confinement of much work within the artificial boundaries of the factory gave industrial workers as well as their masters a sharp sense of time as well as of place and led to greater differentiation between work and non-work than was perhaps evident elsewhere. Clearly matters of class are at issue here too (the Victorians would, after all, style the eighteenth-century aristocracy the 'leisured class', whilst work remained work wherever it was undertaken – not least amongst the 'working class').

Them and us

It is clear by now that the North–South divide in this period was not a straightforward matter of geography: of territoriality and the policing of a boundary which – according to any reasonable criterion – divided two different but internally homogeneous domains. Neither pattern of commerce nor lifestyle, neither wealth nor faith, neither substance nor style set North unambiguously apart from South. Even if we allow that boundaries of this sort are always mutable and insecure and that the spirit rather than the letter of such difference should prevail, any distinctions that might be drawn are unlikely to be coincident nor are they impervious, and any proposed division is compromised by exception, discrepancy and example. More seriously, the concept of an immutable divide is also negated by the social constructions which must necessarily attach to it. Divide the sentient population as we might – by location, class, mobility, knowledge or attitude – the inescapable conclusion remains that any resulting dichotomy is false, precisely because it was the *recognised* dichotomy of no authority and no group, perhaps – rationally – of no individual.

Yet, to return to where we began, a feeling of North–South and of a perceived difference between them seems to have become an abstract commonplace in the late-eighteenth century and, if not from demonstrable realities, from what did this 'structure of feeling' (a term borrowed from Raymond Williams) derive?

In one sense it may have cascaded – particularly for the privileged observer – from a broader (and broadening) sense of geography, the consequences of which became imprintable on landscapes nearer to home. Throughout the later-eighteenth century the wealthier classes enjoyed increasingly secure access to another and very different South. Perhaps agreeing with Lord Byron (1823: 42) that the English winter 'end[s] in July to recommence in August', the more mobile amongst the wealthy voted with their feet and – following Dr Johnson's (1776/77) advice that 'the grand object of travelling is to see the shores of the Mediterranean' – undertook the 'Grand Tour' to the Mediterranean – as desirable as it was educative – which was, in fashionable, circles, the natural adventure of those with the wherewithal to undertake it. Annual journeys to Italy and to Greece (from which Romanticism would derive much of its languid vigour) connected the curious with an Arcadian classical past to which Georgian public rhetoric felt increasingly connected both by instinct and, more importantly, by birthright. Georgian England – not least in its 'Augustan' phase – made much of this in political and social terms. The Mediterranean south was held to be the place from which the civilised world had emerged: an *omphalos* from which 'culture' had first sprung. Certainly those returning from it brought back as much of it as they (or more accurately their bearers) could bear. The physical artefacts were obvious (take, for example, the Elgin Marbles which arrived by the ton, removed from the Parthenon and other ancient buildings in Athens), though far more significant was the simultaneous *invisible* import this implied.

Logically, it might be supposed that, on return, the wider perspectives that travel afforded would easily dissolve the petty distinctions so small a realm as England could sustain; that difference between north and south (Cumbria and Surrey?) would pale beside the obvious foreignness of other places. On the contrary, it appears either to have spawned or to have reinforced strong notions of difference in which the familiar was merely a pawn. This travel broadened the experience but narrowed the mind: ruined Rome was a precocious attempt at a proper London; Venice a precursor of canal-conscious Birmingham; squalid Naples a Mediterranean Manchester gone predictably wrong (Premble 1987). For the most part eighteenth-century travellers returned, it seems, with their prejudices refreshed and their perceptions intact; ready and able to impose their prescriptive perceptions closer to home.

On the other hand, there were also those whose memories embraced another, and different, 'north'. The Jacobite rebellion had been crushed finally at Culloden as late as 1746: it was well within living memory by the end of the century. An ill-defined sense of 'threat' from the North was surely still etched in the consciousness of many – not least those in government – and the temptation to see Scotland's 'savage wildness' as the obverse of the Mediterranean's 'gentle charms' is readily perceivable in the rhetoric of the time (Mason 1994; Devine and Young 1999). That rhetoric was itself becoming more heavily influenced by broadly environmentalist theses which – 'scientifically' derived – began to connect character to context and manner to landscape. With macro-geographies of this type to scale the construction, it makes sense that Georgian 'intellectuals' should perceive – and politically elaborate – a well-found version of its consequences in their own backyard: the closer to Caledonia, the rougher the character, the nearer to Parnassus, the more gentle the nature. As for England itself: the gritty North and the civilized South (Nibelheim and Valhalla?) were convenient constructions waiting to happen.

In part, then, 'North' and 'South' derived from bogus intellectualisations or, more commonly, from pure sentiment and were constructed on a variety of scales. But, in essence (and regardless of their immediate derivation) they were fabrications – insistences – of otherness. In Jane Austen's *Pride and Prejudice* (1813), Mr Bennet got close to it in as polite a respect as was decently allowed: 'For what do we live, but to make sport for our neighbours; and laugh at them in our turn.' Whilst it is true that otherness was not uniquely defined in North–South terms (often northerners were northerners only to southerners and did not feel such in the presence of other 'different' northerners (*and vice versa*)), the distinction appears to have gained an almost 'taken for granted' status in the general currency and thereby an inarticulate potency which stretched beyond logic. In this sense North and South were metaphors, totems, shibboleths.

This does not mean that they were, or are, unimportant. On the contrary, they gave rise (however inarticulately) to the idea of North and South as different and contradictory ecologies: different 'conditions of England'. In consequence, a distinction which could not be widely or accurately drawn in cartographic terms survived as a perception – better a 'structure of feeling' – which would later be elaborated into a set of self-defining, self-protective, self-advancing claims. In time, such readily deployable totems would justify, excuse, explain and even become instruments for the establishment of differences in character between the two, giving rise to a culture of otherness in encounters between them. Later still, these would be formularised: Mrs Gaskell, as we have seen, would juxtapose North and South as contrary entities, exclusive in their parameters and unmixable in their mores: a northern chalk and a southern cheese. But these were little more than distillations of difference and of prejudice to which the everyday perceptions of geography were often forced (or in some cases educated) to conform. It was all in the eye of the beholder. In the end too, North and South came to represent distinctions which increasingly mourn the passing of one era (as well as construct its hagiography) and to celebrate, though with some anxiety, the birth of another, so that what began as a casually locative vocabulary eventually gave shape and coherence to a mutual suspicion the main purpose of which was to articulate an otherwise unsustainable ideological divide.

For many, too, any idea of difference was based, surely, on the ignorance that parochialism fostered. Perhaps, like hell, North and South were simply 'other people', and this other began, not at some arbitrary distance from home, but at the limit of experience, where knowledge dissolved into ignorance and security into threat: ultimately where here became there and us became them. A population which could be convinced that sea monsters existed a bare mile offshore, was not invulnerable to the suggestion that northerners ate domestic animals (perhaps even their children) or that southerners, without exception, lived the life of Riley (Corbin 1995). Arguments prevail today about the merits of northern and southern beer and the kind of 'man' it takes to drink them. They are not different from those that prevailed in the past; only demonstrably more crass, because experientially less tenable.

In this sense, the border between the North and the South was both powerful and real (it might even be claimed that it was productively deployable where the *bête noire* could be invoked to a specific end) but it was real in the imagination (in the consciousness) and not on the ground, not on the map. North and South might not, then, have existed in any incontrovertible sense, but as the Italian saying goes: '*Se non è vero, è molto ben trovato*" (If it's not true, it's well found [invented]).

Over and out

Though it was almost certainly old enough to qualify, the Italian phrase did not find its way into Dr Johnson's *Dictionary*. Naturally; it was not English. But then 'slopston', 'fow', 'faffy' and 'sken' were not there either. They *were* English but not the right kind of English: not Dr Johnson's. They were dialect and not within his ambit, outside his ken, beyond his purview, outwith his experience; unacknowledged, alien: perhaps from just too far north for a man who had famously remarked: 'The noblest prospect a Scotchman ever sees, is the high road that leads him to England.'

Discerning North and South between 1750 and 1830 is much like reading *The Dictionary*. It is a challenging experience, and it offers glimpses of an idea, but, as Giuseppe Verdi once said of an art which attempted 'to copy reality' – 'it is photography not life'. The North–South divide can be made – as almost everything can – an object of definition and, sufficiently hedged, it can be made plausible too. But plausibility is not the issue. Intellectual abstractions are not the stuff of which real geography is made; certainly not the lodestone from which experience is fashioned. The geography of Britain between 1750 and 1830 was not so simple, nor was the diversity it sustained so unimportant, as to be reducible to the formulaic dichotomy of North and South. After all, chalk is $CaCO_3$; whilst cheese is ... 1,934 words in the *Encyclopedia Britannica*.

Note

1. The phrase is the title of a play by Goldoni (1707–93) whose work was widely influential in the eighteenth century and was particularly so in the work of Britain's (actually Ireland's) foremost playwright Richard Brinsley Sheridan (1751–1816).

6

South, North and nation: regional differences and consciousness in an integrating realm, 1550–1750

JOHN LANGTON

Early modernity

Generally known as 'the early modern period', this span of time is identified by the onset of 'modernity': that is, the deployment of instrumental human reason in relationships with nature and people, eventually to create an incomparably more materially productive, intricately ordered and expansive world (Graham and Nash 2000: 1–7). Human lives, livelihoods and geographies began to change profoundly as people and institutions deliberately set out to improve material life and its natural, social and political settings. This quest for improvement required the communication of both abstract and instrumental knowledge, in written and other forms. Modernity is therefore not only a state of being, but also, necessarily, a communicated state of knowing: a text about itself. Because we can only deliberately maintain and sustain, or improve and progress, through the elucidation of relationships between past, present and future, modernity's texts are inevitably historical. People began to recount what others wanted (and what they wanted others) to know about their world as it actually was, and to explain how it was changing for better or worse.

Of course, such profound structural and conceptual changes cannot happen suddenly or synchronously, and a 'late' something else must also have existed in the period: which would be 'feudalism' according to conventional historical tags. What that and its geography were are the subject of the next chapter, but it is necessary in this one to be wary of looking only for the beginnings of what later became general. Now that we are 'post-modern', we must also be wary of taking at face value what contemporaries began to tell themselves (and us) about the geography of their world and how its was changing. 'When we tell it like it is we are also telling it like we are', and so must they have been (Barnes and Duncan 1992: 3).

Real geographies

Historical change and continuity

It is now an orthodoxy that 'revolutionary' economic growth did not come suddenly in the late-eighteenth century, but that development was gradual and began much earlier, cumulating through the whole of the eighteenth century at least (Crafts 1985; Berg and Hudson 1992, 1994; Crafts and Harley 1992; Jackson 1992). Consistent with that, in the 1720s Daniel Defoe depicted a prosperous country at the centre of the known world, fructified by internal and overseas trade, everywhere 'full of good company' (Defoe 1724–6). By 1750 the processes he described had gone much further. Already, convertible husbandry and clover- and root-based crop rotations were diffusing through agriculture (Overton 1996: 99–105 and 116–7), and 'it would appear that the whole of this advance [in agricultural output per head between 1700 and 1800] was achieved before 1750' (Deane and Cole 1964: 75). The fly shuttle of 1733 had added impetus to the industry that already created massive wealth from the wool crop that was God's bounty to his chosen people (Earle 1977: 81). Its inventor's house was burned down by a mob in 1753 in protest against the unemployment it had caused (Mantoux 1961: 206–8). Steam engines were already busy (Hills 1989: 13–36). The coal to which they gave access was used in iron and other smelting processes as well as in domestic and smithy hearths (Flinn and Stoker 1984: 231–41), and the tin, copper and lead ores they opened up were matters of intense speculation and development (Burt, 1995; Pollard 2000a: 225).

A cornucopia of riches surged from the colonies through London to the edges of the realm (Walvin 1997). The 'great transformation' to capitalism brought by the emergence of factor as well as commodity markets was already under way (Polanyi 1957). Fixed-term leasehold tenures reflected the commercialisation of farming and enabled a land market (Brenner 1985). A market in proletarian labour was acknowledged as early as 1563 by the Statute of Artificers, which ordered the annual fixing of wage rates in each county (Woodward 1995: 172–3). Bills of exchange, the consolidated government funds, transferable shares in the permanent stock of corporations, and the Bank of England marked the emergence of a sophisticated money market after 1688 (Dickson 1967; Carruthers 1996). These markets stimulated the search for profit through innovations in techniques of production, distribution and business organisation (Mokyr 1990). They also allowed geographical space to be organised (indeed, produced) through exchanging the products of subdivided labour as well as natural materials specific to particular locales (Dodgshon 1990; Smith 1984). Increasingly, rational economic imperatives could mould that space to their own design as Coke's standardising legal *Institutes* (Blomley 1994), the political principles enunciated by Hobbes (1651) and Locke (1690a and b), and innovations in government practices (Corrigan and Sayer 1985: 43–113) smoothed legal and administrative barriers, blockages and inconsistencies away.

'A national economy is a political space, transformed by the state as a result of the necessities and innovations of economic life into a coherent, unified economic space whose combined activities may tend in the same direction. Only England managed this exploit at an early date' (Braudel 1977: 77). Government was fully imbricated in this before 1550. Henry VIII passed his 'great Arboricultural Act for the Preservation of Woods' in 1543 to ensure the systematic conservation and exploitation of timber resources nationwide (Nisbett and Lascelles 1903: 444), and the 677 statutes of his reign occupy 'almost as much space as all the preceding legislation from Magna Carta onwards' (Corrigan and Sayer 1985: 51). Government excise men coursed around the realm deploying nationally standardised volumetric measures from the late-seventeenth century (Ogborne 1998: 158–200). Defoe depicted in his *Tour* 'the most flourishing and opulent country in the world' (Defoe 1724–6: 43). His *Complete English Tradesman* was a vade-mecum for the harmonious and singular 'polite and commercial people' who had created it, secure and confident in the constitutionally guaranteed freedoms of the Glorious Revolution and the Hanoverian settlement (Langford 1992 and 2000).

In 1549 Sir Thomas Smith had bemoaned the 'manifold complaints of men touching the decay' of an island on the edge of Europe (Dewar 1969: 11). Its husbandmen and their families farmed smallholdings held on customary tenures overwhelmingly for subsistence (Overton 1996: 22). Peasant-like, they made most of the crude manufactures that were worked up from their non-comestible produce in time spare from farming (Grantham 1994; de Vries 1994). Many had recently been dispossessed so that sheep flocks could be increased to produce a bigger wool clip for sale abroad (Dewar 1969: 17). Gold and silver poured out in colonial enterprises and in exchange for foreign coins of base metal. Fewer husbandmen and less specie meant that 'now for lack of occupiers [towns are] fallen to great desolation and poverty' (Dewar 1969: 18). England was a resource-rich appendage of a more economically developed continent: 'they come for their wools, for their clothes, kerseys, corn, tin, lead, yea, their gold and silver, and such substantial and necessary things, [whilst] theirs be to us more to serve pleasure than necessity as tables, cards, perfumed gloves, glasses, gallypots, dials, oranges, pippins and cherries' (Dewar 1969: 68–9). As the proverb had it, 'the stranger buys of the Englishman the case of the goose for a groat and sells him its tail for a shilling' (Chapman 1967: 66). Economic ineffectuality and despondency was accompanied by deep 'division of opinion in matters of religion which hale men to and fro and make them to contend one against another' (Dewar 1969: 37). The state could do nothing to ameliorate these things because it was still, as Smith showed in his *De Republica Anglorum*, essentially feudal (Dewar 1982).

Clearly, more aspects and consequences of modernity existed in 1750 than in 1550: an 'advanced organic economy' was brought into being through the production of a national space of capitalist interaction, and was being supplemented by coal and other minerals (Wrigley 1988; Thomas 1993). But many things did not change: in fact, 'the boundary between the early modern and the modern

British economies is an historiographical bloodbath' (Hoppit 1993: 82). Given the enthusiasm of geographers and historians of all stripes now to see signs of our own world's birth, it is worth remarking on the gulf that still separated England in 1750 from what it became fifty years later. The first industrial canal was not opened until 1757 (Duckham 1983). The chronometer, diagnostic symbol of the English synthesis of science, art, craft skill, trade and war, was not perfected until 1761 (Sobell 1998). Though invented in 1709, coke smelting had hardly diffused from Shropshire by 1750 (Hyde 1977), and crucible steel making had barely been invented (Ashton 1924: 54–9). The impact of the fly shuttle was negligible compared to improvements in spinning made in the 1760s and 1770s: at 2.3 million lb, retained cotton imports in 1750 were less than twice as big as they had been in 1700, compared with 54.3 million lb in 1800 (Wadsworth and Mann 1965: 520–1). Watt's rotative steam engine, which allowed coal to be used to turn machinery, had not yet been invented (Hills 1989: 95–111). Like Arkwright, Priestley and Wedgwood, Watt was still in his teens in 1750, and Crompton was not yet a twinkle in his parents' eyes.

The Jacobite Rebellion of 1745 came just before the end of the period, as the Pilgrimage of Grace had come just before it began, and civil war wracked the seventeenth century even more savagely than it had blighted feudal times. The feudal aristocratic hegemony was as firm in 1750 as it had been in 1550, and its beneficiaries were more concerned with military matters, political placement and blood sports than the improvement of their estates or anything else (Porter 1982: 54–86). In 1750 most selective animal breeding was still probably for hunting hounds and horses, not commercial stock (Birley 1993: 78 and 87; Ponting 1969: 60). It was still illegal to buy and sell game and venison, the culinary symbols of extreme social privilege and the honour its patronage bestowed (Munsche 1981: 22; Whyman 1999: 14–37). A bewildering plethora of weights and measures (Connor 1987; Hoppit 1993; Pollard 2000b) and a severe lack of coinage (Muldrew 1993: 171) limited the extent to which markets could operate in the rural economy generally. Parliamentary enclosure largely came after 1750: vast areas of common land were not yet privatised and subject to commercial imperatives (Turner 1980; Mingay 1997). The makeshift economy they supported allowed the poor to escape both commodity and labour markets (Neeson 1993a and b; Thompson 1991). Protests by the lower orders against economic hardship still took the form of food riots, not wage strikes (Reed and Wells 1990; Randall and Charlesworth 2000). Poor relief expenditure in 1750 was less than half that of 1776, and less than one-thirteenth that of 1813 (King 2000: 80–1). Public spending as a whole grew from £6.2 million in 1715 to £7.2 million in 1750, but was £23.6 million in 1783 and £61.3 million in 1801 (Mathias 1969: 41).

Parish registration of baptisms, burials and marriages started before 1550 (Corrigan and Sayer 1985: 50), but little progress was made before 1750 in the systematic gathering and organisation of information required for rational decision-making and policy-formulation (Headrick 2000). The extent and composition of the Crown Lands was discovered only in the 1790s (Langton forthcoming a), of the human population in 1801 (Glass 1978). In 1750 fact was only just being conceptually separated from fiction and fable in the construction of histories and geographies (Mayer 1987; Sweet 1997). Josiah Tucker had not yet revealed the value of free trade (Schuyler 1931), nor had Adam Smith (1759, 1776) yet shown that the pursuit of private gain might be construed as anything other than the degraded corruption satirised by Bernard Mandeville (Mandeville 1714, 1723; Goldsmith 1978; Winch 1996).

Geographical processes

How might a North–South divide, or any other clear general pattern, have been produced in this *mélange* of novelty and constancy? It cannot simply have been that one had existed at an unmodernised beginning, to be reinforced or dismantled as it passed, or that modernity had produced one by 1750 where none had existed before. We have seen incidentally that the England of Henry VIII looks remarkably modern in some respects. And it is salutary to recollect not only that England's population increased by barely 10 per cent between 1651 and 1751, compared with 50 per cent over the next fifty years, but also that it had increased by 74 per cent between 1551 and 1651 (Wrigley and Schofield 1981: 207–8). The nature and chronology of change were too complicated to allow straightforward geographical trends and outcomes. What might we expect?

Most fundamentally, however 'modern' the period was, it came before the widespread use of mineral fuel lifted the kilocalories of energy available per head of population per year from about 26,000 to about 77,000 (White 1943; Cook 1971). The English were still 'ecosystem people' (Klee 1980: 1–2), dependent for their metabolism, reproduction, movement and recreation on tapping the flow of solar energy as it coursed through nature. Food, clothing, shelter and fuel, the four necessities of life, were derived by harnessing the power of wind and flowing water and, mainly, by growing plants and raising animals. This 'photosynthetic constraint' (Wrigley 1994: 33) did not only mean that little energy was available compared with a century later. Because agriculture has a very high ratio of energy consumed to energy produced, most of it was locked up everywhere in sustaining the flow (Wrigley 1991), and it is unlikely that so much as one-third was free for consumption outside its own production (Langton 1998a: 79–82). The most commonly used manufacturing raw materials were also produced from the land, by people who had to do farm work as well. Industry was limited in extent and capacity because its inputs were organic and produced by human labour that was necessarily unspecialised (Wrigley 1991: 332).

The nature of these biological resource systems would obviously vary according to the physical environment: 'man found natural regions, but . . . made the farming countries' (Kerridge 1973: 73). Social organisation, work routines and quotidian preoccupations varied according to farming system (Langton 1998a).

Table 6.1 *Sheep-corn and wood-pasture regions*

Characteristic	Sheep-corn	Wood-pasture
Land quality	Light	Heavy
Land availability	Shortage	Plentiful commons and wastes
Cash crops	Corn, wool	Dairy products, meat
Field system	Common, open	Several, enclosed
Settlement	Nucleated	Dispersed
Social control	Strong	Weak
Parish size	Small	Large
Population movements	Out-migration	In-migration
Industry	Little	Much
Social structure	Differentiated	Family farms
Politics	Conformist	Radical
Religion	Conformist	Dissenting
Crime	Order	Disorder
Sport	Team games	Individual games

Source: after Overton (1996: 49)

So did beliefs about the world and people's place and role in it: Adam Smith acknowledged that 'the understandings of the greater part of men are necessarily formed by their ordinary employments' (Clayre 1977: 196) and Hardy, echoing Shakespeare, that 'thought's the slave of life' (Orel 1967: 44). Overton's (1996: 49) tabular summary of the starkest of these human ecological differences, between areas where arable and pasture farming were dominant, is reproduced in Table 6.1. A wide array of economic, social and cultural variables were correlatively patterned. We have already seen that these pre-modern human ecological processes, differentiating societies according to the agricultural basis of their subsistence, were supplemented by others. Timber of various kinds, charcoal, dyestuffs and medicines of the woodlands were also part of the suite of resources available to ecosystem people. So were wind and water power: 'if the economy of the nineteenth century rested on coal, that of the eighteenth was closely dependent on water' (Ashton 1959: 8). Even a pre-modern economy would not simply produce a series of geographical cells reflecting agriculture.

If the availability of mineral supplements to agricultural energy and raw materials that were already used by 1750 were strongly patterned, so would be their effects on economic geography. And that is not the only geographical sign of modernity we might expect to find. Because up to a third of output can circulate through exchange even in agrarian economies (more if wood, water power, metals and coal were widely used), the subdivision of labour gives rise to secondary and tertiary economic activities, adding value to output through processes of manufacturing and circulation, which are largely based in and/or organised through towns

(Wrigley 2002). The size and growth rates of urban populations would, therefore, reflect modernity's capacity to organise space into more productive configurations, and their distribution patterns would reflect any geographical differences in that process. Not only that: the greater the extent to which space was organised to allow specialisation through exchange, the more marked would be any geographical differences in what was produced where, in agriculture and industry (Homans 1969). The more complete the hierarchical organisation of the towns within and through which this organisation was occurring, the greater that effect would be, the larger would be the system's primate city, and the greater would be the likelihood of an overall core-periphery pattern across an economic space radiating from that hub (de Vries 1984; Bairoch 1988). 'Thought's life's slave' for everybody, not just peasants, and the effects of modernity would not be confined to economic geography. Economic patterns and changes of these kinds would bring geographical differences and changes in society and culture as well.

In short, then, we would expect a geography that was a conflation of pre-modern human ecological processes bound mainly to agricultural resources, the beginnings of what might be termed 'mechanical modernity' based on water power and mineral resources, and the increased articulation of both through national and international spatial organisation. Did this conflation resolve into a North–South divide at any time during its progress?

Geographical patterns

Unfortunately, it is difficult to tell because what is supposed to be one of modernity's distinguishing features is absent from the early modern period. An almost complete dearth of systematically collected statistical information makes it impossible to construct reliable maps of human geographical patterns. Those that follow are attempts to make something out of very imperfect indicators. This is acknowledged in the cartographic technique used: most maps are plotted on a coarse-grained base of county units, ranks are represented rather than absolute values, and only the twenty extreme values are distinguished.

The geographical distribution of wealth and the way it changed have been used to suggest both a clear divide between wealthy south and poor north in the early-eighteenth century (Darby 1973: 308), and significant geographical change through our period (Buckatzsch 1950). A conflation of lay wealth in 1514 with church wealth in 1535 (Schofield 1965: 504) does seem to be concentrated in the south (Figure 6.1a). Although two of the poorest ten counties were also in the south, Huntingdonshire was the furthest north of the richest ten, and eight of the poorest ten were in the Midlands and north, despite the absence of the four most northerly counties from the data. The richest ten counties were on average more than twice as wealthy as the poorest ten. Figure 6.1b seems to show an even more starkly polarised geography in 1707 (Darby 1973: 308). Again, there was an outlier of a wealthy south in the Midlands, but now all eight counties north of the

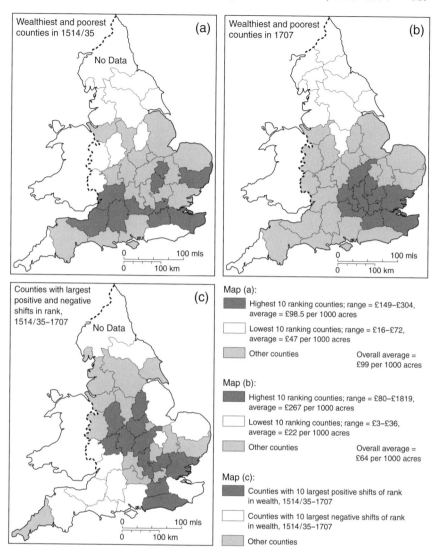

Figure 6.1 The geographical distribution of wealth in 1514/35 and 1707 (after Schofield (1965: 504) and Darby (1973: 308))

Mersey–Humber line were amongst the poorest ten, and the richest ten were ten times richer than the poorest ten. Figure 6.1c suggests that geographical polarisation was also growing: even though they already ranked highly, some southern counties were amongst those that increased their ranks most between the two dates, and some already low-ranking counties in the north were amongst the ten counties whose ranks fell by most. Mainly, though, the largest movements up and down the rankings were amongst middle-ranking counties in the Midlands.

The patterns in Figure 6.1 might seem to suggest that counties where wealth depended on rich agricultural endowments fell in rank. However, that is not consistent with the overall picture of a rich south getting richer, and a north with worse agricultural endowments getting relatively poorer. These patterns are also consistent with increased diffusion of economic stimuli from London. But it would be wrong to make too much of these things. The sixteenth-century taxes were levied on actual assessments of all wealth, whereas that of 1707 was based only on landed wealth. It also represented a total sum set by government needs, apportioned to counties according to quotas set in the seventeenth century (Browning 1953: 317–21 and 458–9; Schofield 1965). Figure 6.1 and its legend do not, therefore, reflect an increase in wealth over the period or the distribution of all wealth in 1707, and if any geographical changes can be inferred from them they happened long before 1700.

Statistics of population are at least as imperfect as those of wealth. John Rickman's county estimates from parish registers have been used throughout for consistency, ignoring improved data for the eighteenth century (Rickman 1843: 36–7; Deane and Cole 1964: 103). Figure 6.2 shows that average densities varied widely: the sparsest county population was 75 persons per 1,000 acres in 1570, falling to 65 in 1670 and 64 in 1750, but the densest (outside Middlesex, which included London) increased from 176 to 249 to 305 persons per 1,000 acres. The wealthiest counties in the south in 1514–35 were amongst the most densely populated in 1570, and the poorest and unassessed counties in the north were amongst the least densely populated. Both wealth and population were concentrated in London and adjacent counties. But there was no simple distance-decay function around the capital. Away to the west, Gloucestershire, Somerset and Wiltshire ranked highly on wealth in 1514/35, though not in 1707; the first two and Devon were relatively densely populated in 1570 and 1670, and the first two and Wiltshire in 1750. The overall correlation between sixteenth-century county rankings on wealth and population density was quite low at +0.47, and deep poverty and dense populations in Lancashire and Herefordshire were not necessarily statistical aberrations: the proportion of total tax in 1514 accounted for by poll payments 'in some counties in the north and west . . . was quite considerably higher than elsewhere, indicating the existence of a much larger proportion of very poor people in this region' (Schofield 1965: 493). The correlation coefficients of wealth in 1707 and population density in 1670 and 1750 were only slightly higher than for the sixteenth century, at +0.51 and +0.52. Certainly, any suggestion of a poor, sparsely populated north and a wealthy, densely populated south is confused by aberrant counties in each region, and by the Midlands, which contained the full national range of county experiences.

The population growth statistics plotted on Figure 6.3 add further complexity. Overall, national population increased by 66 per cent over the period, 42 per cent

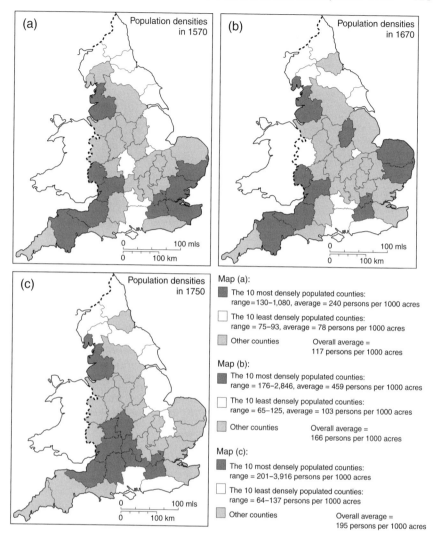

Figure 6.2 Population densities in 1570, 1670 and 1750 (after Rickman 1843: 36–7)

between 1570 and 1670 and 17 per cent between 1670 and 1750. The range of experience narrowed as national growth slowed. Of the ten counties with the fastest growth between 1570 and 1670, four were in the south, four in the Midlands and two in the north. Of the ten slowest growing, three were in the south, two in the Midlands and five in the north. Maybe there is a hint of a North–South difference, but no more than that. Between 1570 and 1670 and between 1670 and 1750 the regional distribution of the twenty counties with the most extreme demographic

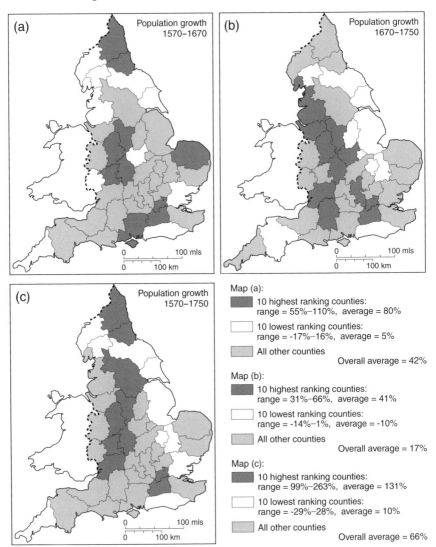

Figure 6.3 Population growth 1570–1670, 1670–1750 and 1570–1750 (after Rickman 1843: 36–7)

movements hardly changed. Relatively slow growth – indeed, decline – occurred across wealthy East Anglia and Lincolnshire, which we would expect to be amongst the most productive agricultural areas, as well as Sussex and Devon in the south and Cumberland and two Yorkshire Ridings in the north. Numbers fell in all ten lowest-ranking counties between 1670 and 1750, but no others, although according to Deane and Cole's (1964: 103) recalculations from Rickman's data, this occurred in sixteen counties between 1701 and 1751. On the other hand, Gloucestershire and Wiltshire had dense populations in 1570 and 1670, which grew rapidly thereafter as they apparently slid down the county rankings of wealth. Strikingly, rapid growth between 1670 and 1750 was heavily concentrated in the Midlands and adjacent western counties: eight of the ten counties with the fastest-growing populations were there. Given that London was already very large in 1550, it is hardly surprising that Middlesex, which had ranked first on every other index plotted so far, was sixth in terms of population growth between 1670 and 1750. Taking the two periods together, as in Figure 6.3c, in the south, metropolitan Middlesex and Surrey were in the ten counties with the fastest-growing populations, and Gloucestershire appears to be a southern extension of the strongly growing Midlands. In the north, three counties east of the Pennines were in the highest echelon of growth, but two west of it were in the lowest. There was certainly no evidence of a North-South divide – unless similar levels of variegation were 'divided' by the Midlands, where growth was more uniform and only Lincolnshire bucked the trend.

Populations for units as small as towns are even less reliable than those for counties. The data presented in Figure 6.4 are based on estimates calculated mainly from hearth taxes levied in the 1660s, 1670s and 1680s (Langton 2000a: 457–62), which show a massively primate city and a repletion of tiny towns. With more than 300,000 people, London contained a quarter of the total urban population; the 791 towns with fewer than 2,500 inhabitants contained more than twice as many, and the 59 of intermediate size all had fewer than 20,000 people and contained only 23 per cent of townsfolk. Towns in all size ranges were quite evenly scattered, implying that a heavily commercialised rural economy existed throughout the country, facilitating local exchange and funnelling goods up to and receiving them back from London, with few hierarchical tiers adding value in between (de Vries 1984; Clark 1995). On average, nearly a quarter of county populations lived in towns. Apart from in Middlesex, where it was 53 per cent, this proportion varied from 11 per cent in Durham to 32 per cent in Gloucestershire; the average for the nine counties below London was 31 per cent, and of the ten least urbanised counties 13 per cent. Although the proportions of county populations living in towns perhaps tended to be lowest in the north and Midlands and highest in the wealthier and more densely populated south-east, the few relatively large towns greatly affected urbanisation figures, increasing those of the counties they sat in and reducing those of neighbouring counties within their hinterlands – hence, the otherwise incongruously high rates of urbanisation in Westmorland and the East and North Ridings of Yorkshire.

No urban population figures exist for the eighteenth century, and so growth can be measured only to 1801, so that an unknown (but certainly high) proportion of the urban growth depicted in Figure 6.5 occurred after our period ended. However, on the assumption that the pattern of growth did not change massively after 1750,

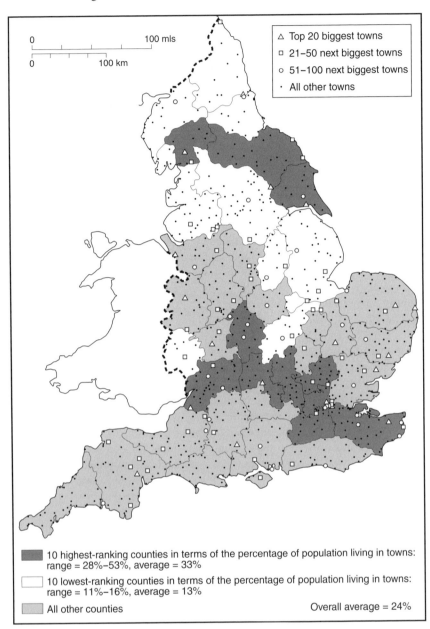

Figure 6.4 The distribution of towns and the proportions of county populations living in towns, 1662/77–1801 (author's own database)

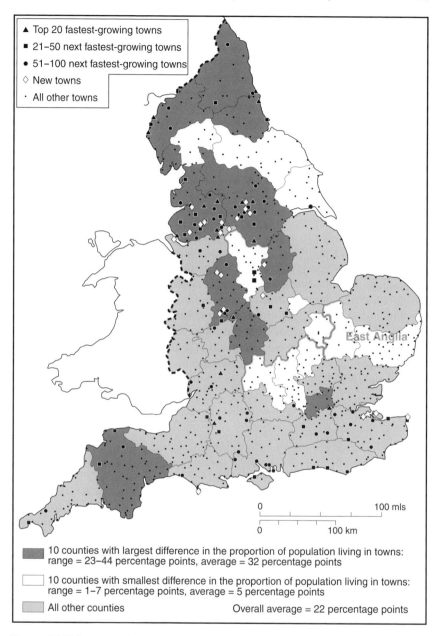

Figure 6.5 Urban growth, new towns and rates of urbanisation of county populations, 1662/77–1801 (author's own database)

Table 6.2 *Regional distribution of the 100 fastest-growing towns and new towns from the late-seventeenth century to 1801*

Region	Ranks 1–20	Ranks 21–50	Ranks 51–100	Total	New towns
North	15	13	19	47	11
South-East	1	7	14	22	3
South-West	2	4	10	16	1
Midlands	2	6	7	15	6
East Anglia	0	0	0	0	0
Totals	20	30	50	100	21

we can see that the proportion of population living in towns increased by only five percentage points on average in the ten counties with the smallest increases, over half of which were in East Anglia and an arc extending inland from it to Oxfordshire. Only two of the ten counties with the largest increases were in the south or East Anglia: Middlesex, reflecting London's continued rapid growth, and Devon, where the statistic is heavily affected by the expansion of Plymouth and Devonport after 1750. Eight of the ten counties where population was urbanising fastest were in the north and Midlands, which also contained most of the fastest-growing and newly emergent towns (Table 6.2). Much of this urban efflorescence must have occurred after our period ended, but it was certainly under way before then (Trinder 1973; Hopkins 1989; Stobart 1996a and b; Stobart and Lane 2000).

These heavy geographical variegations in patterns of wealth, population, towns and their changes were underlain by economic variables. Thirsk's well-known detailed maps of the agricultural systems that provided most energy, raw materials and employment show massive variation, with no neat North–South, or any other clean national divide (Thirsk 1987: 28–9). Overton's maps show that this reflected soil quality (Overton 1996: 58–9). Mixed farming with a strong arable presence had northern salients up the coastal and inland plains of Yorkshire, Lancashire, Cumberland, Durham and Northumberland, whilst there were large areas of open-pasture and wood-pasture farming on marshes, clay plains and sandy heaths in the south, Midlands and East Anglia. No counties had uniform agricultural practices. The scale of differences was much smaller. As Pehr Kalm observed in 1748, 'in England the wholesome custom is much in use, that nearly every district lays itself out for something peculiar in Rural Economy, to cultivate, viz., that which will thrive there best, and leaves the rest to other places' (Overton 1996: 104). It was local exchange of complementary products that generated England's dense network of small central places (Coates 1965).

Figure 6.6a is highly generalised and based on marriage seasonality, with arable farming indicated by an autumn and pastoral farming by a spring peak (Kussmaul

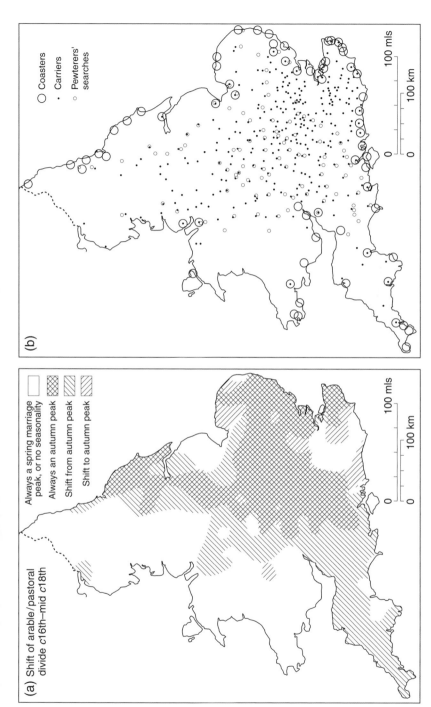

Figure 6.6 (a) Geographical shifts in arable and pasture farming from the sixteenth to the mid-eighteenth century; (b) London contacts in the late-seventeenth and early-eighteenth centuries (after Kussmaul (1990: 2 and 12), Andrews (1970: 205) and Anon. (1667–77)).

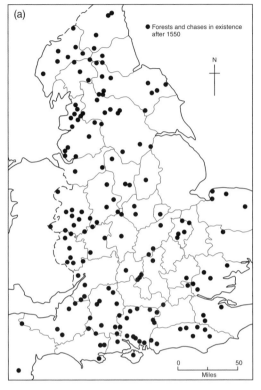

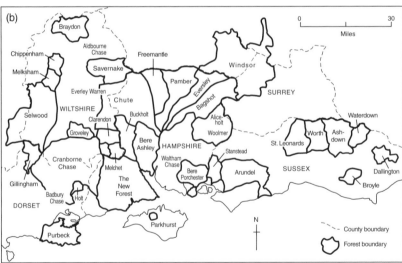

Figure 6.7 Forests and chases *c*.1550 (a) in England as a whole (b) in six southern counties (author's own database)

1990: 2 and 12). It suggests that the boundary between predominantly pasture farming areas and the mainly mixed/arable 'heartland' of English grain production lurched south-eastwards over the period. This is consistent with the innovation of convertible husbandry and clover/root rotations onto better soils within reach of the London market, which could then also supply more marginal areas that no longer needed to produce their own grain. Agricultural labour requirements per acre increased where innovation occurred, but fell where arable gave way to pasture farming (Kussmaul 1990: 103–25). Greater stocking densities in areas where new farming systems were introduced reduced their demand for animal products from predominantly pastoral areas, where people must thenceforth keep body and soul together through non-farming activities, 'thereby making good the old proverb, that a barren soil is an excellent whetstone to promote industry' (Jones 1969; Pollard 1981: 336).

Perhaps this evidence cannot bear that or any other interpretation (Overton 1996: 103–4), although it is at least intriguing that Wrigley and Schofield's map of marriage seasonality (based on a different sample of parish registers and covering a different time from Kussmaul's) shows an area of arable farming in north-west England corresponding to that on Thirsk's map (Wrigley and Schofield 1981: 302). And a comparison of all the maps does seem to show that the areas where mixed arable farming remained predominant through the period were also the wealthiest, with dense populations in 1570 that grew slowest thereafter, and high initial rates of urbanisation which also increased more slowly than elsewhere. Even more striking from a geographical point of view is that the midland heartland of greatest change in other respects, splashing over into adjacent areas of the south-west and north, also experienced the most comprehensive alteration of farming regimes. Perhaps clearest and most widely agreed of all, though, is that the geography of farming and the way it changed were as kaleidoscopically varied as all the other phenomena mapped so far, with a multitude of little fractures between small regions rather than clean divides between large slabs of uniform territory (Kerridge 1973; Everitt 1977 and 1979; Thirsk 1987; Davie 1991; Overton 1996: 46–56).

This effect was heightened by the existence of forests and chases (Langton forthcoming b). Figure 6.7 shows that everywhere, even in the arable south-east, huge areas of land survived in that pre-modern state. Forests managed to facilitate deer hunting by the Crown and aristocracy sustained scrappy woodland, coppices, warrens and lawns on open common 'wastes' (Rackham 1989). Complex intercommoning arrangements and the aristocracy's defence of hunting privileges prevented enclosure (Hann 1999: 67), and the innovation of new crop rotations was impossible because of deer grazing (Hawkins 1980: 77–8). Here were the sources of the game and venison that made meat such a large component of the English diet (Drummond 1939), and here, too, the poor could eke out an independent living (Neeson 1993a and b; Reed and Wells 1990). Although forests were no more heavily wooded than elsewhere (Rackham 1989: 39), their resources were accessible to everyone. Squatters could graze a few cows, sheep and pigs and do craft work, from coal and metal mining, through brick and glass making, charcoal burning, wood turning and hurdle making, to gloving, initially from animal skins. The makeshift forest economy of the poor was actually facilitated by the draconian acts passed after 1660 to protect forest deer and game for the Crown and nobility (Munsche 1981; Thompson 1991). Even where modernity brought disafforestation and enclosure before 1750, as over much of Wiltshire, Hampshire, Oxfordshire, Buckinghamshire and Worcestershire, at least one-third (sometimes much more) of erstwhile forest wastes survived as common, and extensive hunting parks remained (Beresford 1957; Williamson 1995). Forest boundaries, within which market charters could not be granted (Wilson 1958), were strung like necklaces with little towns. Like the open pastures of the north and west, forests supported independent landless people dependent on common resources and commodity markets. Their survival gave a dense scattering of 'little norths' everywhere.

More 'modern' non-agricultural resources were also widely scattered. Wool was ubiquitous: all counties produced over two packs per 1,000 acres in 1700, Berkshire, Dorset, Hertfordshire and Northamptonshire over six (Andrews 1970: 197). The woollen cloth industry was spread in little specialised regions across the whole country (Bowden 1962: 49; Langton 1978: 177). Water power was abundant throughout the rugged west, as well as in heavily corrugated Kent, Sussex, Dorset and Wiltshire. There were pockets of coal there, too, as well as in what later became major coalfields: from Bovey Tracey in Devon, through Nailsea and Vobster in Somerset, Iron Acton in Gloucestershire, Cleobury Mortimer and Pontesbury in Shropshire, and Neston in Cheshire, to Bentham in north Lancashire. The size of reserves was not yet significant. Iron smelting and forging were scattered widely through the south and Midlands; tin ore was limited to the south-west, but lead, copper and iron were more widespread (Burt 1995; Westerfield 1915: map III). Local coincidences of timber, water power and ore, sand or clay gave rise to manufacturing in Kent, Sussex, Dorset, Somerset, Gloucestershire, deepest south and west Shropshire, and vastly numerous other places, as well as in what later became the northern and midland industrial regions. Early industry was as firmly fixed as agriculture to the particular attributes of small localities (Hoskins 1955: 162–5; Everitt 1979; Deacon 1998).

Perhaps it is possible to link the patterns shown by the maps so far presented as follows. First, there was massive variability throughout the country in a mosaic with small *tesserae*. In pre-modern mode, wealth and population still mainly reflected soil fertility, though this was somewhat disturbed by the strong and widespread survival of forests and chases. Greater disposable income in farming provided numerous niches for specialist rural and urban craftsmen locally (Skipp 1978), and also in nearby less agriculturally propitious areas: 'while the inhabitants of the favoured soil raise corn for the support of the community, those who are not blessed in this way, manufacture goods for the comfort and convenience of the happy agriculturalists, and in this manner both equally promote the public good' (Pollard 1981: 336). Secondly, the geography of wealth and population were already changing in response to greater exploitation of non-agricultural resources. Like fertile soils and forests, these were widely scattered: metal ore, charcoal and water power occurred together on the Weald, Mendips, Clee and Stiperstones as well as the Birmingham Plateau and regions to the north.

Thirdly, the maps are unmistakable evidence of spatial sorting around the hub of London. Figure 6.6b shows the capital city's virtually nationwide economic contacts in 1728, with coastal shipping, especially to eastern and southern shores, ameliorating the sharp inland distance-decay of land carriage (Andrews 1970: 205). Freemen and apprentices poured in from everywhere, with little apparent diminution of numbers with distance (Pawson 1979: 36; Wareing 1980), and shopkeepers from as far away as Lancaster stocked up in the capital (Marshall 1967). Not only goods flowed back. Wealth accumulated in London was dispersed nationwide through the charitable endowment of religious, welfare and educational institutions: 'it intervened decisively in order to change the whole social and religious structure of a county like Lancashire, and it lent important aid to Yorkshire' (Jordan 1959: 364). Changes in the geography of agriculture are recognisably a response to the pattern of these links to the massive London market for grain and malt, which fixed prices in a regular distance-decay pattern across the country until after our period ended (Westerfield 1915: maps I and II; Gras 1926; Chartres 1995). Competition for labour from improved farming (Large 1984; Kussmaul 1990), for water power from corn milling (Jones 1960; Short 1989; Zell 1994: 241–6), and for fuel from London itself pushed the industries needing them out beyond the improving farming areas of the south-east: the 'tyranny of wood and water' that drove iron smelting and forging into the more distant provinces (Ashton 1924: 13–25) had powerful allies, and more than one enemy.

The capital's huge demand for fuel kick-started coal mining and related industries on the Tyne (Wrigley 1987), and most other crafts and manufactures serving more than local markets were still connected to the capital. Figure 6.6b shows the extent of the control exercised by the London Pewterers' Company in the late-seventeenth century (Anon. 1667–77; Barker and Hatcher 1974: 255–8). Their provincial searches continued until at least 1723, and similar inspections were conducted by the London Cutlers Company (Hey 1991: 159). Under their monopoly of 1635, Blackwell Hall drapers had a firm grip on the marketing of cloth made almost nationwide (Jones 1972). The Shrewsbury Drapers were an outpost of the London Company (Mendenhall 1953). The London Ironmongers' Company controlled the supply of naval dockyards and the West Indian and North American markets as well as the metropolis itself (Rowlands 1975). Ambrose Crowley, a London ironmonger, introduced factory iron production to Tyneside in 1682 (Westerfield 1915: 242); John Weld, one of the first industrial entrepreneurs of Coalbrookdale, was a London merchant's son and brother-in-law to two others (Trinder 1973). Provincial glass-making was initiated by French craftsmen who entered the country through London (Barker and Harris 1954: 110; Rowlands 1987: 145). In the 1750s London imported more raw cotton than Liverpool (Wadsworth and Mann 1965: 170 and

188–9). 'The greater part of the foreign and home trade in Manchester goods was carried on through London' (Wadsworth and Mann 1965: 236–7), where Lancashire manufacturers had much wealthier mercantile partners, and where roller spinning was invented by Lewis Paul in 1736, and first innovated by a Spitalfields check manufacturer in 1739–40 (Wadsworth and Mann 1965: 173, 236–40 and 419–20).

London was still the nursery where nascent industries were incubated before eventually responding to the lower factor costs of the provinces. Paul's own first factory was in Nottinghamshire, and fustian weaving had already left the capital for north-west England by the end of the seventeenth century (Schwartz 1992: 35). Framework knitting was in the process of doing so: by 1727 there were 2,500 frames in London (where wage costs were 15s. per week) and 5,500 in the provinces, mainly the east Midlands (where wages averaged 10s. per week) (Chapman 1967: 72). Contemporaneously, 'silk throwing drifted from London to the north Midlands . . . and London employers controlled concerns a hundred and fifty miles away, at which the materials for the looms of Spitalfields were prepared' (Wadsworth and Mann 1965: 304). Craftsmen in Birmingham and Sheffield were employed by London goldsmith shopkeepers (Clifford 1995), and in Liverpool and Prescot by London watch and clockmakers (Bailey and Barker 1969; Schwartz 1992: 38–9).

As modernism implies, an integrated economic space was being produced. The consumers, producers and merchants of London were the pivot of a clearly patterned economic geography encompassing agriculture and industry. The subdivision of labour and exchange that created it greatly increased the wealth of what was still very largely an advanced organic economy (Wrigley 1988). Core and periphery relationships that might have created a North–South divide did not do so because of coastal shipping contacts, and because intricately patterned resource endowments could be even more strongly reflected in economic activities. London's tentacles grasped into the midland and northern coalfields, and it is a pity that we cannot know how much of the change shown in Figure 6.5 occurred before our period ended in reflection of that.

However, provincial growth was not wholly dependent on London. Lancashire fustians, out of which the cotton industry grew, were first produced for export to Ireland through Chester and Liverpool (Lowe 1972), and that industry had an impact on the urban system of north-west England before 1750 (Stobart 1996a). The independence from London control to which the expansiveness of the Yorkshire woollen industry has been attributed (Wilson 1973) was also evident amongst the cutlers of Sheffield by 1720 (Hey 1991: 159–62), and the pewterers of Wigan before that (Anon. 1667–77; Moran 1997). Perhaps most intriguingly, the Midlands and west, which show most cartographic evidence of fundamental change before 1750, also seem to have wriggled most free of London by 1750 (Rowlands 1975). Bristol was dealing in exports of metalware from as far afield as Sheffield and textiles from Shrewsbury, Wiltshire, Somerset and Gloucestershire, as well as articulating the movement of capital and goods through the whole of west-central England before 1750 (Minchinton 1951; Morgan 1993: 102–8). The textile and other exports of Lancashire and Yorkshire were already moving out into the Irish Sea and Atlantic trade through Liverpool. Although we do not know how far this process had got by 1750, it is worth remembering that Adam Smith noted in the 1770s that 'all over Great Britain manufactures have confined themselves to the coal countries' (Wrigley 1987: 38). The increased use of mineral fuel can only have brought more geographical variegation (Langton 2000b and 2002). In so far as it affected the Midlands as well as the north, the use of mineral fuel in regional economies increasingly separate from London massively blurred any indication of a North–South divide.

Cultural differences and political movements reflected the complexity of economic geography. Defoe's inability to understand what was being said in Somerset (Defoe 1724–6: 216) must have been general amongst travellers, most bewilderingly so in the large parts of western Shropshire where Welsh was spoken, and in the extreme west in Cornwall, with its own language. Indeed, the perception on both sides of the Tamar of Cornwall's separateness from the rest of England was the most marked regional divide in early modern England, with economic and linguistic roots (Stoyle 1996; Deacon 1998). According to twentieth-century research, the dialects that perplexed Defoe could not have evinced a North–South divide either. Maps of phonological, lexical and morphological features of English dialects show a vast archipelago of islands and promontories bounded by the most sinuous of lines. If there is any sign of a North–South divide on any of them, it runs through the Midlands, or to the north of south Lancashire (Orton, Sanderson and Widdowson 1978).

The Pilgrimage of Grace is sometimes represented as a revolt of the conservative upland north against religious innovation from the lowland south, and the Northern Rising is actually cardinally specified (Hoyle 2001). However, Figure 6.8a shows that Lincolnshire was an epicentre of the former, from which Lancashire conspicuously abstained, and the west, Midlands, East Anglia and the southeast were much more riotous than the north during our period (Barraclough 1979; Charlesworth 1983; Fletcher 1998). Forest areas, wherever they were, and especially if they were being improved, were particularly prone to riot (Langton forthcoming a).

The battle lines of the Civil War were equally convoluted. If a Royalist north existed, Figure 6.8b shows it had long salients down the east and west Midlands through to Oxfordshire and a completely detached locus in Cornwall, whilst parts of Yorkshire and Lancashire were fervently Parliamentarian from the start (Barraclough 1979: 184; Cannon 1997: 1022). The Clubmen who called a plague on both houses were concentrated where fighting was most intense in the southwest and south-west Midlands, though there were none in equally battle-scarred south Lancashire (Lynch 1983). In fact, maps of this size again fail to reflect differences that were sharpest on very small scales. If there was 'an ecology of allegiance' in religious or civil concerns, it was a filigree of intricate patchwork (Underdown 1985; Morrill 1987; Stoyle 1994: 149–61). A divide as profound as any sliced down the middle of south Lancashire, 'the *Cock-pit of Conscience*,

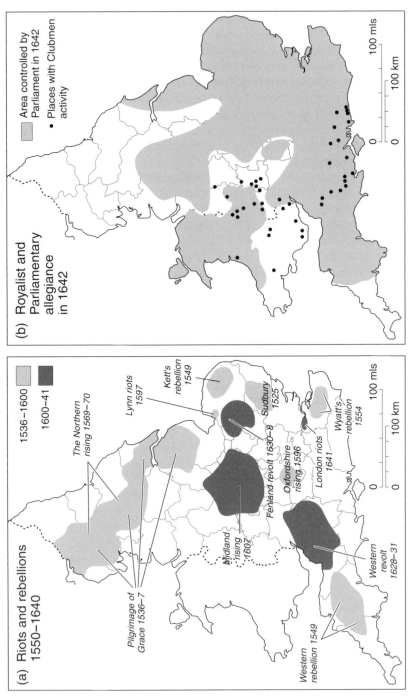

Figure 6.8 (a) Riots and rebellions, 1540–1640; (b) Areas supporting Parliament and the King in 1642 (Barraclough 1979: 185 and 184)

wherein . . . *Antient* and *Modern Fanaticks*, though differing much in their wild Fancies and Opinions, meet together in mutual *madness* and *distraction*' (Fuller 1662: Part 2, 124). Allegiance in the Civil War corresponded closely with these religious dispositions (Morrill 1987). Generally, Catholicism has, like the emergence of Puritanism, been associated with remote and upland areas; but as Bossy (1975: 86) dismissively put it, Catholics were 'not distributed like a species of vegetation'. In Lancashire, where Catholicism tended to be staunchest in areas of relatively rich manorial agriculture and Puritanism in upland pastoral and rural industrial areas, there were obdurate Catholic communities in textile-producing uplands and Puritan communities in the lowlands of the Manchester embayment (Langton 1998b). Through commercial links, the latter was most under the London cultural influence noted earlier (Haigh 1975: 13 and 176; Hardman 1998), and the former was closer through Liverpool to Ireland. It was the same in Devon, where although 'some general trends can be identified . . . time and again, exceptions have been found to the general rules' (Stoyle 1994: 161).

Things were just as multiplicitously complex in the eighteenth century. Maps of the counties that were most Jacobite, and most and least non-conformist, in the late-seventeenth century show the by now familiar confused pattern in which there is rarely uniformity across more than two adjacent counties, let alone over a North or a South (Browning 1953: 255 and 425). So do maps of the county distribution of the most and least commercially minded Members of Parliament in the 1730s (Horn and Ransome 1957: 200). Always, north and south were split into widely contrasting subregions when data are mapped at a county level, overlapping across a central nexus of geographical variegation in the Midlands. Even then, as in the seventeenth century, there must have been enormous variability within counties, with single ones exhibiting the full range of national cultural experience.

Imagined geographies

Textual representations of reality

How was this seething space of contrasts and changes envisioned and depicted at the time? True to the nature of modernity, textual and cartographic description and discourses on improvement proliferated through the period. Smith's discourse of 1549 was supplemented in 1577 by Harrison's description of England, with a second edition in 1587 (Edelen 1968). An efflorescence of detailed evaluative surveys of landholdings came soon after: the office of Surveyor General was instituted, the 'Great Survey' of all Crown lands was initiated in 1608, and the Crown paid nearly £18,000 to surveyors between 1602 and 1611 (Barber 1992; Hoyle 1992b; Thirsk 1992). The government assiduously promoted improvement projects from the 1540s (Thirsk 1978), and manuals on how to improve farms, gardens, woods and other natural resources abounded (Leslie and Raylor 1992). Fuller's description of what was noteworthy in the realm appeared in 1662; Davenant, Graunt, King and Petty tirelessly collected national economic and demographic statistics in that and succeeding decades (Glass 1965; Blaug 1968). The relationships between healthiness, disease, human character and the environment were explored and elucidated (Dobson 1997), and 'by 1700 improvement was a cultural force of major importance for the environment' (Slack 2002: 214).

Explicitly geographical descriptions ran in parallel. The first national topography, written by John Leland between 1535 and 1543, was not published until 1710, but it was quarried extensively for William Camden's *Britannia* of 1586, the first English topography to be widely used and acknowledged as authoritative (Gibson 1695; Chandler 1993). *Britannia* was frequently rewritten and reissued over more than a century, moving from an emphasis on heraldry and genealogy to one more in keeping with the scientific and practical temper embodied by the Royal Society for the promotion of natural knowledge, founded in 1660 (Butlin 1990). By 1700 fourteen county topographies-cum-histories had been written. Most contained information on material concerns and patterns, and some, like those by Robert Plot of Oxfordshire (1674) and Staffordshire (1678), were based on questionnaire surveys (Emery 1958). Recognisable maps of the British Isles exist from the 1530s and 1540s, but the earliest properly surveyed county and national maps were those of Christopher Saxton, published as an atlas in 1579. Lord Burghley was an avid user of maps and atlases and a patron of cartographers (Barber 1992: 68–77): he kept in touch with one of his concerns through a chilling secret map of 'loyal' Protestant and 'disloyal' Catholic houses and the roads between them in fractious Lancashire (Anon. 1907). Corresponding with the efflorescence of Crown surveys (Barber 1992; Delano-Smith and Kain 1999), improved versions of Saxton's maps were published, with maps of some counties by other cartographers, in John Speed's *Atlas* of 1611 (Nicholson 1988). Some more accurate and larger scale cartographic surveys of counties and the country as a whole were undertaken between then and the end of our period (Delano-Smith and Kain 1999: 77–9), and detailed cartographic plans of estates became a common means for landowners, as for Burghley in statecraft, to establish absent observational presence in distant places (Bendall 1992; Fletcher 1998). Burghley wrote lists of places and the distances between them in his atlases, and everyone needed to know how to get to and between the places depicted. Saxton's and Speed's *Atlases* do not show roads. However, 'itineraries' (lists of consecutive places along particular routes), tables of distances between places, and information on market and fair days also began to be published in the early-seventeenth century, and by the end of it maps of post roads were common (Delano-Smith and Kain 1999: 160–72). They represented either a national space of mercantile circulation pivoted on London, or particular routes in 'strip map' form, as in Ogilby's *Britannia* of 1675.

Concurrent with all this geographical depiction, accounts of the past in relation to the present also began to be told in histories that purported to reveal the origins of aspects of the present (Sacks and Kelley 1999). Shakespeare's history plays were part of this process, as were the county and national topographies already mentioned, stuffed with information about the genealogy of landed families and historical monuments (Parry 1995). Speed's atlas was conceived of as part of a projected history of Great Britain from the Anglo-Saxon Heptarchy to the accession of James I, though it was never written (Nicholson 1988: 29). In the early-eighteenth century, histories became noticeably more modern in their scholarly signification of factual accuracy in accounts that were intended as more than collections of genealogical facts mixed with unsubstantiated fable (Mayer 1987; Sweet 1997).

The textual innovations of the sixteenth and early-seventeenth centuries were not separate. All were part of a deliberate political project to 'write England' as a cohesive unitary realm, independent of outside authority (Helgerson 1992; Ellis 1999). Mapping was central to this effort (Barber 1992; Biggs 1999). The dynastic realm was represented in its separateness as an empire – the title of Speed's atlas was *Theatrum Imperii Magnae Britanniae* – and in its cohesive unity as a commonwealth of free people. The burst of mapping and written description during and after the religious, constitutional and administrative upheavals of Henry VIII and Edward VI was a justification of the reforms needed to bring this unitary 'England' into reality. The state of the nation texts of Smith and Harrison emphasise the earnest concern of an unquestionable unifying authority. Speed's map of the Kingdom of Great Britain and Ireland does not show national boundaries; on it, unlike in reality, the four kingdoms are identically subdivided into a common system of county subunits. His map of England also shows a singular realm (including Wales), divided only administratively, again into the county units through which royal authority and local power had since Anglo-Saxon times been articulated by royal sheriffs and lords lieutenant, parliamentary representation, devolved law courts and penal institutions, taxation and military organisation (Keith-Lucas 1980: 40–74; Butlin 1990: 240–1). Speed's mapped spaces are thickly dotted with market towns and, apart from the vividly coloured county boundaries, bleached of other differences. They depict the intended consequences of the administrative and legal reforms of Henry VIII and Edward VI, culminating in the standardised nationwide applicability of Coke's *Institutes* and of Spellman's commentaries on the civil law, all of which gave added prominence to county officers and institutions (Baker 1977; Blomley 1994).

The renewed burst of mapping and topographical writing in the early-seventeenth century was a response to the need to re-emphasise this unity after the accession of James I brought England and Scotland together. But the Civil War, Monmouth's Rebellion, the flight of James II, the Glorious Revolution, the Hanoverian succession and the Jacobite invasions of 1715 and 1745 came thick and fast to emphasise both deep internal divisions and the significance of continental links. The mapping projects of Saxton and Speed, together with the stress on the realm as commonwealth, had actually allowed people to conceive of a nation without a monarch (Morgan 1979; Helgerson 1992: 108). Inadvertently, such texts were politically dangerous. Except for reissues of Saxton's and Speed's maps, cartography was largely discontinued after the reign of Charles I, apart from a brief 'restored royalist geography' of 1660–75 (Mayhew 2000: 66–85), until 'the re-mapping of England' began after our period ends (Harley 1972: 69). Similarly, on a smaller scale, the production of estate maps fell off after the early seventeenth century and was revived by the parliamentary enclosure movement after 1750 (Kain and Baigent 1992: 236–44). Fuller's *Worthies of England* was organised in 1662 county by separate county, each with its own peculiarities but, in fact, very few individual county topographies had been written before 1750, and the age of scholarly county histories came after our period ended (Currie and Lewis 1994). Most of the few that were written before 1750 echoed the tendency of successive re-issues of Camden's *Britannia*: the stress of Aubrey, Plot and Owen on the mundane matters of towns, soils, farming and industry was as much a retreat from old certainties about continuity and cohesion as it was a recognition of new interests.

In the 1720s the prominence of material practicality provided a new viewpoint from which to see national unity and cohesion. Defoe's *Tour* is a paean to the national harmony brought by trade, unified into a single entity by London (Earle 1977: 116–9). He had spied on Jacobites for the government (West 1997: 86–117), and the *Tour* can be read as a propaganda tract for the Whigs and the Hanoverian Succession, their mercantile supporters and their concern with the practical business of exchanging goods to make money (Backscheider 1989: 283–312).

The disruption and dissension caused by the archaic Tory-Jacobite preoccupation with irresolvable non-material questions is hardly mentioned by Defoe, but is as evident as the voice of the dog that didn't bark (Anderson 1941). Mapping and topographical writing began again after the Hanoverian–Whig hegemony was definitively secured in 1745.

Images inherent in practices

Much of what actually happened in the processes of administration and government also contained ideas about geography. The singular realm was divided in many ways for practical purposes, as well as into the counties so beloved of the cartographers. The unitary uniform realm steered by a benign central authority was a complete fiction. 'The government's efforts to promote peace, good rule and "English civility" in the far north by reducing noble power, extending royal government, and building up crown lands and a crown interest among the border gentry proved spectacularly unsuccessful' in Tudor times (Ellis 1999: 121). Throughout the period, statute law was not nearly up to the task of homogenisation. Even Maitland admitted that lawmakers of the eighteenth century seemed 'afraid to rise to the dignity of a general proposition', and most parliamentary statutes were temporary, limited in scope to particular interest groups or places and subject to considerable latitude of interpretation by county magistrates (Hoppit 1996: 131).

The fragmentation of law and administration generally went much further through the existence of numerous separate sets of legal codes and institutions.

Canon Law, outside the control of Crown and parliament, operated through a completely different set of spatial units from the counties of common law (Poole 1902: plate XXI; Cannon 1997: 1021). The strictly bounded forests were administered through Forest Law, codified in 1598 as arbitrarily in the hands of the monarch (Manwood 1717 [1598]). With their own hierarchy of courts and officers, the forests were islands of arbitrary feudalism (Langton forthcoming a). Feudal law and institutions also survived in the four most northerly counties, where chieftains still had to muster, arm and livery troops of retainers to repel Scots border raiders until the union of 1707. Until then, magnates there had more power, and their tenants more tenurial and other freedoms during normal times, than elsewhere in the country (Jewell 1994: 127–8; Ellis 1999). The royal duchies of Lancaster and Cornwall, each comprising a patchwork of estates scattered across the whole country, had their own councils, law courts and exchequers (Somerville 1953 and 2000; Haslam 1992). Numerous other independent civil jurisdictions survived until after our period ended, such as the palatinate counties ruled by their earls (Baines 1836; Holdsworth 1956–72: vol. I, 109–17), or in the case of Durham by its prince-bishop (Lapsley 1900), and smaller private fiefdoms where the royal writ did not run except for suits of treason and error, such as Hexamshire in Northumberland, belonging to the Archbishop of York (Hinds 1896); Purbeck in Dorset, belonging to the Constable of Purbeck Castle (Hutchins 1861: vol. II, 463); Malvern in Worcestershire, belonging to the Constable of Handley Castle (Nash 1781: vol. I, lxxiii); and Exmoor, belonging to its Chief Forester (Macdermot 1973).

The image inherent in these institutional practices is akin to that of the real geographies described earlier: one of massive incoherent fragmentation. Intriguingly, however, the coordination of these institutions sometimes did actually divide North from South. Directly under the king, there were Chief Justices for the Forests North and South of the Trent – or more precisely, for 'this' or 'the other' side of the Trent, depending on where the king happened to be (Turner 1903). The Duchy of Lancaster also divided its forest jurisdictions north and south of the Trent (Somerville 1972). To cope with palpable administrative confusion, remoteness and rebelliousness, The Council of the North was set up by Henry VIII (Reid 1921). But the north was not uniquely distinguished in this way because a similar council was set up for the Welsh Marches in 1543 (Cannon 1997: 252). Moreover, the ducal palatinate county of Lancashire was outside the northern Council's remit, and the Wardenships of the Northern Marches continued alongside until 1603: spatial coherence seems to have been unattainable (Cannon 1997: 252). The dissolution of the Northern and Welsh Marcher councils under the Commonwealth did not signify increased national unity any more than a more comprehensive splitting up of the whole unruly realm 1655–7 into the Provinces of the Major-Generals (Newman 1985: 112–3).

The perceived difference between North and South that was institutionalised in these arrangements carried over into other aspects of life and thought at court. Competitions were organised between northern and southern knights during royal progresses (Nichols 1823). The fact that no progress or any other journey took the monarch outside the south during the whole of our period (apart from James I's passage from Scotland and some of his later hunting expeditions) must have invested the northern cohort with some exoticism. This southern confinement of the court may also have been responsible for the projection of other exotic characteristics onto 'the north' in Tudor and Stuart times. Moral uprightness and freedom from control, defended by a propensity to riot and rebel made 'northern forests . . . the context for stories celebrating the violent but cleansing lives of bandits, outlaws, rustlers and chivalric heroes' (Pollard 1997: 141). However, in the face of the complexities of geographical reality, such a simple dichotomy could never be maintained, even at a court where it gained credence from administrative practices. Maybe in the four northernmost counties of all there was some correspondence between an idealised 'north' and reality. But as we have seen, 'many, if not most parts of the Tudor North were indistinguishable in their economy, wealth, social structure, and doubtless religious practices from southern lowland England' (Hoyle 2001: 29).

The geographical imagination of early modern England

If a geographical imagination is concerned with spatial patterns, the human ecological processes making landscapes, and the interaction between them, then it began to become evident in early modern times (Gregory 1994). We have already seen that Defoe argued that a differentiated space was produced as economic activities were organised around the London market in reflection of the availability of natural resources. Just as vividly and explicitly, Dyer's project in 1749 for 'A plan of a commercial map of England and a discourse on the uses of it' was written 'as if to construct new lines of communication for the circulation of commodities, to make better use of the economic space that is England . . . indeed to make more space' (Barrell 1999: 239 and 241; McRae 1999). Defoe also knew that this internal geographical process was inextricably linked with colonial and other overseas contacts focused through the trading institutions of the city. In his vibrant description of London itself (Defoe 1724–6: 286–336), he showed that massive subdivision of labour within and circulation through the nexus of this space of flows made it uniquely dynamic; a much faster pace of life than elsewhere brought people into constant contact with novelty, opportunity, unpredictability and threat. In current terminology, Defoe showed that a second nature – that is a natural world shaped by human beings (Smith 1984: 32–65) – was being produced by urban growth: that nature was being urbanised, as well as the people of the city itself (Kaïka and Swyngedouw 2000).

In a few colourful vignettes, Defoe also described cultural peculiarities evident in particular places. In Lancashire he commented on the interruption of normal urban life caused by sequestration of the estates of the numerous local supporters of the first Jacobite invasion; in Somerset he could not understand the speech of 'a dextrous dunce' reading the Bible aloud; the wild open country of the Peak District yielded subsistence to a lead miner whose numerous family lived 'like a wild body' in a cave fronted by pigs, a cow and a patch of barley; a 'country fellow' from Wansford rescued from the Nene at Wisbech could say only that his home village was 'in England' (Defoe 1774–6: 548–9, 216, 463–6 and 424). However, Defoe was much more concerned with the harmony brought by spatial interaction than with differences from place to place that were incidental to that process, even though human ecological differences and their expression in landscape had been the subject of speculation – indeed, assertion – for over a century by the time he wrote.

Three aspects of modernity operated together to initiate this: the need for a unitary state to exert social control; the drive for economic improvement associated with it, and enlightened curiosity about empirical relationships. In a realm wracked by division, dearth and dissension, the Tudor ruling elite aimed to ensure abundant food supplies and social order. The encouragement of arable farming provided both: according to Sir Robert Cecil, son of Lord Burghley and later Earl of Salisbury, 'whosoever doth not maintain the Plough destroys this Kingdom' (McRae 1992: 35). Fruitful cornland was the bulwark of England, its proprietors and cultivators the epitome of Englishness (McRae 1996; Ellis 1999). In order to ensure their success, enclosure for sheep pastures was forbidden if it destroyed 'houses of husbandry' (Beresford 1961), and bringing new land into cultivation was vigorously encouraged (Beresford 1961; Hoyle 1992b; Leslie and Raylor 1992). Of course, this cornland also supplied the wealth and sociopolitical niches of the aristocrats and gentlemen who were the local agents of the state, in firm control of tenant farmers through manorial institutions and the pulpits of the established national church.

Some of the differences in human ecology summarised in Table 6.1 were recognised in the sixteenth century. 'Our soil being divided into champaign ground and woodland, the houses in the first lie uniformly builded . . . with streets and lanes, whereas in the woodland countries, they stand scattered abroad, each one dwelling in the midst of his own occupying' (Edelen 1968: 217). This difference was strongly evaluated: a truly English landscape was one of cornfields interspersed with meadows and woodlands, nucleated villages of husbandmen, manor houses and parish churches. As Harrison knew, English soils were generally better suited to pasture than to arable farming (Edelen 1968: 429), and English produce and diet were thought remarkable by foreign observers because of the amount and variety of meat (Williams 1967: 193; Langford 2000: 38–50). But non-corn-producing areas were anathematised. According to the early-seventeenth-century surveyor, cartographer and topographer John Norden, 'where great and spacious heaths are . . . many cottages are set up, the people are given to little or no kind of labour . . . dwelling far from any church or chapel, and are as ignorant of God, or of any civil course of life as the very savages among the infidels' (Thomas 1978: 195). Such places were common in the extreme upland north (Ellis 1999), but were not confined there: Lincolnshire, Essex and Hampshire were full of them, too (Thomas 1978: 194–6). All over southern England, 'the desert forests' were everywhere like that, full of 'idleness, beggary and atheism . . . wherein infinite poor, yet most idle inhabitants have thrust themselves, living covertly without law or religion . . . among whom are nourished and bred infinite idle fry, that coming to ripe grow vagabonds and infect the commonwealth with a most dangerous leprosy'; putting them under cultivation would make 'the commonwealth greatly enriched and bettered by providing of [5,000 dwelling houses] for so many desolate people which do now want places of habitation' (Large 1992: 391).

Of course, it was no accident that these were the views of the surveyor and cartographer of Crown projects to disfranchise and enclose forest land, so that it could be brought into the private possession of wealthy landowners and put under their tenants' ploughs (Hoyle 1992a and b; Thirsk 1992). Nor was it accidental that the Diggers and other Puritanical levellers made exactly the opposite evaluation: for them, the commons signified economic independence and social freedom (Hill 1993; Loewenstein 1999). The Restoration of the Crown restored the old imagery, 'for how should men manure the ground, their minds being choakt with weed?' This could not be done on common land, where 'men mixed with beasts together in one shed' (Turner 1979: 94), but required a properly ordered landscape, where 'no crook-backed tree / Disgraced the place, no foolish rambling shrub, / No wild and careless bush, no clownish stub' (Turner 1979: 97; O'Brien 1999). The empirical science promoted by the Royal Society verified these ideas. John Aubrey attributed causal potency to the physical environment and the farming systems it produced in Wiltshire, contrasting the productive upright obedient people of the corn-growing downlands with their disaffected, disputatious and impious neighbours in the pastoral vales (Ponting 1969: 11). This imagery continued through our period to project improvement and propriety as the epitomes of English life. According to Samuel Johnson, 'affrighted nature shuddered at her own depravity, weakness and misery; and was soon obliged to seek her security and accommodation in the various regulations of political or civil life', although sadly 'the inhabitants of mountainous regions lost that reverence for property, by which civil life is preserved' (Langford 1991: 31 and 33).

The deliberate creation and painting of landscapes to symbolise this ideology did not begin in earnest until after our period ended (Barrell 1980; Bermingham 1987; Cosgrove and Daniels 1988). However, given the widespread currency and power of this vivid imagery, an obvious question arises: why was it so rarely expressed in the geographical descriptions of the time? The frequency and exclusiveness with which Aubrey's human ecological analysis is quoted are, in fact, an eloquent testimonial to its uniqueness. One obvious reason for this dissonance between imagery and observation is that to notice it would have contradicted the picture of uniformity and cohesion that the descriptions were meant to express. Another reason was that whilst the relationship between environment and people was being drawn, Ireland was being claimed for English colonisers because, according to Sir John Davies in 1610, the 'nomadic', 'wild Irish' lived 'by the milk of the cow without husbandry or tillage', were therefore more 'hurtful and wild than wild beasts', and would 'never to the end of the world build houses, make townships or villages, or manure and improve the land as it ought to be; therefore it stands neither with Christian policy nor conscience to suffer so good and fruitful a country to lay waste like a wilderness' (Stallybrass 1989: 205–6). Ireland must be taken over by the English, who, to qualify for the role, must be arable farmers. If Irish pastoralism was to be set in apposition to civilised Englishness, England could not be pastoral too. The 'other' against which Englishness was being defined was conveniently pushed outside the realm.

Not only did the geographical imagery of the time carry profound ideological and political freight – the same burden as the almost invariably negative representations of travel and movement (McRae 1999; Barrell 1999). The highest human achievement was not to be found in the arrangements of material life and its facilitation anyway, but in the apprehension of Christian verities. These were best reached directly through purely mental activity, although *faute de mieux* they might be less surely approached by considering what God had made uniform and universal in and for his people on Earth. Differences from place to place were imperfections. In the great chain of being, humans occupied a single level; what made them human was what they had in common (Mayhew 1997 and 1999). For this reason, Ireland and the forests and open pasture lands of England must be brought nearer to a state of human perfection that was attainable by and desirable for all: differences should be eradicated.

So, it is not surprising that there is very little about human geographical differences in the topographical descriptions of the time. The digressions through which Fuller expresses his alarm at religious differences, by which Defoe amused his readers and with which Aubrey has tantalised modern historians were not thought to be worth serious notice. In 1685 Aubrey separated his statement of the universal truth that 'according to the severall sorts of earth in England (and so all the world over) the Indigenæ are respectively witty or dull, good or bad' from his example of Wiltshire particularities with the remark that 'to write a true account of the severall humours of our own countrey would be too sarcasticall and offensive: this should be a secret whisper in the eare of a friend only . . . Well then! let these Memoires lie conceal'd as a sacred arcanum' (Ponting 1969: 11). Similarly for Defoe, who 'could give many more accounts of the dialects of the people of this country, in some of which they are really not to be understood, but the particulars have little or no diversion in them, they carry it to such a length' (Defoe 1724–6: 217). According to Johnson at the end of our period, 'nothing can please many, and please long, but just representations of general nature. Particular manners can be known to few, and so few only can judge how nearly they are copied' (Mayhew 1997: 11; 1998 and 1999).

It was Romanticism that made the complexities of relations between humankind, nature and society worthy of serious intellectual attention (Moretti 1998; Wiley 1998; Bate 2000), and empirical geographical science that made it possible to pursue that curiosity (Gregory 1994: 16–33). Both emerged after our period ended. Before then, human geographical differences – whether of a North–South divide or the much more variegated reality that existed – could hardly be conceived of or acknowledged, let alone celebrated, while 'the great myth' of singular English nationhood was being written (Jones 1998).

7

North–South dichotomies, 1066–1550

BRUCE M. S. CAMPBELL

Late-medieval England was a land of dichotomies. The most conspicuous were those between upland and lowland, dispersed and nucleated settlement, woodland and champion, weak and strong lordship, free and customary tenants and tenures, remoteness and proximity to major markets, and between the marches and the metropolitan core. Some of these contrasts were inherent in England's climate and topography, others sprang from deep-rooted human institutions such as field systems, manors, and property rights, while yet others derived from the centralising and differentiating forces of governments and commercial exchange. Many of these dichotomies had a strong north–south dimension but this does not necessarily mean that there was such a thing as a 'North–South divide' or that distinctions between the North and the South should be privileged above other spatial and regional differences. The strength and nature of these dichotomies also varied over time, depending upon whether centripetal or centrifugal tendencies were more to the fore. Any systems shift in the balance between these two tendencies was likely to heighten the tensions between core and periphery thereby giving rise to expressions of northern (and southern) consciousness (Jewell 1994). This is what seems to have happened at the close of the Middle Ages. It was then that the dichotomy between North and South in the medieval period was probably at its most pronounced.

A disunited nation? Popular protest North and South

Can there be any clearer symptom of a North–South dichotomy than the rebellion that broke out in autumn 1536, when the north of England rose in protest at policies imposed by a southern-based government? Suppression of the lesser monasteries, religious reforms arising from promotion of the Reformation, the levying of a new lay subsidy, and rising entry fines and rents provided the immediate sources of discontent. Trouble broke out first at Louth in the North Riding of Lincolnshire on 1st October. Incited by the clergy, protest spread to nearby Caistor and Horncastle. Soon rebels in great number had occupied Lincoln, and the movement, supported

145

by many local gentry, had acquired some political coherence. Rumour inflamed an already highly volatile situation. Report of the Lincolnshire rising sparked insurrection in the neighbouring East and West Ridings of Yorkshire, and on 16th October York was occupied. By then the Lincolnshire rebels had dispersed, but north of the Humber and the Ouse the flame of popular protest was not to be so quickly or easily extinguished, not least because in Yorkshire the movement had found a leader. Robert Aske, a country gentleman and London lawyer, gave the 'Pilgrimage of Grace' its purpose and unity and bestowed upon the rebels the name of 'Pilgrims'. Religion provided the 'Pilgrims' with their ideology that the law of God took precedence over the laws of men. Thus legitimated, the rebellion rapidly gathered momentum (Mackie 1952: 385–92; Bush 1996; McCord and Thompson 1998: 86–90).

From Yorkshire, insurrection spread to Cumberland and Westmorland and then to County Durham (Bush 1996: 424–36). In the border counties, political anxieties added fuel to the fire. Here the government was endeavouring to curb the traditional power and influence of those northern magnates upon whom, as wardens of the march, the military and juridical needs of this region – for centuries the scene of conflict between England and Scotland – had long been devolved. By 26th October most of the North had risen and some 30,000 'Pilgrims', including many gentry, had mustered at Doncaster on the principal route south. Their aim was to compel the king to halt and, if possible, reverse the unwanted religious and political changes. Henry VIII (1509–1547) played for time, gave reassurances and, by 8th December, had persuaded the Pilgrims to disperse. It was the single most dangerous crisis of his reign. Had this northern rebellion succeeded the progress of the Reformation in England would have taken a different course. Discontent rumbled on for several months until further protest was quashed and order re-established.

Notwithstanding that the aspirations of the 'Pilgrims' were national rather than regional, it is tempting to interpret the Pilgrimage as an expression of northern patriotism in reaction to unpopular religious, political and fiscal policies imposed by a government based in the South (Beckingsale 1969: 72–3). Nowhere else did these national policies provoke outright rebellion or the Reformation meet with such immediate and organised resistance. Thereafter, Catholicism at all social levels remained far stronger in the North than in the South. Catholicism sparked the ill-fated rebellion of the northern earls of 1569 in support of the claim of Mary Queen of Scots to the English throne and in 1603 it was in the northern dioceses of Chester, Durham, Lichfield and York that recusants were reported in greatest number (Hawkyard 2001: 117). The North's religious conservatism had long been apparent. During the fifteenth century John Wyclif's heretical teachings had attracted few adherents in the North and consequently there had been virtually no northern participants in the Lollard revolt of 1414 (Horrox 2001: 107; Rex 2002: 84–7). Not only was the North remote from the main Lollard centres of Oxford and London, but lower levels of literacy than in the South and the immense power and influence of the northern monasteries reduced the potential for heresy.

The North's lack of involvement in the Lollard revolt was typical. Until the Pilgrimage of Grace, large-scale popular protest was a southern rather than northern phenomenon. Even the greatest of those rebellions, the Peasants' Revolt of 1381, was limited mainly to East Anglia, the south-east, and a sprinkling of mostly urban centres elsewhere (Figure 7.1). What made the latter revolt so dangerous was that the rebels succeeded in occupying London and confronting the king and his councillors directly (something that distance would prevent Aske's northern 'Pilgrims' from achieving) (Dobson 1983: 153–229). Nevertheless, it remained a regional rather than a national rising, with Norfolk (where rural protest would flare again under the leadership of Robert Kett in 1549), Suffolk, Essex and Kent (the focus of Jack Cade's rebellion of 1450) the counties most involved. North of the Trent there was little active participation in the revolt outside the three Yorkshire boroughs of Beverley, Scarborough and York (Dobson 1983: 284–96). The only recorded rural manifestation of revolt occurred on the Wirral peninsula of Cheshire, where the abbot of Chester's villeins briefly and belatedly rose in armed protest (Dobson 1983: 297–9). The elimination of serfdom had been high on the agenda of the southern rebels, along with the fixing of rents, reform of the labour laws, redistribution of church property, curbing of excessive seigniorial powers and removal of unpopular government ministers. The last was one of the few aims shared in common by the rebels of 1381 and 'Pilgrims' of 1536. Beverley and York alone were actively involved in both rebellions. Outside these two towns the contrasting geographies of the Peasants' Revolt and the Pilgrimage of Grace appear to reflect the division between a progressive South seeking to reform or overthrow the old order and a conservative North striving to maintain it.

In the sixteenth century, northern conservatism and traditionalism were also manifest in resentment of and resistance to the political and administrative reforms of a vigorously centralising government keen to assert stronger control over the entire realm and beyond. Old feudal loyalties, especially to the great territorial magnates of the region, died hard. For most of the later Middle Ages, when the monarchy and central government were preoccupied with war abroad and dynastic struggle at home, it was upon these northern magnates – Percies, Nevilles, Dacres, Greystokes and the palatine bishops of Durham – that responsibility for maintaining border security was devolved (Lomas 1992: 86–90; McCord and Thompson 1998: 70–85). By the fifteenth century direct military conflict between England and Scotland had largely given way to localised violence and raiding. Security lay in the patronage of a powerful lord, the means, readiness and ability to fight, and the protection afforded by a strongly built peel tower or other defensive structure. Central government was too remote to provide much practical help and had little interest in doing so. In the sixteenth century, however, a strong Crown, expansionist state and rapidly advancing artillery-based military technology beyond the financial resources of individual aristocrats together necessitated a change of policy. Commencing with Henry VIII, the Tudor monarchs determined to bring the

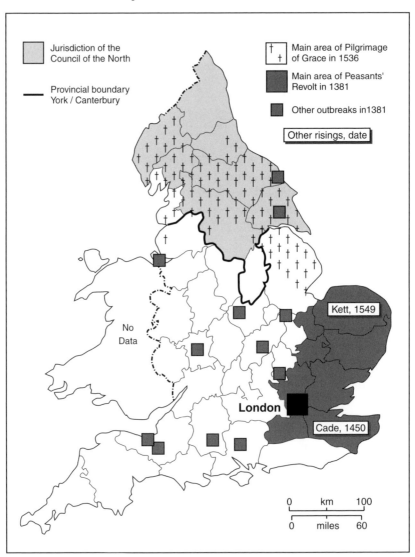

Figure 7.1 The geography of popular rebellion: the Peasants' Revolt of 1381 and the Pilgrimage of Grace of 1536 (Dobson (1983: 38–44); Bush (1996: 3); Hawkyard (2001: 114–17))

North more directly under their authority. That meant 'the rule of the South over the North' (Bindoff 1950: 107).

Administrative divisions between North and South

The administrative status of the North was characterised by a mixture of subservience and autonomy. The subservience naturally arose from the location of the seat of government in London. The autonomy derived from the periodic need of that government to devolve certain responsibilities and powers to the North, together with the distinctive status of the palatine counties of Durham, Cheshire and Lancashire. These powers tended to be jealously guarded. It was mistrust of central government and opposition to political interference and rule from Westminster that encouraged many to join the Pilgrimage of Grace. Nor were northern fears unjustified. In January 1537, immediately following suppression of the rebellion, Henry VIII formally established the Council in the North thereby firmly extending his own power to the northern limit of his realm. The great northern magnates were deprived of their former influence and even the mighty bishop of Durham suffered some loss of autonomy. Administrative authority was bureaucratised. Power was handed over to 'a hard-working, middle-class committee, paid a regular salary and in constant touch with the council at Westminster' (Mackie 1952: 393). In October 1537 the Council held its first meeting at York. It had jurisdiction over the five northernmost counties of Yorkshire, Durham, Northumberland, Cumberland and Westmorland (Lancashire, because it belonged to the Duchy of Lancaster, was excluded). Within these counties it had the highest administrative power, could inflict any penalty short of death and, although itself it might appeal to the privy council for advice, its suitors had no appeal from its decision. Henceforth, England south and west of the Humber and the Duddon would be administered from London, and England north and east of that line, from York; with the northern administration always subservient to the southern.

This administrative division between the North and the South mirrored the ancient ecclesiastical division of England into northern and southern provinces. East of the Pennines the Province of York encompassed all of England north of the Trent, plus the diocese of Whithorn in south-west Scotland. West of the Pennines the river Ribble marked the southern limit of the Province, which included the northern half of Lancashire (once part of Yorkshire), Westmorland and Cumberland. York had long exercised jurisdiction over these last two counties, since in the eleventh and twelfth centuries it had claimed metropolitan authority over Glasgow. In 1133, however, Henry I (1100–1135) forcibly detached them from the diocese of Glasgow and established the diocese of Carlisle (Wilson 1905: 11–14; Thompson 1913: 15; McCord and Thompson 1998: 58). In the eleventh century the archbishop of York had also claimed the sees of Lichfield, Worcester and part of Lincoln, but this was successfully resisted by Lanfranc, the powerful

Norman archbishop of Canterbury (Chibnall 1986: 40). As a result the southern province of Canterbury extended as far north as mid Lancashire. Moreover, it was Lanfranc who insisted that York should acknowledge the primacy of Canterbury. Instead, he had to be satisfied with a clear acknowledgement that as archbishop of Canterbury he took precedence over the archbishop of York. Throughout the Middle Ages, Canterbury was the larger, richer and more populous of the two provinces; in 1535 the fourteen southern sees accounted for almost 80 per cent of all episcopal revenues (Hoskins 1976: 127).

The separate but subordinate ecclesiastical jurisdiction of the North had its secular counterparts. In the 1230s the Trent became the titular boundary for the divisions of the Crown's forest administration. At about the same time, in 1236, separate escheators were appointed for England north and south of the Trent (these were the officials who policed the Crown's proprietorial rights and who supervised all escheats and wardships of the king, answering for their issues at the Exchequer). This arrangement persisted until 1275, after which the number and jurisdiction of the escheators were subject to periodic reform. Nevertheless, throughout all these reforms the Trent tended to persist as an administrative fault line. Yorkshire, Westmorland, Cumberland and Northumberland were almost always treated as a single administrative unit, sometimes with the inclusion of Lancashire (which, when not grouped with Yorkshire, was coupled with Derbyshire) and, from 1332, sometimes with the exclusion of Holderness in the East Riding of Yorkshire (Campbell and Bartley forthcoming). From 1293 England north of the Trent, but also including Derbyshire and Nottinghamshire, also constituted one of the four assize circuits. When, from 1328, the number of assize circuits was increased to six, England north of the Trent and Mersey (i.e. excluding Derbyshire and southern Nottinghamshire) remained a separate circuit (Cockburn 1968: 118–22; Musson 1996: xii–xiv, 85–122).

The sole exceptions to these arrangements were the county palatines of Durham and Cheshire, which, although subject to the royal law, enjoyed administrative and legal autonomy. This was because of the key role discharged by the bishops of Durham in defence of the eastern march against Scotland and the strategic importance of the former earldom of Chester respecting the Principality of Wales. Already by the twelfth century the bishop of Durham had come to exercise quasi-regalian rights in his own territory, which included large parts of Northumberland. His was the greatest franchise in medieval England (Bayley 1907: 137–8, 144, 146). Cheshire acquired its palatine status later, in the second half of the thirteenth century, and soon became subsumed into the Crown estate. Like Durham, it was exempt from national taxation, the jurisdiction of sheriffs and escheators, and did not send members to parliament (Harris 1979: 5–6, 9–35). Eventually, from 1351, Lancashire also became a county palatine and this was confirmed in 1377. In due course the county's administration became absorbed into that of the Duchy of Lancaster, which, from 1399 (like that of Cheshire before it), became incorporated into the Crown estate (Tait 1908: 205–12). Lancashire, however, lacked the higher regalities possessed by the bishop of Durham and earl of Chester (from 1301 the Prince of Wales), remaining liable to taxation and continuing to send members to parliament. No southern county enjoyed the administrative, juridical and fiscal autonomy exercised by these three northern county palatines.

The medieval North thus comprised three distinct administrative zones. First, there were the four northernmost counties of Cumberland, Westmorland, Northumberland and Durham. Not until 1092 were these fully incorporated into the realm. In 1086 the Domesday commissioners had extended their enquiries no further north than the river Tees in the east and river Duddon in the west (Darby 1977: 2). At that time Cumbria had yet to be conquered from the Scots, Durham – known as the land of St Cuthbert (a saint as much venerated by the Scots as by the English) – was an independent liberty, and the old earldom of Northumberland was still contested between the English and the Scots. All four were also shired late. It was from 1174 that county government was consolidated in Northumberland (McCord and Thompson 1998: 35). The county of Cumberland is first referred to by name in a pipe roll of 1177 (Wilson 1905: 239). Westmorland also appeared as a fiscal unit at that time but until 1190 was treated as a subdivision of Yorkshire (Wilson 1905: 310). Durham always remained a separate liberty in its own right, administered from Durham by its bishop, who held his own courts, issued writs and appointed justices (Bayley 1907: 146). Owing to the immediate proximity of the Scottish border these four counties were organised on a war footing for much of the Middle Ages. From the early-fourteenth century until 1537 Northumberland came under the jurisdiction of the warden of the eastern march and Cumberland and Westmorland under that of the warden of the western march. Under this arrangement these counties were very much a law unto themselves. The holders of these offices were invariably local magnates who, within the marches, enjoyed great authority, which the Crown periodically attempted to curb (McCord and Thompson 1998: 70; Ellis 2001a).

Second, and lying immediately to the south, there was the core northern county of Yorkshire, far greater in territorial extent than all four northernmost counties combined. Until the second half of the twelfth century it incorporated the Amounderness district north of the river Ribble in what would later become Lancashire. At that time it was the sole northern county equipped with the administrative and fiscal attributes of a shire. Moreover, York, located where the East, North and West Ridings met, was more than just a county town: it was the metropolitan capital of the North and its administrative, political and military key. In the early-tenth century York had been the capital of the independent Kingdom of York, whose southern boundary extended from the Humber in the east to the Mersey in the west. From 1537 it would become the seat of the Council in the North, whose jurisdiction encompassed much of the same area. Between 1283 and 1335 York was the venue of fourteen parliaments and royal councils (Figure 7.2). On the Gough Map of

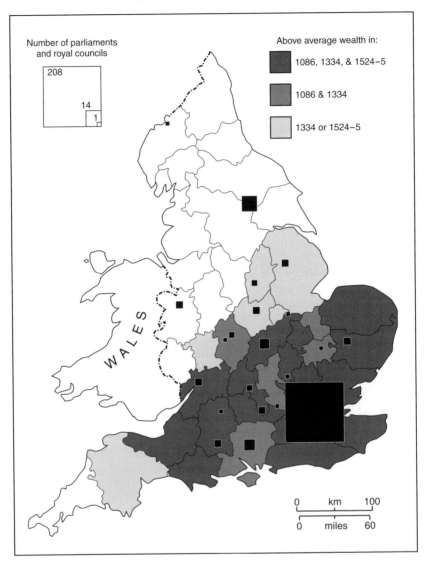

Figure 7.2 The venues of parliaments and royal councils, 1258–1545 (Powicke (1939: 342–50); Darby (1977: 359); Sheail (1998: 438); Campbell and Bartley (forthcoming))

*c.*1360 it is represented as second only to London in size and significance, and the map implies that York was then seen as the capital of the North (Parsons 1958: 9). Administratively, the four northernmost counties and Yorkshire together belonged unequivocally to the North. All lay within the Province of York and in due course would fall within the jurisdiction of the Council in the North.

A third group of counties – Lancashire, Cheshire, Derbyshire, Nottinghamshire and Lincolnshire – also possessed northern attributes even though administratively they were not always included within the jurisdiction of the North. Geographically, Lancashire marched with Yorkshire and lay emphatically within the North. That part of the county north of the Ribble had once been part of Yorkshire and was always included within the Province of York. Lancashire 'between the Ribble and Mersey', however, lay within the Province of Canterbury and was included with Cheshire by the Domesday commissioners, since both were once part of the old Anglo-Saxon kingdom of Mercia (Darby 1977: 2). Lancashire became a county in its own right only in the second half of the twelfth century. By 1168 it had been divided into wapentakes and by the 1190s it was being treated as a separate fiscal unit parallel with the older shires (Tait 1908: 187, 191). South of the Mersey, Cheshire originated as a territorially consolidated earldom that extended westwards into present-day Flintshire, and in official documents is not referred to as a county until after 1237 when it was taken into the king's hands (Harris 1979: 2–3). Cheshire tended to look west, towards Wales, rather than north. Nevertheless, like Durham and Lancashire it acquired palatine status and, along with Lancashire south of the Ribble and Derbyshire, belonged to the Mercian diocese of Lichfield (which also included Staffordshire, north Shropshire, and north-east Warwickshire), to which the archbishop of York had attempted to lay claim in the eleventh century. The Crown also sometimes grouped Derbyshire with Lancashire, for the two counties shared a short common boundary and both lay 'north of the Trent', which was the normal division between northern and southern forest jurisdictions and escheatries. It was more usual, however, to group Derbyshire with Nottinghamshire, its immediate neighbour to the east. Ecclesiastically, Nottinghamshire belonged emphatically to the North, for it always lay within the Province of York. In the eleventh century the archbishops of York had also attempted to lay claim to the northern part of the vast diocese of Lincoln. When the Domesday survey had been undertaken, Lincolnshire and adjacent Rutland, Nottinghamshire, Derbyshire and Yorkshire were included within the same northern administrative circuit (there were seven circuits in total) (Darby 1977: 7). This territory coincided in large part with the northern Danelaw and its counties were subdivided into wapentakes rather than hundreds.

There was therefore no single, clear-cut, administrative boundary between North and South. Ecclesiastical and secular jurisdictions sometimes coincided and sometimes overlapped with each other. The most generous definition of the North would include the ten counties comprising Cumberland, Westmorland, Northumberland and Durham (Zone 1); Yorkshire (Zone 2); and Lancashire, Cheshire, Derbyshire, Nottinghamshire and Lincolnshire (Zone 3). A tighter definition would exclude Cheshire and Lincolnshire and limit the North to the eight counties north of the Humber, Trent and Mersey. *Circa* 1500 these eight counties had a common linguistic identity, in so far as it was within this area that English was spoken with a predominantly Northumbrian dialect (Ellis 2001b: 153). Nevertheless, the real administrative core of the North comprised the five-and-a-half counties north of the Humber, Ouse and Ribble. Yet in the eleventh century, as far as the Domesday commissioners were concerned, the North extended no further than the Tees in the east and Duddon in the west, since everything to the north comprised a frontier zone disputed between England and Scotland. Scottish kings maintained a technical claim to these lands until 1237, although de facto everywhere as far as the Tweed and Solway had been English since 1157.

War and peace: the Anglo-Scottish border

Remoteness from the seat of power in London was not by itself responsible for the North's distinctive administrative history and character, for the south-western counties of Cornwall and Devon were equally distant. At least as important was the proximity of Scotland. Until 1237 the Scots laid claim to significant parts of the North and under David I (1124–53) they were temporarily successful in shifting the border southwards from the Tweed and Solway to the Tees and Ribble. Since at least 1066 English kings had claimed lordship over their Scottish counterparts and Edward I (1272–1307) attempted military conquest of his northern neighbour. Thereafter, raiding and counter-raiding became facts of northern life. War, and the threat of war, affected the North far more directly than the South, and those who lived near the border became accustomed to levels of violence and insecurity of which southerners had almost no experience (Tuck 1985). Of necessity, the North was always more heavily fortified than the South, with castles, walled towns and peel towers. Berwick-upon-Tweed became the northernmost and most strongly walled town in England. Originally Scottish, it had been captured and refortified by Edward I in 1296. Thereafter, it was successively lost and recovered by the English (McNamee 1997: 216–19; Paterson 1997: 88–108). Between 1558 and 1569, following what proved to be England's last war with Scotland, it was provided with a wholly new set of walls designed to withstand siege by artillery (McCord and Thompson 1998: 92–3). No other English town was as strongly defended.

It was William II (1087–1100) who, in 1092, wrested Cumbria from Scotland and established the Tweed–Solway line as the border (Kapelle 1979: 150–4; Barrow 1989: 2–4). Until then the Scottish kingdom of Strathclyde had extended as far south as Stainmore on the boundary between Westmorland and Yorkshire, where it is still marked by the Rere Cross (Kapelle 1979: 130–1). Castles at Durham and Newcastle-upon-Tyne defended the eastern march and to secure the western march William II erected the castle at Carlisle. Henry I (1100–35) further defined and reinforced the border through the creation of powerful lordships and the establishment in 1133 of the diocese of Carlisle (Kapelle 1979: 191–230; Chibnall 1986: 48–53). The discovery of rich veins of silver in the fells of eastern Cumberland c.1130 gave him an added incentive to secure these borderlands for England and provided the resources for the completion of Carlisle's cathedral and city walls

(Blanchard 1996: 27). The discovery of such fabulous mineral wealth in territory that had de facto so recently been Scottish led David I of Scotland (1124–53) to cast covetous eyes across the newly realigned border. In 1136 the outbreak of civil war in England between Stephen and Matilda gave him his opportunity. He invaded northern England, occupied Carlisle, reannexed Cumbria to Scotland and claimed the English earldom of Northumberland for his son (from whom, in 1152, it would pass to his second grandson). For a time the Scottish king held sway over the whole of northern England north of the Ribble and north of the Tees, thereby reinstating the political situation that had prevailed under Malcolm II (1005–34) in 1006 (Gillingham 1995: 52–3). Yorkshire became once more a border county, with York just two days, ride from Scottish-held territory. Not until 1157, following the deaths of both David I and Stephen, did the English under Henry II (1154–89) succeed in reclaiming this territory, thereby re-establishing the 1092 line of the border.

For the next 140 years peaceful coexistence between the two realms became increasingly the norm (Barrow 1989: 17–21). Intermarriage between the two royal families helped. The destruction wrought by brief episodes of conflict was followed by fairly rapid recovery. When, in 1174, William I of Scotland (1165–1214) invaded Northumberland in a vain effort to recover the lost earldom of Northumberland, he was captured and forced to acknowledge Henry II's overlordship of Scotland. There were further hostilities in 1215–16. Then, under the Treaty of York in 1237, the Scots formally renounced their claim to northern England (Stringer 1995: 86). For the next sixty years the border ceased to be disputed and almost ceased to matter. A string of English and Scottish monastic estates helped neutralise and stabilise the borderlands. Peace encouraged a build-up of settlement and increasing economic interaction took place between northern England and southern Scotland. Berwick-upon-Tweed and Newcastle-upon-Tyne both profited from expanding trade and commerce. 'People spoke the same language, and landowners inter-married and acquired property in the other kingdom' (Lomas 1992: 42).

It was the failure of the Scottish royal line in 1290 coupled with the imperial ambitions of Edward I (1272–1307) that brought this happy state of affairs to an end, for the resultant succession dispute (there were thirteen rival claimants) provided Edward with the pretext to subjugate Scotland. Edward I had already conquered and annexed Wales, when, in 1296, he attempted to extend English rule to the whole of Britain. He came closer to fulfilling that ambition than did any other English monarch (Prestwich 1980: 42–53). During the latter years of his reign the North became the focus of intense military activity: southern troops, southern expenditure and southern victuals poured into the North. The region thereby became more directly exposed to the effects of protracted and large-scale armed conflict than any other part of the realm. While the war went England's way the North profited but when the tide turned, especially following the crushing English defeat at Bannockburn in 1314, it was the North that bore the brunt of retaliatory Scottish raids intent upon plunder and destruction.

Between 1314 and 1322 these raids penetrated ever deeper into England. Amounderness in mid-Lancashire was raided in 1318, the Aire Valley of the West Riding of Yorkshire in 1319 and the East Riding of Yorkshire in 1322 (McNamee 1997: 85–105). Not until the second Jacobite rising in 1745 would a Scottish army advance so far south of the border. The aim of these raids was to undermine the capacity of the English to wage war by inflicting as much economic damage as possible across a wide area of the North. In this they were remarkably effective. The tactic was hit and run. Castles and walled towns were avoided. Instead, the raiders targeted farms, villages, small towns and monasteries. If protection money was not paid – Durham, visited eight times by the Scots between 1311 and 1327, paid a total of approximately £4,000 to escape physical damage – buildings and crops were destroyed and livestock driven off (Tuck 1985: 33–7; McNamee 1997: 135).

The impact of these Scottish raids was all the greater because their period of greatest intensity between 1314 and 1322 coincided with years of abnormal weather, serious harvest failure and devastating outbreaks of cattle plague and sheep murrain. Simultaneously, a Scottish army was inflicting similar damage upon the English Lordship of Ireland, thus depriving north-west England of its main source of relief grain (McNamee 1997: 169–86). As a result, no part of England suffered more during the Great European Famine of 1315–22 than the North (Kershaw 1973). Here, if not in the South, the famine represents a demographic and economic turning point. During the ensuing period of emergency, parliament met eleven times at York. Then, from the late 1330s, English military and territorial ambitions shifted from Scotland to France. In 1333 the Scots had been massively defeated at the battle of Halidon Hill: four years later, with the North seemingly secure, Edward III (1327–77) declared war on France. Henceforth the North would have to fend for itself for English kings were preoccupied elsewhere. On 26th May 1335 the last medieval parliament was held north of the Humber (Powicke 1939: 346–50).

Under Edward III England eventually regained the military upper hand. The North had nevertheless paid dearly for his grandfather's imperial ambitions. Right across the northern counties a wide array of documentary sources bear witness to the extensive destruction of property and massive reduction in the volume and value of economic activity (McNamee 1997: 105–15; Campbell and Bartley forthcoming). The Scots had done most harm but English troops had also blighted some areas. Exposure to repeated raiding naturally gave rise to the most lasting damage, not least because of the depopulation which resulted. More generally, warfare destabilised the region's economy by sapping it of capital, disrupting markets and undermining commercial confidence. Human and financial resources had to be diverted to reconstruction and too often these proved inadequate. Recovery, when it occurred, was rarely complete. Revenues, rents and tithes remained permanently below the peak levels of the late-thirteenth century (Tuck 1985: 40–3; Lomas 1992: 54–74). In the border counties, the breakdown in security proved lasting, and extortion, ransom and plunder replaced the peaceful pursuit of profits. Here there was a permanent retreat of settlement and everywhere a heightened emphasis upon defence. Those who could moved to more trouble-free areas.

In many parts of the North, therefore, demographic and economic contraction was already well established before the Black Death struck. The first half of the fourteenth century was a difficult period everywhere but contrasting circumstances ensured that the North suffered in ways that barely affected the South. The North also fared less well during the centuries that followed, for tax revenues demonstrate that the contraction of the later Middle Ages was most pronounced in the counties north of the Trent. Their estimated share of the nation's taxable lay wealth fell from approximately 15.0 per cent in 1334 to 7.5 per cent in 1524–5 (Sheail 1998: 438; Campbell and Bartley forthcoming). The North's ongoing political and military problems compounded its environmental disadvantages and exacerbated its remoteness. From 1314, therefore, the South gained in political and economic power relative to the North. Above all, London gained in relative size, wealth and influence and so, too, did the counties around it (Darby *et al.* 1979: 257–8).

After 1284 the Scottish border was England's only land border with a rival state. From 1326 until 1560 it was the more dangerous because of the alliance formed between Scotland and France in mutual resistance to a common enemy. This provided that 'the French would aid and counsel the Scots in any Anglo-Scottish war, and that the Scots would attack England in any Anglo-French war' (Grant 1984: 16). The 'auld alliance', as it became known, lasted until 1560, when lasting peace finally broke out between the two countries, allowing a return to the settled conditions of the mid-thirteenth century. Since the English invasion of 1296, raiding by both English and Scots had remained endemic, with consequences for settlement, society and the economy across a wide area. This was something, some French attacks upon the south coast apart, of which the South had virtually no experience. To Matthew Paris in the peaceful thirteenth century and the maker of the Gough Map in the more violent fourteenth century, the border with Scotland was the most crucial north–south divide of all (Parsons 1958: 11–14; Delano-Smith and Kain 1999: 45). No other was as contested.

North and South: periphery and core?

When medieval monarchs visited the North it was generally to wage war. Typically this was against the Scots, although in the fifteenth century, during the internecine dispute between the rival houses of York and Lancaster, it became dynastic (Jewell 1994: 45–52; Horrox 2001: 107–9). Between 1296 and 1307, Edward I, the so-called 'hammer of the Scots' probably spent more time in the North than any other king and was the only English king to die there (at Burgh-by-Sands, just a few miles south of the border). During his reign, councils to which representatives of the commons were summoned were held at York in 1283, 1298 and 1303. In mid-Lent 1304 – at the climax of English power in Scotland – a parliament was even held at St Andrews and in 1307 parliament met at Carlisle. Never again would parliament meet further north than York, and after 1336, it would never meet further north than Leicester and Shrewsbury (Powicke 1939: 344–50). More than any subsequent English monarch, Edward I knew the North at first hand. A reconstructed itinerary of his travels demonstrates just how much of the North he saw in the course of his repeated campaigns against the Scots. Even so, he seems never to have visited Lancashire and to have spent most of his time on the eastern rather than the western side of the Pennines (Hindle 1976: 214). The same was true of other kings. After Cornwall and Devon in the equally remote south-west, Lancashire was the county least visited by medieval monarchs. The main route north, as depicted on Matthew Paris's thirteenth-century map of Britain and the fourteenth-century Gough Map, had long lain to the east of the Pennines, where it was served by a number of substantial towns and monastic houses (Stenton 1958: 17–19; Harvey 1992: 117–8; Delano-Smith and Kain 1999: 47).

Except when at war, it was in the Midlands and the South that medieval kings spent the greater part of their time. This was where the principal royal palaces were located, along with the forests in which kings preferred to hunt. The venues of royal councils and parliaments held between 1258 and 1547 define this core area of the English medieval state. London and Westminster, of course, were its joint nerve centre and it was here that three-quarters of all councils and parliaments met. Moreover, the importance of the capital grew over time. In the first half of the fourteenth century only two-thirds of all councils and parliaments were held there, but after 1350 this proportion rose to 85 per cent and, after 1500, to 90 per cent (Powicke 1939: 342–50). The other twenty venues where medieval councils and parliaments met were scattered across the centre of England (Figure 7.2). Of these, councils and parliaments were only ever held at all regularly at York, and then only between 1314 and 1335. Even so, fewer than 7 per cent of all medieval councils and parliaments were held north and west of the Humber, Trent and Severn, and then usually only because war, directed by the king, was being waged against the Welsh or the Scots. With these few exceptions (none occurring after 1400) the North was ruled from the South. The same applied even more to the south-west, for Cornwall, Devon, Somerset and Dorset also lay outside the charmed circle of power. Here there was no border to give 'territorialising' monarchs cause to visit.

The North, of course, sent representatives to parliament, but these never amounted to more than about a tenth of the commons. Durham and Cheshire as county palatines were unrepresented. Parliamentary boroughs were also thinner on the ground in the North than in the South, since urbanisation came later to the North than the South (Britnell 1996). In 1546 the eight northern counties contained only eight of the 126 parliamentary boroughs. In parliament's infancy several other northern boroughs had occasionally sent representatives to royal councils and to parliaments but following the Black Death, for one reason or another, these all lapsed (Willis 1730: viii–xiv, xix–xxxiv). The absence, after 1349, of any parliamentary boroughs in either Lancashire or Cheshire meant that the north-west, in particular, had very little say in government.

In Lancashire and the four northernmost counties urbanisation was an exclusively post-Conquest phenomenon. Here, as elsewhere in the North, there was much catching up during the twelfth and thirteenth centuries, when trade and commerce were expanding everywhere. The new territorial lords of the region were active founders of boroughs (Beresford and Finberg 1973; Beresford 1981; Britnell 1996: 65–7). Of these borough foundations, however, only a handful took vigorous root and grew to significant proportions. Foremost among these were the east-coast ports of Newcastle-upon-Tyne, Scarborough and Kingston-upon-Hull, which benefited from the thriving trade along the east coast and across the North Sea. York, too, owed part of its prosperity to the fact that it was located at the tidal limit of the river Ouse. According to the 1327 and 1332 lay subsidies, York had half as many tax-payers as London but only a seventh of the capital's taxable wealth. In tax-payers York ranked as the second city and in taxable wealth the third (after Bristol) (Campbell and Bartley forthcoming). The compiler of the Gough Map was nevertheless in no doubt that York was next in importance to London (Parsons 1958: 9). At its medieval peak, York probably had a population of at least 20,000 against the 70,000 of London (Campbell 2000: 405).

Within the North, Newcastle-upon-Tyne was the second wealthiest and, by implication, second largest borough and *c.*1330 ranked among the ten wealthiest and largest towns in the kingdom, with a population of around 10,000 (Campbell and Bartley forthcoming). Strongly fortified and never taken or sacked by the Scots, it had undoubtedly profited from the military provisioning trade and was already shipping coal to ports along the east coast and across the North Sea (Pelham 1936: 321–2; Blake 1967). Penrith, Nottingham, Kingston-upon-Hull, Derby and Newark were the next highest-ranking northern boroughs and the only others to rank among the fifty wealthiest and largest boroughs in 1334 (Campbell and Bartley forthcoming). In the Middle Ages the South was more urbanised than the North. York and Newcastle excepted, the South contained all the largest towns (including London, the largest, wealthiest and most important of them all), the lion's share of the nation's urban population (probably 90 per cent of that living in towns of at least 10,000 inhabitants), and almost certainly proportionately more people in the South lived in towns than did so in the North.

Trade was the life-blood of all the most substantial medieval towns, and in the Middle Ages it was southern rather than northern ports that handled the bulk of the nation's overseas trade. In 1204 ports south of the Humber had contributed 85 per cent of a tax of one-fifteenth levied on trade (Miller and Hatcher 1995: 196). A century later the ports from Kingston-upon-Hull northwards still accounted for only about 16 per cent of English overseas trade (less than half that of London) (Carus-Wilson and Coleman 1963: 40–1; Lloyd 1982: 210–26). In the late-thirteenth century foreign-owned vessels dominated the shipping that frequented these north-ern ports and of the native-owned vessels a significant proportion belonged to southern merchants (Pelham 1936: 306–10). This meant that the bulk of the profits of trade accrued to merchants from outside the region, many of them aliens. Even so, the North's share of alien trade was relatively small. In 1304–5 only 3 per cent of the alien trade in cloths, 9 per cent of that in general merchandise, 26 per cent of that in hides and 29 per cent of that in wool was shipped through the five northern customable ports of Kingston-upon-Hull, Ravenser, Scarborough, Whitby, Hartle-pool and Newcastle-upon-Tyne (Lloyd 1982: 210–26). Collectively, the northern ports never handled more than a fifth of English trade, whereas by 1300 Lon-don alone probably handled well over a third and by the opening of the sixteenth century that proportion had doubled (Keene 1989: 99).

These patterns of trade reflected the nation's economic geography. Throughout the Middle Ages the thirty-one counties south of the Humber, Trent and Mersey always contained at least four-fifths of the country's tax-paying population and five-sixths of its taxable wealth. Not only was the South wealthier and more popu-lous by far in aggregate, it was also wealthier and more populous per unit area. The highest densities of plough-teams, population and wealth were all to be found in the South (Figure 7.2). Here, too, were the most intensive, developed and produc-tive farming systems (Campbell and Bartley forthcoming). Although many horses were bred in the North, southern farmers and carriers made greater use of horse-power (Campbell 2000: 123–31). The North contained extensive upland grazings, but it was the South that produced the bulk of the nation's wool and nearly all of the highest-grade wool that commanded the best prices on the international market (Campbell 2002: 1–30). On these criteria the South would appear to have been economically more advanced than the North.

The South's demographic and economic advantage over the North appears to have been most pronounced in the late-eleventh century. In 1092 when William II first established the Tweed–Solway line as the northern limit of the realm, barely 10 per cent of the population lived north of the Humber, Trent and Mersey and, on the evidence of the enigmatic Domesday valuations, the North contributed only about 6 per cent of the nation's wealth (Darby 1977: 359). This was when the economic fortunes of the North were at their lowest ebb, for the region had not yet recovered from the scorched-earth policy employed in the winter of 1069–70 by William I when he brutally reduced the whole of the North to submission (Darby 1977: 248–52; Higham 1993: 244–7). Recovery and reconstruction took several generations and often involved the complete replanning of settlements and deliberate recruitment of colonists (Bishop 1962; Shepherd 1976). Discovery and exploitation of the region's mineral wealth – silver, lead, iron and coal – was a further lure to settlers, Cumberland and Northumberland experiencing a veritable silver rush between c.1130 and c.1200 (Blanchard 1996: 27–39). After much making good of lost ground the North began to catch up. The prolonged Anglo-Scottish peace helped. By 1290 the North had probably reached its apogee of medieval prosperity. On the evidence of the 1327–34 lay subsidies, the region had increased its shares of population and wealth to approximately an eighth of the total (Campbell and Bartley forthcoming).

By the 1330s, however, following forty years of bitter and violent warfare, the North's fortunes were once more in decline and they would continue to wane for the remainder of the Middle Ages. Many of the relative gains made during the preceding century or so of peace were lost during the ensuing 250 years of war and border reiving. In 1524–5 the North accounted for only about 8 per cent of the country's moveable lay wealth (Sheail 1998: 438). In contrast, the seven counties closest to London – with less than half the North's area – contributed 29 per cent of the country's wealth in 1086, paid 17 per cent of the lay subsidy of 1334, and paid approximately 21 per cent of the lay subsidy of 1524–5 (Darby 1977: 336; Campbell and Bartley forthcoming; Sheail 1998: 438). By the opening of the sixteenth century the south-east was already firmly established as the nation's political and economic centre of gravity. By comparison, the North lagged far behind and remained not only more thinly peopled but conspicuously poorer, except where manufacturing provided employment and stimulated trade. Herein lay the seeds of some of the economic developments that would eventually transform the commercial fortunes of the region, especially when exploited by mercantile capitalists from the South.

The unequal distribution of economic and demographic power

That the economy of the South should so consistently have eclipsed that of the North is hardly surprising. In an agrarian age, it was in the south and east that the bulk of the land best suited to mixed arable husbandry was located. Trade and commerce also flowed from the west and north to the east and south-east, for the bulk of England's overseas trade was with mainland Europe, especially Flanders and northern France. As yet the Irish Sea and Atlantic had limited commercial potential. With the exception of Bristol, whose main trading partners were Gascony, Iberia and Ireland, all the most important and active English ports faced east (Campbell 2001: 101). The demand of these ports and the overseas markets they serviced stimulated economic development within their hinterlands. Accordingly, wealth and population attained their medieval maxima in northern Kent, in eastern Norfolk and in the recently reclaimed fenlands immediately inland from the busy ports of Kings Lynn and Boston. In 1291 clerical wealth per unit area was likewise greatest in the dioceses of Canterbury, Ely and Norwich (Campbell 2001: 101).

Whether in 1524–5, 1334, 1291 or 1086, it was in the counties and dioceses that lay to the south and east of a line from the Humber to the Severn, and thence to the Tamar, that the highest levels of assessed wealth were to be found (Figure 7.2). This predominantly lowland, south-eastern half of the realm consistently contributed at least three-quarters of the nation's wealth. Within this broad zone the areas of greatest wealth shifted over time. In the early-sixteenth century there were conspicuous concentrations of wealth in the counties closest to London as well as in the textile-producing regions of the West Country (Sheail 1972: 120). These were relatively recent developments (Darby *et al.* 1979: 256–62). In the first half of the fourteenth century, at the climax of medieval demographic and economic expansion, the main focus of wealth had been the closely settled and intensively farmed countryside of East Anglia and the east Midlands. Taxable wealth per unit area and per tax-payer and the density of tax-payers per unit area all attained their maxima in a wedge of countryside stretching inland from the Wash as far as Oxford (Campbell and Bartley forthcoming). The fertile and recently reclaimed silt fenlands of East Anglia were the single most populous and wealthy area of all. Two hundred and fifty years earlier, when the enigmatic Domesday valuations were made, these fenlands had been largely empty and of little value and the ports of Boston and Kings Lynn had yet to be founded. At that time the main focus of wealth had been in central southern England – in Oxfordshire, Berkshire, Wiltshire and Dorset – together with Kent. In these same counties, plus Gloucestershire and Buckinghamshire, values per man were also at a maximum (Darby 1977: 359). Nevertheless, no matter how the geography of wealth shifted over time, the highest levels of wealth always lay south and east of the Humber–Severn–Tamar line.

In economic terms, the administrative division into England north and south of the Humber, Trent and Mersey was an artificial divide. Instead, the most pronounced and persistent contour was that which ran diagonally across the country from Flamborough Head in the north-east, via the Trent, the Warwickshire Avon and the lower Severn, across Devon to the Tamar in the south-west (Figure 7.3). Throughout the Middle Ages levels of wealth and densities of population were consistently lower to the north and west of that contour than they were to the south and east. If, in the Middle Ages, there were two Englands, this was the line that divided them. Analysis of the combined distribution of lay and clerical taxable wealth in the early-sixteenth century shows that Yorkshire and Lancashire ranked among England's poorest counties, together with Derbyshire, Staffordshire, Shropshire and, by implication, Cheshire, plus – in the extreme south-west – Cornwall (Schofield 1965: 506). The last was in cultural terms probably the most distinctive English county of them all, with its Celtic saints and Cornish language, absence of any large town, and a physical remoteness from the seat of power so great that it was rarely if ever visited by any reigning monarch. More detailed analysis of the lay subsidies of 1524 and 1525 confirms this basic pattern, while bringing the geography of lay wealth into sharper focus (Sheail 1972: 120). The essential difference between North and South was that, whereas in the south and east low levels of taxable wealth were confined to specific localities that were environmentally poor, in the north and west such low levels of wealth were decidedly the norm.

In 1524–5 the fourteen counties (including Cornwall and Devon) lying north and west of the Humber–Severn–Tamar line accounted for less than a fifth of all assessed lay wealth (Sheail 1998: 438). In 1334 the equivalent proportion had

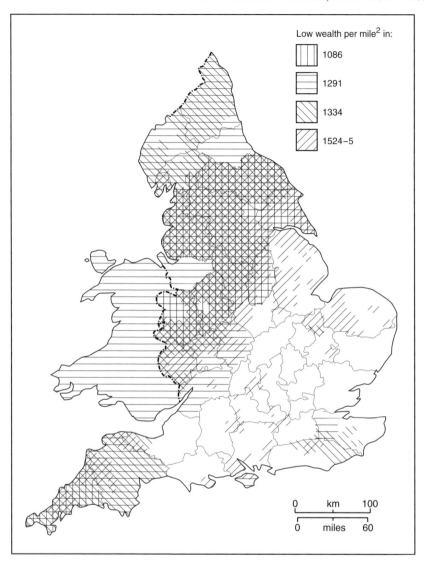

Figure 7.3 Areas of lowest wealth in 1086, 1291, 1334 and 1524–5 (Sheail (1972: 120); Darby (1977: 359); Campbell and Bartley (forthcoming))

been just over a fifth, for the centrifugal forces of the preceding age of expansion had displaced population and economic activity to the north and west (Campbell and Bartley forthcoming). Even so, Lancashire, Yorkshire (the North and West Ridings), Derbyshire, Staffordshire, Shropshire and Worcestershire, together with Devon and Cornwall, stand out as the poorest counties in terms of their combined lay and clerical wealth (Schofield 1965: 506). In 1291 Exeter had the lowest unit wealth of any English diocese, closely followed by Lichfield in the north-west Midlands, and then Carlisle in the extreme north-west. The next poorest dioceses – Hereford, Worcester, York and Durham – were all similarly located in the north and west. In fact, the high unit wealth of the diocese of St Andrews in eastern Scotland demonstrates that northerliness per se was not necessarily a disadvantage (Campbell 2001: 101). Rather, the key geographical difference was between east and west. In 1334 it was in the north-west, the west Midlands and the south-west that taxable lay wealth per unit area, wealth per tax-payer, and tax-payers per square mile were all consistently at their lowest (Campbell and Bartley forthcoming). At that time the fourteen northern and western counties contained only a quarter of all those deemed wealthy enough to pay tax and contributed less than a quarter of the total tax subsidy. In 1086 the relative poverty of these fourteen counties had been even more pronounced, for they contained approximately 23 per cent of the population south of the Tweed–Solway line and accounted for merely 15 per cent of valued wealth (Darby 1977: 359). In Yorkshire, Lancashire, Cheshire, Staffordshire, Derbyshire and Cornwall values per unit area, per man and per plough-team were only a fraction of those that prevailed south and east of the Humber, Severn and Tamar. The pronounced economic contour that the latter represented was as real in the eleventh as it would be in the sixteenth century (Figure 7.3).

Both from the Trent to the Severn and in the extreme south-west, this economic contour closely followed the boundary between a 'northern and western province' of predominantly dispersed settlement and a 'central province' within which nucleated settlement prevailed (Roberts and Wrathmell 2000: 2). The latter was a largely treeless and champion landscape where closely regulated common-field agriculture was the norm. This contrast is exemplified by the Felden country of southern Warwickshire, with its nucleated villages, two- and three-field systems and relatively high unit levels of taxable wealth, and the wooded Arden district of the north of the county, with its more scattered and dispersed settlement, irregular field systems and lower unit levels of taxable wealth (Harley 1958). The scenic contrast that these two landscape types provided was instantly recognisable to those who, like John Leland in the 1530s and 1540s, travelled between them (Tomlin Smith 1907). In 1334 this 'central province', from Lincolnshire to Somerset, was associated with levels of taxable lay wealth that were well above average. From Yorkshire northwards, however, the patterns of wealth and of settlement diverged, for whereas high levels of taxable wealth did not persist north of the Humber, the 'central province' of nucleated settlement extended right up the lowland corridor that extended to the east of the Pennines as far as Northumberland. In terms of settlement, the key divide was east–west rather than north–south.

In the alluvial fenlands of East Anglia and in much of East Anglia and the Home Counties, mixed patterns of settlement again predominated, comprising some villages and many lesser dispersed settlements. Commonfields, when they occurred, were irregular rather than regular (Baker 1973a; Postgate 1973). In Suffolk and

Essex, the Chiltern Hills and the Weald of Surrey, Kent and Sussex, there was also much woodland (Roberts and Wrathmell 2000: 31; Campbell and Bartley forthcoming). In terms of settlement and landscape this 'south-eastern province', therefore, bore much in common with the 'northern and western provinces'. Levels of taxable wealth were, nevertheless, for the most part much higher, and in the fens, in eastern Norfolk and in north-eastern Kent levels of wealth and densities of population exceeded those prevailing anywhere in the 'central' or the 'northern and western provinces' (Campbell and Bartley forthcoming). All three localities were naturally fertile and each had evolved husbandry systems that made the most of their respective environmental advantages (Power and Campbell 1992: 233–42). They were also strategically located with regard to major domestic and overseas markets and were characterised by weak and fragmented lordship and a predominance of free over customary tenures.

These profound contrasts in the pattern of rural settlement can be shown to have existed in broad outline since at least the Norman Conquest (Roberts and Wrathmell 2000: 27–36). The same was true of the geographies of field systems and common rights. Both were further complemented in the Middle Ages by the geographies of lordship and tenure (Figure 7.4). In the greater part of the south-eastern settlement province in the first half of the fourteenth century the value of free rents exceeded that of customary rents by a factor of at least two. Since free rents per unit area were typically only half those of customary rents, at least four times as much tenanted land must have been held by free tenures as by servile tenures (Kanzaka 2002: 611). This was most conspicuously the case in Kent and eastern Essex, where villein tenure was virtually unknown. Significantly, free rents and tenures also prevailed over customary rents and tenures in that part of the 'northern and western settlement province' lying south of the Duddon in Cumbria and west of the Severn, Warwickshire Avon and Trent. In this respect there was a strong affinity between the south-east and the north-west. Between these two zones dominated by free tenures lay the wealthy 'central province' of nucleated commonfield villages, where customary rents either equalled or exceeded free rents. This was symptomatic of stronger lordship and is a further manifestation of the distinctive institutional history of this central region. Significantly, customary rather than free rents also predominated in the south-western counties of Devon and Cornwall, as well as in the north-eastern counties of Yorkshire, Durham and Northumberland. Here, therefore, the affinity was between the south-west and the north-east and a real contrast again existed between the eastern and western sides of the Pennines. Customary rents and tenures were, above all, most prevalent in the border counties of Cumberland, Westmorland and Northumberland. Here, very likely, they were a product of Henry I's creation of powerful territorial lordships following his conquest and settlement of Cumbria and redefinition of the Anglo-Scottish border at the end of the eleventh century.

With tenure, as with settlement, a tripartite rather than bipartite division prevailed at a national scale that cut right across the administrative divisions between

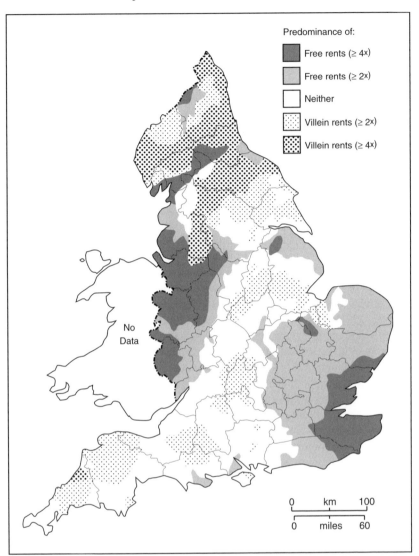

Figure 7.4 The relative importance of free and customary rents, 1300–49: the value of free and assize rents relative to the value of customary rents on lay manors (Campbell and Bartley (forthcoming))

North and South. One very clear tenurial contrast did, nevertheless, exist between North and South. Irrespective of whether tenures were free or customary, by the early-fourteenth century, everywhere north and west of a line from the Humber to the Severn, as well as in Devon and Cornwall, money rents far outweighed labour rents and other payments in kind (Figure 7.5). Kent was the only southern county in which a comparable situation prevailed. Indeed, from Shropshire to Northumberland, services are recorded on less than a quarter of manors (Campbell and Bartley forthcoming). In this important respect, the North is conspicuously different from the South. Paradoxically, money rents were most prevalent in what, seemingly, was the most remote and underdeveloped part of the country. Evidently, manorialism took a different form in the north-west Midlands and the north-west from that prevailing in the midland and southern heartland of England.

This deep-rooted institutional difference undoubtedly helps to explain why parts of the north and west proved so fruitful to the growth of proto-industry in the form of mineral extraction, metal working, leather manufacture and the production of textiles. Weak lordship, free tenures, small holdings, wood-pasture economies, cheap land and victuals, and the local availability of industrial raw materials in the form of oak bark for tannin, wood, charcoal, coal, iron, lead, hides, wool, flax and hemp all nurtured and facilitated the development of craft production (Thirsk 1961). Water power was also more abundant and fully exploited here than in most of the rest of the country and it was in the extreme north-west, where water power was available in greatest abundance, that it was earliest extensively applied to the fulling of cloth (Campbell and Bartley 2003: 000). Per capita, there were probably already more people with an understanding of cogs and gears in the North than in the South. This was a harbinger of things to come. Low levels of taxable wealth within the north and north-west should not, therefore, be mistaken for a lack of economic enterprise. In fact, in the 1330s wealth per tax-payer in the North bore relatively favourable comparison with that in much of the South (Campbell and Bartley forthcoming).

Uniting the nation: convergence versus divergence between North and South

For those who seek them, differences between North and South are not hard to find (Jewell 1994). Whether these differences divided more than they united is, however, a moot point, for environmentally and economically the two parts of the realm complemented each other. Certainly, there is nothing to suggest that there was any contemporary concept of a 'North–South divide'. Rather, the period is notable for the emergence of a growing sense of national consciousness, which overrode older regional identities (Davies 2000: 195–9). The idea of England as one country and the English as one nation is manifest in the creation of the first national maps. Matthew Paris produced a succession of them in the mid-thirteenth century, possibly based upon a lost Roman original, contemporary *mappa mundi*,

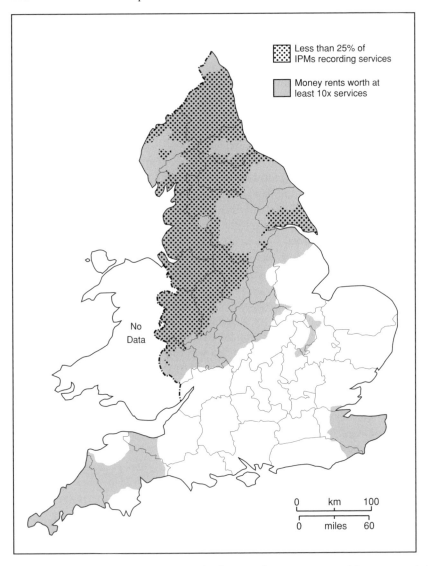

Figure 7.5 Areas with the greatest predominance of money rents and fewest recorded services, 1300–49 (Campbell and Bartley (forthcoming))

and a written itinerary of places and river crossings between Berwick in the north and Dover in the south (Harvey 1992: 110–6). These maps show the whole island of Britain, *nunc dicta Anglia*, and the last and most accomplished of them depicts with great emphasis both the Anglo-Scottish border and Hadrian's Wall. South of these vital boundaries there is nothing to suggest that England was anything other than a unified realm. The same is true of the later and fuller Gough Map, produced *c*.1360, which celebrates a united kingdom within a divided island (Parsons 1958). Neither map is, of course, 'true' in its outline and proportions. The distortion is nevertheless greater between east and west than between north and south, and greatest of all in the case of the non-English parts of the island – Wales and Scotland (Parsons 1958: 5–14; Delano-Smith and Kain 1999: 45–8). This is consistent with prevailing levels of geographical knowledge but also with a growing differentiation – cultural, administrative and legal – between those who were English and those who were not. Although there is some literary evidence of regional stereotyping within medieval England, this was of little consequence in an age which saw pronounced and prolonged conflict between the English and the Irish, the Welsh, the Scots and the French. War, in fact, was a great cultural leveller. The armies of soldiers and craftsmen mustered by Edward I to fight the Welsh and the Scots were melting pots of northerners, southerners and many others (Prestwich 1972: 67–107). These armies saw the North at first hand.

Opposition to the Welsh and the Scots helped forge a sense of Englishness (Davies 2000: 194–7). Thus, when Scots raided the north of England it served to remind northerners that first and foremost they were English (Gillingham 1995: 54–5). Since the twelfth century, as national self-confidence grew and the English state developed, there had been a growing belief in the superiority of English law, English governmental order and English norms. Henceforth, attitudes towards the Welsh, the Irish and the Scots hardened. 'The Anglo-Normans saw themselves, therefore, from an early date as purveyors of good governance and sound laws to the backward people of the British Isles. The novelty of their mission in the thirteenth century is that it acquired a much sharper and more intolerant aspect' (Davies 1990: 114). In order to extend and define the borders of their realm and extend their power throughout the whole island, English kings from William I to Richard II devoted much attention to the North and spent significant amounts of time there. The marches of both Wales and Scotland took on a significance and reality that they would lose once these borderlands ceased to be disputed (after 1284 in the case of Wales and 1560 in the case of Scotland). In the 1270s Chester became, briefly, the seat of king and court, as did Carlisle in the 1090s and 1290s. At Michaelmas 1283, during the second Welsh campaign, parliament met at Shrewsbury and in 1307 the Hilary session of parliament was held at Carlisle (Powicke 1939: 344–5). Royal neglect of the North was a post-medieval phenomenon. In the Middle Ages it was the extreme south-west, not the North, that lay beyond the cognisance of most monarchs. Cornwall was the English county least known to medieval kings and medieval cartographers and the most foreign in its language and beliefs.

In the fourteenth century northern accents and dialects may have been lampooned by southern writers but such humour arose from the recognition and toleration of differences (Jewell 1994: 191–4). Outsiders were generally treated more harshly. 'Foreigners' everywhere were suspect. Attitudes towards Jews and alien merchants mattered far more than attitudes of southerners towards northerners and vice versa. Ignorance, suspicion and prejudice could turn into aggression and hostility. During the thirteenth century Jews became the victims, first, of pogroms and eventually, in 1290, of expulsion (Rigby 1995: 296–301; Stacey 1995: 97–101). Foreign merchants typically sought protection and licence from the Crown (Lloyd 1982: 3–5, 9–34). Even so, in 1381, during the Peasants' Revolt, Flemings became the targets of xenophobia (Dobson 1983: 162, 175, 188–9, 201, 210). As the dramatic and violent events of that summer highlight, the key divisions within English society at that time were based more upon class and gender than upon region, although expression of those divisions did have a strong regional dimension (Rigby 1995: 181–283). Among great lords, class loyalty undoubtedly counted for more than regional allegiance. It was the gentry who, by the close of the Middle Ages, were likely to identify most strongly with their county and their region (Bennett 1973). They were also the group most actively involved in local government. In 1536 they played a key role in the Pilgrimage of Grace.

At the level of government and administration it is the precocious unity of medieval England that is most striking: 'there is no doubt that it was a unified country by 1066' (Campbell 1995: 43). It was Anglo-Saxon kings who had united the realm, developed a national system of taxation – the Danegeld – and established the shire as the key unit of local government. The Anglo-Saxons, too, had instituted the writ as the instrument for issuing royal instructions and authorising action by royal representatives. All that was left to the first of the Norman kings was to complete and consolidate the process in the North. Thereafter, under Henry II (1154–89), shire government, royal government and the king's justice were vigorously extended to the furthest limits of the realm. By the early-fourteenth century royal writs were acted upon with alacrity by escheators and sheriffs throughout England and in the English lands beyond. Distance from London meant that the lag time was greater in the North than the South, but not on average by more than a week or two (Campbell and Bartley forthcoming). Until war made the far North too risky, justices went on circuit in the North just as they did in the South (Cockburn 1968: 120–2). Even within the palatinate of Durham it was royal justice that the bishops dispensed, not their own, for their regalian rights did not extend to the enactment of laws. Fines were paid in the coins of the realm, the minting of which was a jealously preserved royal prerogative. The quality and reliability of English silver coins boosted commercial confidence while, from the middle of the twelfth century, massive transfusions of northern silver greatly increased the quantity in circulation (Mayhew 1995). Money early possessed a unity of value matched by no other commodity and thereby provided the one standardised measure of quantity.

At this early stage of national development uniformity in all things is not to be expected. Land-use, farming systems, field systems, common rights, settlement forms, tenures, manorial structures, lord-tenant relations, building materials and styles, and even the preferred architectural aesthetic, all displayed much regional diversity (Hallam 1988; Miller 1991; Roberts and Wrathmell 2000; Campbell and Bartley forthcoming). Differences of dialect and speech were pronounced and posed real problems of communication. It was because clerks, the clergy and the learned classes used Latin rather than the vernacular that administrative instructions could be discharged in all corners of the realm. Latin also provided an international means of communication, which greatly facilitated the growth of trade and commerce (Mann 1986: 379). The latter were to prove a powerful medium for the diffusion of national norms and erosion of regional differences. Thus, whereas enactment of the Assize of Measures in 1196 established the principle that there should be national uniformity of weights and measures, the use of statute measures depended upon the willingness of people to employ them (Britnell 1993: 90–1). By the early-fourteenth century, for instance, the use of acres to measure land had made most progress in the commercialised east and south-east and least progress north of the Trent, where allegiance to a range of customary measures – the carucate, bovate and oxgang – remained strong (Campbell and Bartley forthcoming). If, in this respect, the South led the North it was because of its closer proximity to the capital and its stronger exposure to the unifying influences of national and international trade and commerce.

From the twelfth century the gravitational pull of the metropolis began to be felt throughout the realm. This was when London supplanted Winchester as the political capital and became in every respect the country's first city (Keene 1989: 101). In 1086 Londoners had comprised approximately one in 90 of the population, by 1180 this had risen to approximately one in 75, by 1300 it was one in 60, by 1500 it was one in 50, and by 1600 it would rise to one in 25. The metropolis grew in relative size because it gained in political and economic influence. During the thirteenth century, for instance, it doubled its share of the expanding volume of English overseas trade, to approximately 35 per cent of the total by 1300 (Miller and Hatcher 1995: 196, 214–5). Over the same period it grew to become the second largest Christian city north of the Alps after Paris, with a population of perhaps 70,000. The city's demographic expansion was sustained by the recruitment of migrants from all parts of the country. Between 1270 and 1350 there was no English county that did not supply London with migrants, although the flow of migrants naturally decayed with distance from the city and was weakest of all from Cheshire, Lancashire and Westmorland in the north-west and Somerset, Dorset, and Devon in the south-west (Donkin 1973: 133).

The north-west and the south-west were the two least urbanised parts of the country. Although there was no shortage of small boroughs, especially in the south-west, Chester was the only city of size and note in the north-west, as was Exeter in the south-west. Both of these regions therefore occupied a relatively lowly place in the developing urban hierarchy that London headed and which provided the framework within which migrants were recruited. It was through that hierarchy that goods, services, fashions and information were distributed and disseminated. As the country's primate city, London offered the widest range of high-quality wares and thus became the landed elite's preferred place to shop (Dyer 1989: 308–10). Lords, north and south alike, bought from the medieval equivalents of Harrods. Top-of-the-range goods commanded a national market.

Tax assessments show that the wealthiest London merchants were almost without peer in the provinces and often had business interests that extended to the furthest corners of the land (Lloyd 1982: 227–33). Londoners were therefore an important source of capital and credit. By the early-fifteenth century the capital's networks of credit and commerce were national in scope, although the intensity of those networks increased with proximity to the city. Links between London and the immediate Home Counties and the east Midlands appear to have been particularly strong. Links with the North were weaker. There was, however, no sharp divide; rather, a continuum characterised by distance-decay (Keene 2000: 70; Centre for Metropolitan History 2001: 5–9).

As London gained in influence within the nation's affairs so it became the principal medium through which powerful spatial forces of economic integration and differentiation were expressed, with far-reaching consequences for proximate and remote parts of the country. By 1300 an integrated national economy was in the making (Campbell 2000: 424–30). Live animals, hides, wool, minerals and coal produced in the North were already objects of national and international trade (Fraser 1969; Campbell 2002). By 1500 the region was beginning to become a significant supplier of cheap manufactures (Baker 1973b: 218–36). This would prove to be a far more effective means of turning the North's cheap land to economic gain, but it was contingent upon the growth of southern and overseas markets and a steady supply of working capital from the South. In part, the reciprocal relationship evolving between the metropolis and the North was that of core and periphery. The economic activities that developed and prospered in the North were a function of the region's relatively low economic rent. But the comparative advantage derived by the North from its particular factor endowments of land, labour and enterprise was also important. It was fortuitous that the North was better endowed than the South with minerals (silver, lead, iron and coal), that environmentally it was better suited to pastoralism, and that, for historical reasons, the region's agrarian institutions nurtured enterprise and the growth of proto-industry. The seeds of the North's later manufacturing success were mostly sown in the later Middle Ages.

The medieval North may therefore have been poorer and less populous than the South. It may also have possessed its own linguistic and administrative identity. Nevertheless, to stereotype it as backward, conservative and reactionary is misleading (Beckingsale 1969). In the late-eleventh century the destruction inflicted by William I had presented the North with a major task of recovery and reconstruction. Thereafter, during the twelfth and thirteenth centuries, the region grew faster in population and wealth than the South, aided, no doubt, by the silver rush of the mid-twelfth century. This was when trading institutions were established throughout the region and when it became fully integrated into the nation's urban network. Progress was impressive. Newcastle-upon-Tyne, a new urban foundation, rose to prominence and York became the nation's second city, much visited by kings and, for a time, a regular venue for councils and parliaments.

The North also proved more receptive than the South to the arrival of the Cistercian Order and the twelfth century witnessed the foundation of a number of important Cistercian monasteries (Donkin 1978: 29–36). Thereafter these played an active role in developing the region's agricultural resources and exercised a powerful influence upon prevailing architectural styles (Waites 1997). Already at the close of the eleventh century Europe's first high-rib vaults had been constructed at Durham cathedral and, towards the end of the following century, Gothic principles of construction were introduced almost simultaneously at the collegiate church of Ripon and the Cistercian abbey of Roche in Yorkshire and at Canterbury cathedral in Kent (Pevsner 1967: 23–6; Pevsner 1983: 19). Nor was the region a laggard in the development of water- and wind power. By the early-fourteenth century it had capitalised upon its natural advantages and was better provided with water power than the South. The twelfth and thirteenth centuries were therefore a dynamic time for the North. During these centuries the region was regularly visited by kings and their retinues and by royal justices. The gap between North and South, which had been so wide at the time of the Domesday survey in 1086 (from which a significant part of the North had been excluded), had narrowed significantly by 1296.

It was the renewal of hostilities between England and Scotland in 1296 coupled with the general contraction in the international medieval economy that reversed this favourable pattern of development (Munro 1991). Armies and raiders again punished the North. Security along the border disintegrated and settlement retreated from the most exposed and vulnerable areas. Contraction appears to have commenced earlier in the North than in the South and to have progressed much further. Between c.1330 and 1525 the North declined relative to the South in its shares of tax-payers and taxable wealth. The North also began to lag behind the South in adopting the prevailing architectural fashions of the day. Meanwhile, the influence and relative importance of London continued to advance both economically and politically, thereby cementing but also downgrading the North's place within the national polity (Keene 2000; Centre for Metropolitan History 2001). The number of northern parliamentary boroughs dwindled (Willis 1730: viii–xiv, xix–xixxxiv). After 1400 no council or parliament was held in the North and the incidence of royal visits declined (Powicke 1939: 348–50). Defence was increasingly delegated to those local magnates appointed as wardens of the march (Ellis 2001a). As yet, however, direct interference by the South in the affairs of the North remained limited.

It was the Reformation that brought the latent conflict between these processes of convergence and divergence to a head and ignited the Pilgrimage of Grace. If that rebellion was a manifestation of northern consciousness, that consciousness was a product of the specific political, military and economic circumstances pertaining in the fourteenth and fifteenth centuries (Jewell 1991: 24–5). As such it was a relatively recent development. In 1536 the mutual dependence between North and South was not in dispute, it was the subordinate relationship of North to South that was at issue. Such subordination was unavoidable given the North's status as periphery and the South's status as core within the nation state that was England. The whole of the North had first become fully integrated into that state in 1092 and since 1157 that status had remained unchallenged. Four hundred years later, the political, cultural and economic fortunes of North and South had become yet more inextricably bound together. 'The very early institutional maturity and self-definition of the English state and the tight weave of its power structures, ethnic self-profile, and historical mythology gave it a remarkable resilience and cohesion' (Davies 2000: 201). To both northern and southern English, it was the Scots, the Welsh and the Irish who always remained the 'significant others'. By 1560, as in 1066, the one North–South divide that was as real as it was imagined was that between England and Scotland (Barrow 1966).

8

Cultural constructions of England's geography and history

ALAN R. H. BAKER AND MARK BILLINGE

Standard questions about the nature of any North–South divide in England during particular historical periods have not produced standard answers. This is hardly surprising, given the country's changing geography during the last millennium and the differing intellectual baggages brought to this project by its contributors. Nonetheless, it is possible to unravel some common threads running throughout these essays and we want here to identify a few of them. Both the character and the historical status of England's North–South divide have been explored. The concept of such a divide is deeply embedded in today's popular culture and frequently brought to the surface by today's media, which feeds on oppositions and conflicts. But it has also been shown to have deep historical roots.

A negative image of the North has been cultivated in recent decades in travel writing, in television documentaries, in novels and in films. Reflecting upon recent such works, Raphael Samuel concluded:

In any of these literatures, the North of England is apt to fare badly. As the original home of many of this country's staple industries it is peculiarly vulnerable to the charge of being economically moribund. Gastronomically, the people are accused of being overweight and addicted to an unhealthy diet. Environmentally, the North was the great victim of the planning disasters of the 1960s, having more than its fair share of multi-storey car parks, express throughways and 'peripheral' council estates. Medically, as the statistics on lung cancer, heart disease and infant mortality never fail to record, it lags behind the rest of Britain. The people of the North famously smoke more and die younger than those of the South, and they are also – as the Labour Party is discovering in its attempt to promote all-women short lists of parliamentary candidates – more wedded to patriarchal ways. Even the scenery of the North – the hardness and the harshness which made so striking a contrast to the enervating softness of the South – Wuthering Heights vs. Thrushcross Grange – seems to have lost its allure. An age which has made a fetish of the cottage garden and the village green, and which promoted the Cotswolds as England's imaginary heart, has perhaps less taste than Emily Brontë for the solitudes of the moors. (Samuel 1998: 160–1)

Samuel pointed out that the North has been portrayed as being both backward and in decline, differing from the South not only economically but also politically and culturally. For example, Paul Theroux (1983) in his *Kingdom by the Sea* emphasised the – for him – 'dispirited', 'sad','sick' and 'horrible' character of England's northern coastal towns and Robert Chesshyre (1987) in his *The Return of a Native Reporter* stressed the ruination of societies and landscapes wrought by de-industrialisation in many northern towns. The contrast between North and South was stated starkly by Ian Jack (1987) in his *Before the Oil Ran Out: Britain 1977–1986*:

> Money has always tended to move south in Britain, as though it were obeying some immutable Newtonian law, but now it is not just the cream off the top, a case of Bradford profit being spent in Bond Street. The actual generation of wealth has moved south, as well the spending of it . . . Ninety-four per cent of *all* jobs lost since 1979 were north of a line drawn between the Wash and the Bristol Channel. This is a new frontier, a successor to Hadrian's Wall and the Highland Line. Above it, wealth and population dwindle; beneath it, both expand. (Jack 1987: ix)

Although Jack makes a valid general point, he is clearly mistaken in believing that what he calls a 'frontier' was new in the 1980s. He was merely reinventing a North–South divide whose roots have to be unearthed in a much deeper history.

It is extraordinary that the line drawn by Ian Jack – that between the Wash and the Bristol Channel – dividing England into two distinct zones in the 1980s corresponded almost exactly to the line drawn here by Bruce Campbell – that between the Humber and the Severn and thence to the Exe – in the 1080s, with the zone to the south being wealthier and economically healthier than that to the north. It is astonishing that the Industrial Revolution, which involved a major and long-lasting restructuring of England's economy and society, seems not to have involved also a similarly major and enduring restructuring of the geographical distribution of its wealth. That is, of course, a gross generalisation but the fact that it can be made even as a caricature of the situation means that it is genuinely and literally remarkable. There does appear to have been a structural continuity of some kind underpinning the North–South divide, whether as reality or as myth.

For most of the period covered collectively by these essays, England had dominantly an agricultural, organically based and low-technology economy. The human geography of England was thus more closely tied to, or at least reflective of, its physical geography in the earlier part of this millennium than it was to be in later centuries. Furthermore, England's physical geography exhibits a clear north–south divide, or perhaps more accurately a clear north-west and south-east divide. A line drawn not from the Wash or Humber but from the Tyne to the Severn, fringing the eastern Pennines on the way, and thence to the Exe divides England – indeed, Britain – into two zones. Geologically, to the north and west of that line lie Carboniferous and older strata, while to the south and east the rocks are post-Carboniferous. Physiographically, in the former zone are to be found many hills, plateaux and mountains over 200 metres above sea level; in the latter zone there are hardly any (in effect only Dartmoor and the North York Moors) and the relief is comprised instead of lowlands and valleys, and of low hills and low plateaux (Warwick 1964). The fundamental significance of this basic division into a highland and a lowland Britain in prehistoric times was recognised by Cyril Fox (1943) in his classic work, *The Personality of Britain*. It has also been recognised as a basic feature of the rural settlement pattern of Britain in historic times, with nucleated villages being characteristic of lowland England and dispersed settlement with isolated farmsteads and hamlets being associated more with northern and western, highland England and with Wales, Scotland and Ireland (Darby 1964). These statements are the broadest of generalisations and exceptions can be found at regional and, more especially, at local scales. But they capture a basic feature of the identity of England: its fundamentally split personality. The physical division of England into highland and lowland zones has certainly underpinned and probably encouraged a cultural division of England into North and South. We are obviously not arguing here for any kind of environmental determinism, merely for recognition of this basic and enduring geological and physiographical contrast within England (and Britain) and acceptance that this has provided a structural continuity within the country's changing history and geography. On these terms, there has always been and must always be a North and a South in England's history.

But of course a text of cultural history has to be written on the embossed paper of physical geography. The essays in this volume indicate, however, that there has been not just one but many narratives of North and South and of the North–South divide in England. Playing a powerful and enduring role in all of them has been London. The capital's dominance in England's economy and society was already established by the end of the Middle Ages. Campbell (Chapter 7) emphasises that the South was much more urbanised than the North and that London was easily the largest and wealthiest town in medieval England. The second most important – York – was of course located in the North but it fell far short of London's stature. In the early-fourteenth century, York had only half as many tax-payers as London and only one-seventh of the capital's taxable wealth; at its medieval peak, York probably had a population of about 20,000 but London had about 70,000 and was, after Paris, the second largest Christian city north of the Alps. From the twelfth century, when London replaced Winchester as the political capital, the impact of the metropolis diffused increasingly through the country. No doubt at first the process of spatial diffusion was largely contagious, because of the limitations of the transportation networks; but they gradually also became hierarchical, as contacts improved within the settlement system. London was the motor generating geographically uneven development. By the mid-fourteenth century, every English county was supplying London with migrants, although the flow expectedly decayed with distance from the city. By the early-sixteenth century, the North accounted for only about 8 per cent of the country's moveable lay wealth but the seven counties closest to London, together comprising less than half of the North's area, contributed 21 per cent. London had by then become firmly established as England's primate city, playing a dominant role in the circulation of people, goods, capital and information through-out the country – movements which shaped and reshaped England's history and geography.

The central role of London in that process becomes even more evident in the post-medieval period. Langton (Chapter 6) emphasises the key part played by London's consumers, producers and merchants in the spatial organisation of early modern England and that role is also acknowledged in all of the chapters addressing later periods. It would thus be possible to interpret the historical geography of England since 1066 in terms of the concept of metropolitanism. This envisages the emergence of a city of outstanding size and its developing dominance not only over its immediately adjacent hinterland but also over other cities and their hinterlands, with the entire area coming to be organised by the metropolis through its control of the networks of communications, trade, finance and power into a single economic and social unit. The concept of metropolitanism was elaborated by historian Norman S. B. Gras (1922) and was paralleled by geographer Walter Christaller's formulation of central place theory (1933). In these present essays, both Campbell and Langton identify an intentional project to develop a national consciousness and see that project as being effected from London, as England's metropolis, as its most central place within the settlement system. They both see that project as being more important than any contemporary awareness of, or debate about, a North–South divide.

The metropolitan dominance of London persisted throughout the whole of the post-medieval period, despite the upheavals of the Industrial Revolution. Indeed, it could be argued that London increased its dominance during this period. Wrigley (1967) has provided an elegant model of the role of London in transforming English society and economy between 1650 and 1750 and the principal processes which he identified can also be seen operating to varying degrees from that period through to the present day. We might, therefore, perhaps expect any spatial tension to have been expressed in terms of a divide between London and the provinces rather than between North and South. Billinge (Chapter 5) shows that London's growth as the nation's economic, social and political focus between 1750 and 1830 did lead to some provincial suspicion, not only in the north but also in the south of England. In many ways, London stood apart from the rest of the country; it was neither of the north nor of the south. Howell (Chapter 4) argues that the economic upheavals between 1830 and 1918 left the dominance of London unchallenged and even saw it reinforced, with the growth of central state control through social legislation emanating from the metropolis. He also identifies the growth of a distinctive and robust provincialism which aligned both region and nation against the capital. The coarser optic employed by Dorling (Chapter 3) does not enable us to look into the status and role of London during the interwar years but Martin's (Chapter 2) does so for the second half of the twentieth century. During this period London witnessed – along with northern regions – a major de-industrialisation, with the loss of many manufacturing jobs. But it was also able to adjust, reshaping its economic structure by building on its historic role of dominance in the service sector and especially by expanding into the new information or knowledge economy. In many ways, London at the end of the twentieth century still stood apart from the rest of the country, from the provinces.

There are, therefore, grounds for expecting more signs of conflict between London and the provinces than are provided in the foregoing essays. Although they provide hints of such a tension, these essays offer little evidence to suggest that the division between London and its provinces was anything like as deep as has been historically that between, for example, Paris and its provinces (Corbin 1996). This might be because provincial France covered a much greater area than did England and Paris was much more remote than was London from many of their respective provincial regions. It might also be because the centralising intentions and accomplishments of French national governments, especially since 1789, have been more powerful and effective – and thus provocative – than those of Britain.

Despite the persistent dominance of the metropolis over the English provinces since the Middle Ages, a 'London versus the provinces' discourse has been less prominent and less influential than has that of a North–South divide. The essays presented here also suggest that the concept of a North–South divide emerged only with the geographical restructuring of England during the Industrial Revolution. Although Campbell (Chapter 7) acknowledges the existence a number of north–south dichotomies in the Middle Ages, he argues that they did not enter into popular – or even elite – consciousness as a formal North–South divide. He identifies instead a reduction of English regional differences and an enlargement of national consciousness, encouraged by a growing awareness of a differentiation between the English on the one hand and the Welsh, Scots and Irish on the other. For the early modern period, Langton (Chapter 6) identifies the reality of a complex regional mosaic within an idealised national harmony. The twin processes of areal differentiation and specialisation and of spatial integration and harmonisation did not, in his view, find expression or recognition in any North–South divide. Langton considers that the 'other' against which the southern English stereotype set itself was not northern Englishmen but the non-English 'heathen' (meaning Catholic) Irish and the 'uncivilised natives' of overseas colonies.

It was not until the eighteenth century that the idea of an internalised North–South divide gradually entered into popular consciousness. Billinge (Chapter 5) argues that the economic and social transformation of England between 1750 and 1830 brought about a greater regional diversity within a framework of a broadly homogenising culture, a sharpening of the dichotomy between country and city, and a growing awareness of the dominance of London. But it also saw a reworking of ideas and attitudes, the emergence of two different cultures in Georgian England and a developing awareness of internal geographical differences, of geographical 'others', within England. If the idea of a North–South divide was only embryonic before 1750, it came to be born between then and 1830. Its subsequent maturation and incorporation into the popular imagination is traced by Howell (Chapter 4) through to 1918. This was the crucial period during which the idea of a North–South divide became common currency. The interwar years 1918–39 were, according to Dorling (Chapter 3), something of a hiatus, a period in which a deep North–South divide can be recognised with hindsight even though it was hardly noticed at the time. Be that as it may, Martin (Chapter 2) makes it abundantly clear that the idea came to the fore again in academic, political and journalistic debates for two generations after 1950 and it continues to be debated to this day – as witnessed by this book!

The process of uneven economic and social development in England during the period since the Norman Conquest, involving both differentiation and integration, meant that its regional geography was fundamentally transformed. But so too was the geographical consciousness of its people, although that process must have been similarly uneven among social groupings and among individuals within a social grouping. The changing regional geography of England during the last one thousand years has been very complex, as has also the changing knowledge of that changing geography. In order to make some sense of those complexities, both contemporary actors and historical observers have found it necessary to simplify them.

One such simplification, as we have already suggested, might have been provided by the notion of metropolitan dominance. Some contemporary actors and historical observers have made partial use of the nexus of ideas contained within the concept. Among the latter are the classic study by Gras (1926) on the evolution of the English corn market during the medieval and early modern periods and the more recent modelling by Wrigley (1967) of London's role in changing English society and economy between 1650 and 1750. But the concept is itself a complex one and to be fully illuminating is dependent upon detailed information about the flows of people, goods, capital and ideas. The basic concept itself is simple enough but identifying its workings in historical contexts – and even at the present day – is quite the opposite. The fundamental principle underpinning the concept of metropolitan dominance might be little more than common sense but demonstrating it in practice is uncommonly difficult. The role of London in transforming England's geography has been remarked upon frequently but analysed rarely. The notion remains at the surface of the historiography of England's historical geography; it has not become deeply embedded within it.

A seemingly more straightforward concept has been employed (unknowingly) by contemporary actors and (knowingly) by historical observers as a more acceptable way of simplifying, of managing, the complexity of England's historical geography. A multiplicity of local and regional differences within a national framework has been collapsed into a binary contrast between the economies, societies and cultures of the South and the North. Many of the authors of the essays presented here engage with that contrast in terms of a core-periphery concept, a model of the spatial organisation of human activity most closely associated with the work of John Friedmann (1966). This model assumes an unequal distribution of power in an economy and society, with the core dominating a dependent periphery through the relations of exchange between them. Friedmann's model envisaged the development of a pre-industrial economy and society into one characterised by core and periphery, with subsequent development involving the dispersion of economic activity and social control into parts of the periphery and then the emergence of an interdependent spatial integration. It might be that discussion of the North–South divide in England has been underpinned since the 1960s by Friedmann's core-periphery model but its basic principle had been implicit in debates about the condition of England since the 1760s.

The North–South divide is thus best seen as a metaphor, or as Martin puts it 'a discursive device for simplifying what in reality is necessarily a complex socioeconomic landscape'. The device has been in use for more than two hundred years. Moreover, it has also been a rhetorical device. As Howell emphasises, Paul Goetsch (1996) claims that the contrast between the industrial and modern North and the rural and traditional South was never more rhetorically salient than in the Victorian years and various representations of what Robert Shields (1991) calls 'the space-myth of Northern Britain' continue to position the 'industrial North' on the nation's cultural periphery. Inevitably, such a binary characterisation can be shown – through the many local exceptions to it – to have been no more than a caricature. As Martin points out, some authors complicate the simple picture of a North–South divide in the late-twentieth century by identifying an inner and an outer core as well as an inner and an outer periphery, while others argue for a complex archipelago of wealth in the North and of poverty in the South which defies the simple portrayal of a 'poor North' and a 'rich South'. The identification of geographical regions is well known not be an exact science, even as practised by professional geographers let alone popular imaginations. Diverse views flourish because different geographical scales and different social and economic indicators are employed in the process of identifying regions.

The North–South divide – like all such regionalisation – has to be seen as a cultural construction, as a space-myth which could nonetheless be the basis for real thought and action. If people believe in the existence of a North–South divide, then such a belief becomes the basis for action. Historical geosophy – the geographical ideas, both true and false, held by all manner of people in the past – has contributed significantly to the making of England's historical geography. But so too has historical geopiety – the attachment of people to particular places, the identification of individuals and groups with particular locations, environments and landscapes. In combination, historical geosophy and geopiety lead to two other related issues: the possibility of multiple geographical imaginings and attachments, and the probability of a distinction being made between 'insiders' belonging to a particular place and 'outsiders' not so belonging.

As communications improved through the centuries and flows of information were facilitated, so levels of geographical knowledge and potentially of allegiance were enhanced. Individuals became increasingly aware of their being situated within a nested hierarchy of places which went from the locality through the region and the nation to the continent of Europe and to the colonies and the world. Imagining a North–South divide was just one way of coping with the developing complexity of a geographical knowledge and experience. But of course even the concept of a nested hierarchy of connected places is itself a simplification, a theoretical model of a more complex real world. Regions have long been thought of as occupying continuous sections of the earth's surface, so that those such as the North and the South can be differentiated 'on the ground'. But some geographers are now advocating a new approach to regional geography, one which sees regions as constituted of spatialised social relations, and narratives about them, which not only lay down ever-new regional geographies but also work to reshape social and cultural identities and how they are represented. Thus conceived a region may be viewed as being a series of open, discontinuous spaces constituted by social relationships which stretch across spaces in a variety of ways (Allen *et al.* 1998). All of which serves to emphasise the extent to which today the North–South metaphor must be a simplification – a persistent cultural myth increasingly removed from social reality.

The new regional geographers also insist that regional studies are always produced for a purpose, with a specific aim in view, there being multiple ways of seeing 'one' region (Allen *et al.* 1998: 1–5). Regions and regional knowledges are socially constructed, both by 'insiders', those living in them, and by 'outsiders', those living beyond them (Buttimer *et al.* 1999). The North–South divide in England was – and to a considerable extent remains – a representation of two different cultures. It was recognised within both of them but was produced essentially by the southern, metropolitan, South as a way of differentiating itself from northern 'others'. Distinguishing 'self' from 'other' geographically has been a common cultural practice throughout history. It has been applied at a range of spatial scales, from the local to the global. It is remarkable that the concept of a North–South divide has been applied even to the international economic system (see, for example, Adams 1993) but the national scale is the most relevant one here, so we will refer briefly to three European examples for comparative and illustrative purposes. Belgium's North–South divide corresponds broadly to the linguistic and cultural division between the Flemish and Walloon communities but it is also identifiable on economic criteria, with Belgium's South sharing many of the characteristics of England's North (Thomas 1990). For Italy, the classic picture of an advanced North and a backward South has been rendered more complex first by the recognition of a 'Third' Italy between those two regions and more recently by the recognition of a resurgence of significant localisms (Stannard 1999). In France, a line running from St Malo to Geneva was recognised in the early-nineteenth century as dividing an 'enlightened' or modernising North and East from a 'dark' or traditional South and West. That cultural fault line has come to be seen as a structural feature in the historical geography of France, having both long antecedents and enduring relevance (Chartier 1978, 1996). In all of these three cases, of course, contrary to the English case, the North has been the core and the South the periphery. But in all such cases both the precise location of the dividing line and indeed the very existence of a real, material, division have been contested. Such positivist questioning misses the fundamental point: real or not, the imagined geographies of these countries have played significant roles in their histories.

References

Ackroyd, P. 2000 *London: The Biography* (London)

Adams, N. A. 1993 *Worlds Apart*: *The North–South Divide and the International System* (London)

Allen, G. C. 1976 *The British Disease* (London)

Allen, J., Massey, D. and Cochrane, A. 1998 *Rethinking the Region* (London)

Anderson, H. H. 1941 'The paradox of trade and morality in Defoe' *Modern Philology* 39, 23–46

Anderson, M. 1990 'The social implications of demographic change' in F. M. L. Thompson (ed.) *The Cambridge Social History of Britain 1750–1950* Vol. I: *People and their Environment* (Cambridge) 1–70

Andrews. J. H. 1970 'Some statistical maps of Defoe's England' in A. R. H. Baker, J. D. Hamshere and J. Langton (eds.) *Geographical Interpretations of Historical Sources* (Newton Abbot) 196–207

Anon. 1667–77 'Country searches of the Worshipful Company of Pewterers' Guildhall Library, MS 7105, Vol. 2

Anon. 1907 'Lord Burghley's Map of Lancashire, 1590' *Catholic Record Society* 7

Ashton, T. S. 1924 *Iron and Steel in the Industrial Revolution* (Manchester)
　1959 *Economic Fluctuations in England 1700–1800* (Oxford)

Association for Planning and Regional Reconstruction 1945, *Maps for the National Plan* (London)

Austen, J. 1811 *Sense and Sensibility* (London)
　1813 *Pride and Prejudice* (London)
　1815 *Emma* (London)

Backscheider, P. 1989 *Daniel Defoe* (Baltimore)

Bailey, F. A. and Barker, T. C. 1969 'The seventeenth-century origins of watchmaking in southwest Lancashire' in J. R. Harris (ed.) *Liverpool and Merseyside* (London) 1–15

Bainbridge, B. 1987 *Forever England: North and South* (London)

Baines, E. 1836 *History of the County Palatine and Duchy of Lancaster* (London)

Bairoch, P. 1988 *Cities and Economic Development* (London)

Baker, A. R. H. 1973a 'Field systems of southeast England' in A. R. H. Baker and R. A. Butlin (eds.) *Studies of Field Systems in the British Isles* (Cambridge) 377–429

1973b 'Changes in the later Middle Ages' in H. C. Darby (ed.) *A New Historical Geography of England* (Cambridge) 186–247

Baker, A. R. H. and Gregory, D. 1984 'Some *terrae incognitae* in historical geography: an exploratory discussion' in A. R. H. Baker and D. Gregory (eds.) *Explorations in Historical Geography* (Cambridge) 180–94

Baker, J. H. 1977 *The Reports of Sir John Spelman* Vol. I (London)

Balls, E. 2000 'Britain's new regional policy: sustainable growth and full employment for Britain's regions' in E. Balls and J. Healey (eds.) *Towards a New Regional Policy* (London)

Barber, P. 1992 'England II: monarchs, ministers and maps, 1550–1625' in D. Buissert (ed.) *Monarchs and Maps* (Chicago) 57–98

Barker, T. C. and Harris, J. R. 1954 *A Merseyside Town in the Industrial Revolution: St Helens, 1750–1900* (Liverpool)

Barnes, J. 1998 *England, England* (London)

Barnes, T. J. and Duncan, J. S. (eds.) 1992 *Writing Worlds: Text, Discourse and Metaphor in the Representation of Landscape* (London)

Barnett, C. 1972 *The Collapse of British Power* (London)

1986 *The Audit of War: The Illusion and Reality of Britain as a Great Nation* (London)

Barraclough, G. (ed.) 1979 *The Times Atlas of World History* (London)

Barrell, J. 1980 *The Dark Side of the Landscape* (Cambridge)

1999 'Afterword moving stories, still lives' in G. Mclean, D. Landry and J. P. Ward (eds.) *The Country and the City Revisited: England and the Politics of Culture, 1550–1850* (Cambridge)

Barrow, G. 1989 'Frontier and settlement: which influenced which? England and Scotland, 1100–1300' in R. Bartlett and A. MacKay (eds.) *Medieval Frontier Societies* (Oxford) 3–22

Barrow, G. W. S. 1966 'The Anglo-Scottish border' *Northern History* 1, 21–42

Bate, J. 2000 *The Song of the Earth* (London)

Bayley, K. C. 1907 'Political history' in W. Page (ed.) *The Victoria County History of Durham* Vol. II (London) 133–74

Beatty, C., Fothergill, S., Gore, T. and Herrington, A. 1997 *The Real Level of Unemployment* (Sheffield)

Beckingsale, B. W. 1969 'The characteristics of the Tudor North' *Northern History* 4, 67–83

Bendall, A. S. 1992 *Maps, Land and Society: A History, with a Carto-bibliography of Cambridgeshire Estate Maps, c.1600–1836* (Cambridge)

Bennett, M. J. 1973 'A county community: social cohesion amongst the Cheshire gentry, 1400–1425' *Northern History* 8, 24–44

Beresford, M. 1957 'A journey through parks' in M. Beresford, *History on the Ground* (London) 186–236

1961 'Habitation versus improvement: the debate on enclosure by agreement' in F. J. Fisher (ed.) *Essays in the Economic and Social History of Tudor and Stuart England* (Cambridge) 40–69

1981 'English medieval boroughs: a hand-list: revisions, 1973–81' *Urban History Yearbook 1981*, 59–65

Beresford, M. and Finberg, H. P. R. (eds.) 1973 *English Medieval Boroughs: A Hand-List* (Newton Abbot)

Berg. M. 1985 *The Age of Manufactures: Industry, Innovation and Work in Britain 1700–1820* (London)

Berg, M. and Hudson, P. 1992 'Rehabilitating the industrial revolution' *Economic History Review* 45, 24–50

1994 'Growth and change: a comment on the Crafts–Harley view of the industrial revolution' *Economic History Review* 47, 147–9

Bermingham, A. 1987 *Landscape and Ideology* (London)

Biggs, M. 1999 'Putting the state on the map: cartography, territory and European state formation' *Comparative Studies in Society and History* 41, 374–405

Billinge, M. D. 1984 'Hegemony, class and power in late Georgian and early Victorian England: towards a cultural geography' in A. R. H. Baker and D. Gregory (eds.) *Explorations in Historical Geography* (Cambridge) 28–67

Bindoff, S. T. 1950 *Tudor England* (Harmondsworth)

Birley, D. 1993 *Sport and the Making of Britain* (Manchester)

Bishop, T. A. M. 1962 'The Norman settlement of Yorkshire' in E. M. Carus-Wilson (ed.) *Essays in Economic History* Vol. II (London) 1–11

Black, I. S. 1989 'Geography, political economy and the circulation of finance capital in early industrial England' *Journal of Historical Geography* 15, 366–84

1995 'Money, information and space: banking in early-nineteenth-century England and Wales' *Journal of Historical Geography* 21, 398–412

1996 'The London agency system in English banking, 1780–1825' *London Journal* 21, 112–30

Blackaby, D. H. and Murphy, P. D. 1995 'Earnings, unemployment and Britain's North–South divide: real or imaginary?' *Oxford Bulletin of Economics and Statistics* 57, 487–512

Blake, J. B. 1967 'The medieval coal trade of northeast England: some fourteenth-century evidence' *Northern History* 2, 1–26

Blanchard, I. 1996 'Lothian and beyond: the economy of the "English empire" of David I' in R. Britnell and J. Hatcher (eds.) *Progress and Problems in Medieval England: Essays in Honour of Edward Miller* (Cambridge) 23–45

Blaszac, B. J. 2000 'The gendered geography of the English co-operative movement at the turn of the nineteenth century' *Women's History Review* 9, 559–83

Blaug, M. 1968 *Economic Theory in Retrospect* 2nd edn (London)

Blomley, N. K. 1994 'Legal territories and "The Golden Metewand" of the law' in N. K. Blomley *Law, Space and the Geographies of Power* (London) 67–105

Bossy, J. 1975 *The English Catholic Community 1570–1850* (London)

Botham, F. W. and Hunt, E. H. 1987 'Wages in Britain during the industrial revolution' *Economic History Review* 40, 380–99

Bowden, P. J. 1962 *The Wool Trade in Tudor and Stuart England* (London)

Braudel, F. 1977 *Afterthoughts on Material Civilisation and Capitalism* (Baltimore)

Brenner, R. 1985 'Agrarian class structure and economic development in pre-industrial Europe' in T. H. Aston and C. H. E. Philpin (eds.) *The Brenner Debate* (Cambridge) 10–63

Britnell, R. 1993 *The Commercialisation of English Society 1000–1500* (Cambridge)

1996 'Boroughs, markets and trade in northern England, 1000–1216' in R. Britnell and J. Hatcher (eds.) *Progress and Problems in Medieval England: Essays in Honour of Edward Miller* (Cambridge) 46–67

Browning, A. 1953 *English Historical Documents 1660–1714* (London)

Bryson, J. 1996 'Small-firm creation and growth, regional development and the North–South divide in Britain' *Environment and Planning A* 28, 909–34

Buckatzsch, E. J. 1950 'The geographical distribution of wealth in England, 1086–1843: an experimental study of certain tax assessments' *Economic History Review* 3, 180–202

Burt, R. 1995 'The transformation of the non-ferrous metal industries in the seventeenth and eighteenth centuries' *Economic History Review* 48, 23–45

Bush, M. L. 1996 *The Pilgrimage of Grace* (Manchester)

Business 1987 (September) 'Across the north–south divide' 45–58

Butlin, R. A. 1990 'Regions in England and Wales, c.1600–1914' in R. A. Dodgshon and R. A. Butlin (eds.) *An Historical Geography of England and Wales* 2nd edn (London) 223–54

Buttimer, A., Brunn, S. and Wardinga, U. (eds.) 1999 Text and image: social construction of regional knowledges, *Beiträge Zur Regionalen Geographie* 49

Byron (Lord), G. G. N. 1823 *Don Juan* canto xiii (London)

Cabinet Office 1999 *Sharing the Nation's Prosperity: Variations in Economic and Social Conditions Across the UK* (London)

CACI 2001

Cain, P. J. and Hopkins, A. G. 1993 *British Imperialism 1688–1914* (London)

Campbell, B. M. S. 2000 *English Seigniorial Agriculture 1250–1450* (Cambridge)

2001 'The medieval economy' in *The Penguin Atlas of British and Irish History* (London) 100–4

2002 'The sources of tradable surpluses: English agricultural exports 1250–1349' in L. Berggren, N. Hybel and A. Landen (eds.) *Cogs, Cargoes and Commerce: Maritime Bulk Trade in Northern Europe 1150–1400* (Toronto) 1–30

Campbell, B. M. S. and Bartley, K. forthcoming *England on the Eve of the Black Death: An Atlas of Lay Lordship. Land and Wealth, 1300–49* (Manchester)

Campbell, J. 1995 'The United Kingdom of England: the Anglo-Saxon achievement' in A. Grant and K. J. Stringer (eds.) *Uniting the Kingdom? The Making of British History* (London) 31–47

Cannadine, D. 1980 *Lords and Landlords: The Aristocracy and the Towns, 1774–1967* (Leicester)

1983 'The context, performance and meaning of ritual: the British monarchy and the invention of tradition, *c.* 1820–1977' in E. Hobsbawm and T. Ranger (eds.) *The Invention of Tradition* (Cambridge) 101–64

Cannon, J. (ed.) 1997 *The Oxford Companion to British History* (Oxford)

Carruthers, B. G. 1996 *City of Capital* (Princeton)

Carus-Wilson, E. M. and Coleman, O. 1963 *England's Export Trade 1275–1547* (Oxford)

Castells, M. 1996 *The Rise of the Network Society* (Oxford)

Centre for Metropolitan History 2001 *Annual Report 1999–2000* (London)

Champion, T. and Green, A. 1988 *Local Prosperity and the North–South Divide: Winners and Losers in 1980s Britain* (Coventry)

1991 'Britain's economic recovery and the North–South divide' *Geography* 76, 249–54

Chandler, J. 1993 *John Leland's Itinerary* (Stroud)

Chapman, S. D. (ed.) 1967 *Felkin's History of the Machine-Wrought Hosiery and Lace Manufactures: Centenary Edition* (Newton Abbot)

Charlesworth, A. (ed.) 1983 *An Atlas of Rural Protest in Britain 1548–1900* (London)

1986 'Labour protest 1780–1850' in J. Langton and R. J. Morris (eds.) *Atlas of Industrializing Britain 1780–1914* (London) 185–9

Chartier, R. 1978 'Les deux Frances: histoire d'une géographie' *Cahiers d'Histoire* 23, 393–415

1996 'The Saint-Malo-Geneva line' in P. Nora (ed.) *Realms of Memory: The Construction of the French Past* Vol. I: *Conflicts and Divisions* (New York) 467–496

Chartres, J. 1995 'Market integration and agricultural output in seventeenth-, eighteenth- and nineteenth-century England' *Agricultural History Review* 43, 117–38

Chesshyre, R. 1987 *The Return of a Native Reporter* (London)

Chibnall, M. 1986 *Anglo-Norman England* (Oxford)

Christaller, W. 1933 *Die zentralen Orte in Süddeutschland* (Jena). Trans. 1966 *Central Places in Southern Germany* (London)

Clark, A. 1995 *The Struggle for the Breeches: Gender and the Making of the British Working Class* (London)

Clark, J. C. 1985 *English Society 1688–1832* (Cambridge)

Clark, P. (ed.) 1995 *Small Towns in Early Modern Europe* (Cambridge)

Clarke, P. and Trebilcock, C. (eds.) 1997 *Understanding Decline* (Cambridge)

Clayre, A. 1977 *Nature and Industrialisation* (Cambridge)

Clifford, H. 1995 ' "The King's Arms and Feathers": a case study exploring the networks of manufacture operating in the London Goldsmiths' trade in the eighteenth century' in D. Mitchell (ed.) *Goldsmiths, Silversmiths and Bankers* (Stroud) 84–95

Coates, B. E. 1965 'The origins and distribution of markets and fairs in medieval Derbyshire' *Derbyshire Archaeological Journal* 85, 92–111

Coates, D. 1994 *The Question of Decline* (London)

Cobbett, W. 1821 *Rural Rides* (London)

Cockburn, J. S. 1968 'The northern assize circuit' *Northern History* 3, 118–30

Collins, M. 1991 *Banks and Industrial Finance in Britain 1800–1939* (London)

Colls, R. 1986 'Englishness and political culture' in R. Colls and P. Dodd (eds.) *Englishness: Politics and Culture 1880–1920* (London) 29–61

Connor, R. D. 1987 *The Weights and Measures of England* (London)

Cook, E. 1971 'The flow of energy in an industrial society' *Scientific American* 225, 135–45

Corbin, A. 1995 *The Lure of the Sea: The Discovery of the Seaside in the Western World, 1750–1840* (London)

1996 'Paris-Province' in P. Nora (ed.) *Realms of Memory: Rethinking the French Past* Vol. I: *Conflicts and Divisions* (New York) 427–64

Corfield, P. J. 1982 *The Impact of English Towns 1700–1800* (Oxford)

Corrigan, P. and Sayer, D. 1985 *The Great Arch: English State Formation as Cultural Revolution* (Oxford)

Cosgrove, D. 1984 *Social Formation and Symbolic Landscape* (London)

Cosgrove, D. and Daniels, S. (eds.) 1988 *The Iconography of Landscape* (Cambridge)

Cottrell, P. L. 1980 *Industrial Finance, 1830–1914: The Finance and Organisation of English Manufacturing Industry* (London)

1986 'Banking and finance' in J. Langton and R. J. Morris (eds.) *Atlas of Industrializing Britain 1780–1914* (London) 145–55

Coyle, D. 1999 'Richer and poorer: Britain's cities have their own north–south divides' *Independent* 23 August

Coyle, D. and Quah, D. 2002 *Getting the Measure of the New Economy* (London)

Crafts, N. F. R. 1985 *British Economic Growth During the Industrial Revolution* ((Oxford)
1994 'The industrial revolution' in R. Floud and D. McCloskey (eds.) *The Economic History of Britain Since 1700* Vol. I: *1700–1860* (Cambridge) 44–59

Crafts, N. F. R. and Harley, C. K. 1992 'Output growth and the British industrial revolution: a restatement of the Crafts–Harley view' *Economic History Review* 45, 703–30

Critchfield, R. 1987 'Britain: a view from the outside' *Economist* 21 February, 1–26

Cross, S. 2002 'Geographies of Owenite socialism in Britain, 1830–1840: public lecturing, the social institution and the production of associational knowledges' (unpublished PhD dissertation, University of Cambridge)

Crowther, M. A. 1981 *The Workhouse System 1834–1929* (London)

Currie, C. R. J. and Lewis, C. P. (eds.) 1994 *English County Histories: A Guide* (Stroud)

Darby, H. C. 1964 'Historical geography from the coming of the Anglo-Saxons to the Industrial Revolution' in J. W. Watson (ed.) *The British Isles: A Systematic Geography* (Edinburgh) 198–220
1973 'The age of the improver: 1600–1800' in H. C. Darby (ed.) *A New Historical Geography of England* (Cambridge) 302–88
1977 *Domesday England* (Cambridge)

Darby, H. C., Glasscock, R. E., Sheail, J. and Versey, R. 1979 'The changing geographical distribution of wealth in England 1086–1334–1525' *Journal of Historical Geography* 5, 247–62

Daunton, M. J. 1989 'Gentlemanly capitalism and British industry 1820–1914' *Past and Present* 122, 119–58
1995 *Progress and Poverty: An Economic and Social History of Britain* (Oxford)
2000 'Introduction' in M. Daunton (ed.) *The Cambridge Urban History of Britain* Vol. III: *1840–1950* (Cambridge) 1–56

Davey Smith, G., Dorling, D. and Shaw, M. 2001 *Poverty, Inequality and Health, 1800–2000: A Reader* (Bristol)

Davie, N. 1991 'Chalk and cheese? "Fielden" and "forest" communities in early modern England' *Journal of Historical Sociology* 4, 1–31

Davies, C. S. L. 1968 'The Pilgrimage of Grace reconsidered' *Past and Present* 41, 54–76

Davies, R. R. 1990 *Domination and Conquest: The Experience of Ireland, Scotland and Wales 1100–1300* (Cambridge)
2000 *The First English Empire: Power and Identities in the British Isles 1093–1343* (Oxford)

Davis, J. 2000 'Central government and the towns' in M. Daunton (ed.) *The Cambridge Urban History of Britain* Vol. III: *1840–1950* (Cambridge) 261–86

Daysh, G. H. J., Caesar, A. A. L., Edwards, K. C., Geddes, A., Houston, J. M., O'Doll, A. C. and Spaven, F. D. N. 1949 *Studies in Regional Planning* (London)

Deacon, B. 1998 'Proto-regionalisation: the case of Cornwall' *Journal of Regional and Local Studies* 18, 27–41

Deane, P. and Cole, W. A. 1964 *British Economic Growth 1688–1959* (Cambridge)

Defoe, D. 1971 *A Tour Through the Whole Island of Great Britain (1724–26), Abridged and Edited with an Introduction by P. Rogers* (Harmondsworth)

Delano-Smith, C. and Kain, R. J. P. 1999 *English Maps: A History* (London)

Dellheim, C. 1982 *The Face of the Past: The Preservation of the Medieval Inheritance in Victorian England* (Cambridge)

1986 'Imagining England: Victorian views of the North' *Northern History* 22, 218–9

Department of Health 1999 'The widening gap' *Department of Health Press Release 1999/0726* (London)

Devine, T. M. and Young, J. R. (eds.) 1999 *Eighteenth-Century Scotland: New Perspectives* (East Linton)

De Vries, J. 1984 *European Urbanisation 1500–1800* (London)

1994 'How did pre-industrial labour markets function?' in G. Grantham and M. Mackinnon (eds.) *Labour Market Evolution* (London) 39–63

Dewar, M. (ed.) 1969 *A Discourse of the Commonweal of this Realm of England Attributed to Sir Thomas Smith* (Charlottesville)

1982 *De Republica Anglorum by Sir Thomas Smith* (Cambridge)

Dickens, C. 1854 *Hard Times* (London)

Dickens, R. and Ellwood, D. 2001 'Welfare to work: poverty in Britain and the US' *New Economy* 8, 98–103

Dickson, P. G. M. 1967 *The Financial Revolution in England* (London)

Dinwiddy, J. 1979 'Luddism and politics in the northern counties' *Social History* 4, 33–63

Disraeli, B. 1845 *Sybil or The Two Nations* 3 vols. (London)

Dobson, M. 1997 *Contours of Disease and Death in Early Modern England* (Cambridge)

Dobson, R. B. 1983 *The Peasants' Revolt of 1381* 2nd edn (London)

Dodd, P. 1986 'Englishness and the national culture' in R. Colls and P. Dodd (eds.) *Englishness: Politics and Culture 1880–1920* (London) 1–28

Dodgshon, R. A. 1990 'The changing evaluation of space 1500–1914' in R. A. Dodgshon and R. A. Butlin (eds.) *An Historical Geography of England and Wales* 2nd edn (London) 255–83

Donkin, R. A. 1973 'Changes in the early Middle Ages' in H. C. Darby (ed.) *A New Historical Geography of England* (Cambridge) 75–135

1978 *The Cistercians: Studies in the Geography of Medieval England and Wales* (Toronto)

Dorling, D. 1995 *A New Social Atlas of Britain* (Chichester)

Dorling, D. and Shaw, M. 2001 'The geography of poverty: a political map of poverty under New Labour' *New Economy* June, 87–91

Doyle, B. 1986 'The invention of English' in R. Colls and P. Dodd (eds.) *Englishness: Politics and Culture 1880–1920* (London) 89–115

Driver, F. 1993 *Power and Pauperism: The Workhouse System 1834–1884* (Cambridge)

Drummond, J. 1939 *The Englishman's Food* (London)

Duckham, B. F. 1983 'Canals and river navigations' in D. Aldcroft and M. Freeman (eds.) *Transport in the Industrial Revolution* (Manchester) 100–41

Duffy, H. 1987 'Regional development' *Financial Times (Survey)* 19 January

Dummett, R. E. (ed.) 1999 *Gentlemanly Capitalism and British Imperialism: The New Debate on Empire* (London)

Dunford, M. and Perrons, D. 1982 *The Arena of Capital* (Basingstoke)

Dyer, C. C. 1989 'The consumer and the market in the later Middle Ages' *Economic History Review* 42, 305–27

Earle, P. 1977 *The World of Defoe* (Newton Abbot)

Eatwell, J. 1982 *Whatever Happened to Britain?* (London)

Economist, The 1962 'North to Elizabetha' December 8, 989–90

Edelen, G. (ed.) 1968 *The Description of England by William Harrison* (Ithaca)

Elbaum, B. and Lazonick, W. 1986 (eds.) *The Decline of the British Economy* (Oxford)

Elliott, A. 1982 'Municipal government in Bradford in the mid-nineteenth century' in D. Fraser (ed.) *Municipal Reform and the Industrial City* (Leicester) 111–61

Ellis, S. 2001a 'The Anglo-Scottish border' in *The Penguin Atlas of British and Irish History* (London) 120–1

   2001b 'Languages 1500–1800' in *The Penguin Atlas of British and Irish History* (London) 152–3

Ellis, S. G. 1999 'Civilising Northumberland: representations of Englishness in the Tudor state' *Journal of Historical Sociology* 12, 103–27

Emery, F. V. 1958 'Regional studies from Aubrey to Defoe' *Geographical Journal* 124, 315–25

Evans, E. 1995 'Englishness and Britishness: national identities, *c*.1790–*c*.1870' in A. Grant and K. J. Stringer (eds.) *Uniting the Kingdom? The Making of British History* (London)

Everitt, A. 1977 'River and wold: reflections on the historical origins of regions and *pays*' *Journal of Historical Geography* 3, 1–20

   1979 'Country, county and town: patterns of regional evolution in England' *Transactions of the Royal Historical Society* 24, 79–108

Financial Times, The 1987 'Thatcher says north of England thriving' 4 January, 6

Firth, G. 1990 *Bradford and the Industrial Revolution: An Economic History, 1760–1840* (Halifax)

Fitton, R. S. and Wadsworth, A. P. 1958 *The Strutts and the Arkwrights, 1758–1830: A Study of the Early Factory System* (Manchester)

Fletcher, D. 1998 'Map or terrier? The example of Christ Church, Oxford, estate management, 1600–1840' *Transactions of the Institute of British Geographers* 23, 221–37

Flinn, M. W. and Stoker, D. 1984 *The History of the British Coal Industry* Vol. II: *1700–1830* (Oxford)

Floud, R. 1997 *The People and the British Economy 1830–1914* (Oxford)

Fox, C. 1943 *The Personality of Britain* (Cardiff)

Fraser, C. M. 1969 'The pattern of trade in the northeast of England, 1265–1350' *Northern History* 4, 44–66

Fraser, D. 1982 'Introduction: municipal reform in historical perspective' in D. Fraser (ed.) *Municipal Reform and the Industrial City* (Leicester) 2–14

Freeman, M. J. 1980 'Road transport and the English Industrial Revolution: an interim reassessment' *Journal of Historical Geography* 5, 17–28

   1986 'Transport' in J. Langton and R. J. Morris (eds.) *Atlas of Industrializing Britain 1780–1914* (London) 80–94

Friedmann, J. 1966 *Regional Development Policy: A Case Study of Venezuela* (London)

Fuller, T. 1662 *The History of the Worthies of England* (London)

Gallagher, C. 1985 *The Industrial Reformation of English Fiction: Social Discourse and Narrative Form, 1832–1867* (Chicago)

Garside, P. L. 1990 'London and the Home Counties' in F. M. L. Thompson (ed.) *The Cambridge Social History of Britain* Vol. I: *Regions and Communities* (Cambridge) 471–539

Garside, R. 2000 'The political economy of structural change: Britain in the 1930s' in C. Bucheim and R. Garside (eds.) *After the Slump: Industry and Politics in 1930s Britain and Germany* (Frankfurt) 9–32

Gaskell, E. 1855 *North and South* (London)

George, D. 1951 *London Life in the Eighteenth Century* (London)

Gibson, E. 1695 *Camden's Britannia, Newly Translated into English: With Large Additions and Improvements* (London)

Giddens, A. 1994 'Living in a post-traditional society' in U. Back, A. Giddens and S. Lash (eds.) *Reflexive Modernisation: Politics, Tradition and Aesthetics in the Modern Social Order* (Cambridge) 56–109

Gilbert, D, Matless, D. and Short, B. (eds.) 2003 *Geographies of British Modernity* (Oxford)

Gilbert, D. and Southall, H. 2000 'The urban labour market' in M. Daunton (ed.) *The Cambridge Urban History of Britain* Vol. III: *1840–1950* (Cambridge) 553–92

Giles, J. and Middleton, T. 1995 *Writing Englishness: An Introductory Sourcebook on National Identity* (London)

Gillingham, J. 1995 'Foundations of a disunited kingdom' in A. Grant and K. J. Stringer (eds.) *Uniting the Kingdom? The Making of British History* (London) 48–64

Gissing, G. 1903 *The Private Papers of Henry Ryecroft* (London)

Glass. D. V. 1965 'Two papers on Gregory King' in D. V. Glass and D. E. C. Eversley (eds.) *Population in History* (London) 159–220

1978 *Numbering the People* (London)

Goetsch, P. 1996 'North and South in Victorian fiction' *Journal for the Study of British Cultures* 3, 15–29

Goldsmith, M. M. 1978 'Mandeville and the spirit of capitalism' *Journal of British Studies* 17, 63–81

Goodway, D. 1982 *London Chartism 1838–1848* (Cambridge)

Graham, B. and Nash, C. (eds.) 2000 *Modern Historical Geographies* (Harlow)

Grant, A. 1984 *Independence and Nationhood: Scotland 1306–1469* (Edinburgh)

Grantham, G. 1994 'Economic history and the history of labour markets' in G. Grantham and M. MacKinnon (eds.) *Labour Market Evolution* (London) 1–26

Gras, N. S. B. 1922 *An Introduction to Economic History* (New York)

1926 *The Evolution of the English Corn Market from the Twelfth to the Eighteenth Century* (Cambridge, Mass.)

Gray, R. 1996 *The Factory Question and Industrial England, 1830–1860* (Cambridge)

Green, A. E. 1988 'The North–South divide in Great Britain: an examination of the evidence' *Transactions of the Institute of British Geographers* 13, 179–98

Green, S. J. D. 1992 'In search of bourgeois civilisation: institutions and ideals in nineteenth-century Britain' *Northern History* 28, 228–47

Greenleaf, W. 1975 'Joshua Toulmin Smith and the British political tradition' *Public Administration* 53, 25–44

1987 *The British Political Tradition* Vol. III: *'A Much-Governed Nation'* (London)

Gregory, D. 1982 *Regional Transformation and Industrial Revolution: A Geography of the Yorkshire Woollen Industry* (London)

1987 'The friction of distance? Information circulation and the mails in early-nineteenth century England' *Journal of Historical Geography* 13, 130–54

1988 'The production of regions in England's industrial revolution' *Journal of Historical Geography* 14, 50–8

1994 *Geographical Imaginations* (Oxford)

Grieve-Smith, J., Anyadike-Danes, M., Fothergill, S., Glyn, A., Kitson, M. Martin, R. L., Rowthorn, R. E., Turok, I., Tyler, P. and Webster, D. 2000a *The Jobs Gap* (London)

2000b *Labour's New Regional Policy* (London)

Gunn, S. J. 1988 'The "failure" of the Victorian middle class: a critique' in J. Wolff and J. Seed (eds.) *The Culture of Capital: Art, Power and the Nineteenth-Century Middle Class* (Manchester)

Haigh, C. 1975 *Reformation and Resistance in Tudor Lancashire* (Cambridge)

Hallam, E. E. (ed.) 1988 *The Agrarian History of England and Wales* Vol. II: *1042–1350* (Cambridge)

Hann, A. G. 1999 'Kinship and exchange relations within an estate economy: Ditchley, 1680–1750' (unpublished DPhil. thesis, University of Oxford)

Hardman, M. 1986 *Ruskin and Bradford: An Experiment in Victorian Cultural History* (Manchester)

1998 *A Kingdom in Two Parishes* (London)

Harley, J. B. 1958 'Population and agriculture from the Warwickshire Hundred Rolls of 1279' *Economic History Review* 11, 8–18

1972 *Maps for the Local Historian* (London)

Harling, P. 1992 'The power of persuasion: central authority, local bureaucracy and the New Poor Law' *English Historical Review* 107, 30–53

Harris, B. E. 1979 'Administrative history: the Earldom of Chester' and 'Administrative history: the Palatinate 1301–1547' in B. E. Harris (ed.) *The History of the County of Chester* Vol. II (Oxford) 1–8 and 9–35

Harris, J. 1993 *Private Lives, Public Spirit: Britain 1870–1914* (Harmondsworth)

Harrison, R. 1983 *Bentham* (London)

Hartnell, R. 1995 'Art and civic culture in Birmingham in the late-nineteenth century' *Urban History* 22, 229–37

Harvey, D. 1987 *The Condition of Postmodernity* (London)

Harvey, P. D. A. 1992 'Matthew Paris's maps of Britain' in P. R. Cross and D. S. Lloyd (eds.) *Thirteenth Century England* Vol. III: *Proceedings of the Newcastle-upon-Tyne Conference 1992* (Woodbridge) 118–21

Haslam, G. 1992 'The Elizabethan Duchy of Cornwall, an estate in stasis' in R. Hoyle (ed.) *Estates of the English Crown 1558–1640* (Cambridge) 88–111

Hatcher, J. and Barker, T. C. 1974 *A History of British Pewter* (London)

Hatton, T. 1994 'Unemployment and the labour market in inter-war Britain' in R. Floud and D. McCloskey (eds.) *The Economic History of Britain since 1700* Vol. II: *1860–1939* (Cambridge) 359–85

Hawkins, D. 1980 *Cranborne Chase* (London)

Hawkyard, A. 2001 'The age of the Reformation' in *The Penguin Atlas of British and Irish History* (London) 114–17

Headrick, D. R. 2000 *When Information Came of Age* (Oxford)

Heffernan, M. and Gruffudd, P. 1988 *A Land Fit for Heroes: Essays in the Human Geography of Inter-War Britain* (Loughborough)

Helgerson, R. 1992 *Forms of Nationhood* (Chicago)

Hennock, E. P. 1982 'Central/local government relations in England: an outline 1800–1950' *Urban History Yearbook* 9, 38–49

Hey, D. 1991 *The Fiery Blades of Hallamshire* (Leicester)

Higham, N. J. 1993 *The Kingdom of Northumbria AD35-1100* (Stroud)

Hill, C. 1993 *The English Bible and the Seventeenth-Century Revolution* (Harmondsworth)

Hills, R. 1989 *Power from Steam* (Cambridge)

Hindle, P. 1976 'The road network of medieval England and Wales' *Journal of Historical Geography* 2, 207–22

Hinds, A. B. 1896 'Hexamshire: history of the regality' in A. B. Hinds *A History of Northumberland* Vol. III (Newcastle-upon-Tyne) 20–66

Hitchens, P. 1999 *The Abolition of Britain* (London)

HM Government: Department of Trade and Industry 2000 *Biotechnology Clusters* (London)

Hobbes, T. 1651 *Leviathan* (London)

Hobsbawm, E. 1977 *The Age of Capital, 1848–1875* (London)

Hobson, D. 1999 *The National Wealth: Who Gets What in Britain* (London)

Holdsworth, W. 1956–72 *The History of English Law* 7th edn (London)

Homans, G. C. 1969 'The explanation of English regional differences' *Past and Present* 42, 18–34

Hopkins, E. 1989 *The Rise of the Manufacturing Town: Birmingham and the Industrial Revolution* (London)

Hoppen, K. T. 1998 *The Mid-Victorian Generation 1846–1886* (Oxford)

Hoppit, J. 1990 'Counting the industrial revolution' *Economic History Review* 43, 173–93
    1993 'Reforming Britain's weights and measures, 1660–1824' *English Historical Review* 108, 82–104

Horn, D. B. and Ransome, M. 1957 *English Historical Documents 1714–1783* (London)

Horne, D. 1970 *God is an Englishman* (London)

Horrox, R. 2001 'The later Middle Ages' in *The Penguin Atlas of British and Irish History* (London) 106–9

Hoskins, W. G. 1955 *The Making of the English Landscape* (London)
    1976 *The Age of Plunder: The England of Henry VIII 1500–1547* (London)

Howarth, C., Kenway, P., Palmer, G. and Moirelli, R. 1999 *Monitoring Poverty and Social Exclusion, 1999* (York)

Howell, P. 1995 ' "Diffusing the light of liberty": the geography of political lecturing in the Chartist movement' *Journal of Historical Geography* 21, 23–38

Hoyle, R. 1992a ' "Shearing the hog": the reform of the estates *c.*1598–1640' in R. Hoyle (ed.) *The Estates of the English Crown 1558–1640* (Cambridge) 204–62
    1992b 'Disafforestation and drainage as entrepreneur?' in R. Hoyle (ed.) *The Estates of the English Crown 1558–1640* (Cambridge) 353–88
    2001 *The Pilgrimage of Grace and the Politics of the 1530s* (Oxford)

Hudson, B. J. 1982 'The geographical imagination of Arnold Bennett' *Transactions of the Institute of British Geographers* 7, 365–79

Hudson, P. 1986 *The Genesis of Industrial Capital: A Study of the West Riding Wool Industry, c.1780–1850* (Cambridge)
    1989 'The regional perspective' in P. Hudson (ed.) *Regions and Industries: A Perspective on the Industrial Revolution in Britain* (London)
    1992 *The Industrial Revolution* (London)

Hudson, R. 2000 *Production, Places and Environment* (London)

Huggins, R. 2000 *An Index of Competitiveness in the UK: Local, Regional and Global Analysis* (Cardiff)

Hunt, E. H. 1973 *Regional Wage Variations in Britain, 1850–1914* (Oxford)

1986a 'Wages' in J. Langton and R. J. Morris (eds.) *Atlas of Industrialising Britain 1780–1914* (London) 60–8

1986b 'Industrialisation and regional wage inequality: wages in Britain 1760–1914' *Journal of Economic History* 46, 935–66

Hutchins, J. 1861 *The History and Antiquities of the County of Dorset* 3rd edn (Westminster)

Hutton, W. 1996 *The State We're In* (London)

Hyde, C. K. 1977 *Technological Change and the British Iron Industry 1700–1870* (Princeton)

Ingham, G. 1984 *Capitalism Divided? The City and Industry in British Social Development* (London)

Jack, I. 1987 *Before the Oil Ran Out: Britain 1977–1987* (London)

Jackman, R. and Savouri, S. 1999 *The State of Working Britain* (London)

Jackson, G. 1983 'The ports' in D. H. Aldcroft and M. Freeman (eds.) *Transport in the Industrial Revolution* (London) 177–209

Jackson, J. V. 1992 'Rates of industrial growth during the industrial revolution' *Economic History Review* 45, 24–50

Jacobs, J. 1961 *The Death and Life of Great American Cities* (New York)

Jessop, B., Bonnett, K., Bromley, S. and Ling, T. 1988 *Thatcherism: A Tale of Two Nations* (Cambridge)

Jewell, H. M. 1991 'North and South: the antiquity of the great divide' *Northern History* 27, 1–25

1994 *The North–South Divide: The Origins of Northern Consciousness in England* (Manchester)

Johnson, S. 1755 *Dictionary of the English Language* (London)

1776/77 *Of Literary Criticism* (London)

Johnston, R. J. 1987 'A growing North–South divide in British voting patterns, 1979–1987' *Geoforum* 20, 93–106

Jones D. 1975 *Chartism and the Chartists* (London)

Jones, D. W. 1972 'The "hallage" receipts of the London cloth markets, 1562–*c.*1720' *Economic History Review* 25, 567–87

Jones, E. 1998 *The English Nation: The Great Myth* (Stroud)

Jones, E. L. 1960 'The agricultural origins of industry' *Past and Present* 40, 58–71

1969 'Agriculture and economic growth in England, 1660–1750: agricultural change' *Journal of Economic History* 25, 1–18

Jordan, W. K. 1959 *Philanthropy in England 1480–1660* (London)

Joseph Rowntree Foundation 1995 *Inquiry into Income and Wealth* (York)

Joyce, P. 1980 *Work, Society and Politics: The Culture of the Factory in Late-Victorian England* (Brighton)

1991 *Visions of the People: Industrial England and the Question of Class, 1840–1914* (Cambridge)

1994 *Democratic Subjects: The Self and the Social in Nineteenth-Century England* (Cambridge)

Kaïka, M. and Swyngedouw, E. 2000 'The environment of the city or the urbanisation of nature' in G. Bridge and S. Watson (eds.) *A Companion to the City* (Oxford) 567–80

Kain, R. J. P. and Baigent, E. 1992 *The Cadastral Map in the Service of the State* (Chicago)

Kaletsky, A. 1999 'This Government's guff will not close the great divide' *The Times* 7 December

Kanzaka, J. 2002 'Villein rents in thirteenth-century England: an analysis of the Hundred Rolls of 1279–80' *Economic History Review* 55, 593–618

Kapelle, W. E. 1979 *The Norman Conquest of the North: The Region and its Transformation 1000–1135* (London)

Keene, D. J. 1989 'Medieval London and its region' *London Journal* 14, 99–111
    2000 'Changes in London's economic hinterland as indicated by debt cases in the Court of Common Pleas' in J. A. Galloway (ed.), 'Trade, urban hinterlands and market integration' *Centre for Metropolitan History Working Papers Series 3*, 59–82

Keith-Lucas. B. 1980 *The Unreformed Local Government System* (London)

Kennedy, W. P. 1987 *Industrial Structure, Capital Markets and the Origins of British Economic Decline* (Cambridge)

Kerridge, E. 1973 *The Farmers of Old England* (London)

Kershaw, I. 1973 'The Great Famine and agrarian crisis in England 1315–22' *Past and Present* 59, 3–50

King, S. 2000 *Poverty and Welfare in England 1700–1850* (Manchester)

Kirk, N. (ed.) 2000 *Northern Identities: Historical Interpretations of 'The North' and 'Northernness'* (Aldershot)

Klee, G. A. (ed.) 1980 *World Systems of Traditional Resource Management* (London)

Koditschek, T. 1990 *Class Formation and the Urban-Industrial Society: Bradford, 1750–1850* (Cambridge)

Kramnick, J. 1975 *Is Britain Dying?* (Ithaca)

Kuhn, T. 1970 *The Structure of Scientific Revolutions* (Chicago)

Kuhn, W. 1987 'Ceremony and politics: the British monarchy, 1871–1872' *Journal of British Studies* 26, 133–62

Kussmaul, A. 1990 *A General View of the Rural Economy of England 1538–1840* (Cambridge)

Lane. P. 1981 *Georgian England* (London)

Langford, P. 1991 *Public Life and the Propertied Englishman 1689–1798* (Oxford)
    1992 *A Polite and Commercial People: England 1727–1783* (Oxford)
    2000 *Englishness Identified: Manners and Character 1650–1850* (Oxford)

Langton, J. 1978 'Industry and towns 1500–1730' in R. A. Dodgshon and R. A. Butlin (eds.) *An Historical Geography of England and Wales* (London) 172–237
    1984 'The industrial revolution and the regional geography of England' *Transactions of the Institute of British Geographers* 9, 145–67
    1998a 'The historical geography of European peasantries, 1400–1800' in T. Scott (ed.) *The Peasantries of Europe from the Fourteenth to the Eighteenth Centuries* (London) 372–400
    1998b 'The continuity of regional culture: Lancashire Catholicism from the late-sixteenth to the early-nineteenth century' in E. Royle (ed.) *Issues of Regional Identity* (Manchester) 82–101

2000a 'Urban growth and economic change: from the late-seventeenth century to 1841' in P. Clark (ed.) *The Cambridge Urban History of Britain* Vol. II: *1540–1840* (Cambridge) 453–90

2000b 'Town growth and urbanisation in the Midlands from the 1660s to 1841' in J. Stobart and P. Lane (eds.) *Urban and Industrial Change in the Midlands 1700–1840* (Leicester) 7–47

2002 'Prometheus prostrated?' in P. Slack and R. Ward (eds.) *The Peopling of England* (Cambridge) 242–54

forthcoming a 'Forests in early modern England' in J. Langton (ed.) *The Forests in Early Modern England* (Cambridge)

forthcoming b 'How many and where were the forests?' in J. Langton (ed.) *The Forests in Early Modern England* (Cambridge)

Langton, J. and Morris, R. J. (eds.) 1986 *Atlas of Industrializing Britain 1780–1914* (London)

Lapsley, G. T. 1900 *The County Palatine of Durham* (London)

Large, P. 1984 'Urban growth and agricultural change in the west Midlands during the seventeenth and eighteenth centuries' in P. Clark (ed.) *The Transformation of English Towns 1600–1800* (London) 169–89

1992 'From swanimote to disafforestation: Feckenham Forest in the early seventeenth century' in R. Hoyle (ed.) *The Estates of the English Crown 1558–1640* (Cambridge) 389–417

Lawton, R. 1986 'Population' in J. Langton and R. J. Morris (eds.) 1986 *Atlas of Industrialising Britain 1780–1914* (London)

Lawton. R. and Pooley, C. G. 1992 *Britain 1740–1950: An Historical Geography* (London)

Leadbeater, C. 1999 *Living on Thin Air: The New Economy* (London)

Lee, C. H. 1979 *British Regional Employment Statistics 1841–1971* (Cambridge)

1981 'Regional growth and structural change in Victorian Britain' *Economic History Review* 34, 438–52

1984 'The service sector, regional specialisation and economic growth in the Victorian economy' *Journal of Historical Geography* 10, 149–53

1986 *The British Economy Since 1700: A Macroeconomic Perspective* (Cambridge)

1994 'The service industries' in R. Floud and D. McCloskey (eds.) *The Economic History of Britain Since 1700* Vol. II: *1860–1939* (Cambridge) 117–44

Lees, L. H. 1998 *The Solidarities of Strangers: The English Poor Laws and the People, 1700–1948* (Cambridge)

Leslie, M. and Raylor, T. (eds.) 1992 *Culture and Cultivation in Early Modern England* (Leicester)

Levine, A. L. 1967 *Industrial Retardation in Britain, 1880–1914* (New York)

Lewis, J. and Townsend, A. (eds.) 1989 *The North–South Divide: Regional Change in Britain in the 1980s* (London)

Livingstone, D. N. and Withers, C. W. J. (eds.) 1999 *Geography and Enlightenment* (Chicago)

Lloyd, T. H. 1982 *Alien Merchants in England in the High Middle Ages* (Brighton)

Locke, J. 1690a *Essay on Human Understanding* (London)

1690b *Two Treatises on Civil Government* (London)

Loewenstein, D. 1999 'Digger writing and rural dissent in the English Revolution repre-
senting England as a common treasury' in G. Mclean, D. Londry and J. P. Ward (eds.)
The Country and the City Revisited: England and the Politics of Culture, 1550–1850
(Cambridge) 74–88

Lomas, R. 1992 *Northeast England in the Middle Ages* (Edinburgh)

Lowe, N. 1972 *The Lancashire Textile Industry in the Sixteenth Century* (Manchester)

Lynch, G. 1983 'The risings of the Clubmen in 1644–5' in A. Charlesworth (ed.) *An Atlas
of Rural Protest in Britain 1548–1900* (London)

Macdermot, E. T. 1973 *The History of the Forest of Exmoor* 2nd edn (Newton Abbot)

Mackie, J. D. 1952 *The Earlier Tudors 1485–1558* (Oxford)

Macleod, D. S. 1996 *Art and the Victorian Middle Class: Money and the Making of Cultural
Identity* (Cambridge)

Maddison, A. 1982 *Phases of Capitalist Development* (Oxford)

Mandeville, B. 1714 and 1723 *Fable of the Bees* (London)

Mandler, P. 1987 'The making of the New Poor Law redivivus' *Past and Present* 117,
131–57

Mann, M. 1986 *The Origins of Social Power* Vol. I: *A History of Power from the Beginning
to AD 1760* (Cambridge)

Manser, W. A. P. 1971 *Britain in Balance* (London)

Mantoux, R. 1961 *The Industrial Revolution in the Eighteenth Century* (London)

Manwood, J. 1717 [1598] *Treatise of the Forest Laws* 4th edn (London)

Marshall, J. D. 1978 *The Old Poor Law, 1790–1930* (London)

Marshall, J. D. (ed.) 1967 *The Autobiography of William Stout of Lancaster, 1665–1752*
(Manchester)

Martin, R. M. L. 1988 'The political economy of Britain's North–South divide' *Transactions
of the Institute of British Geographers* 13, 389–418

    1992 'Has the British economy been transformed? Critical reflections on the policies of
    the Thatcher era' in P. Cloke (ed.) *Policy and Change in Thatcher's Britain* (Oxford)
    123–58

    1993a 'Remapping British regional policy: the end of the North–South divide?' *Regional
    Studies* 27, 797–805

    1993b 'Reviving the economic case for regional policy' in R. T. Harrison and M. Hart
    (eds.) *Spatial Policy in a Divided Nation* (London) 270–90

    1995 'Income and poverty inequalities across regional Britain: the North–South divide
    lingers on' in C. Philo (ed.) *Off the Map: The Social Geography of Poverty in the UK*
    (London) 189–210

    1997 'Regional unemployment disparities and their dynamics' *Regional Studies* 31, 235–
    50

    2001 'The geographer as social critic: getting indignant about income inequality' *Trans-
    actions of the Institute of British Geographers* 26, 267–72

Martin, R. L., Sunley, P. and Wills, J. 1996 *Union Retreat and the Regions: The Shrinking
Landscape of Organised Labour* (London)

Mason, R. A. (ed.) 1994 *Scots and Britons: Scottish Political Thought and the Union of
1603* (Cambridge)

Massey, D. 1979 'In what sense a regional problem?' *Regional Studies* 13, 231–41

    1985 'Geography and class' in D. Coates, G. Johnson and R. Bush (eds.) *A Socialist
    Anatomy of Britain* (Cambridge) 76–96

Mathias, P. 1969 *The First Industrial Nation* (London)

Matless, D. 1998 *Landscape and Englishness* (London)

Mayer, A. J. 1981 *The Persistence of the Old Regime: Europe to the Great War* (New York)

Mayer, R. 1987 *History and the English Novel* (Cambridge)

Mayhew, N. J. 1995 'Modelling medieval monetisation' in R. H. Britnell and B. M. Campbell (eds.) *A Commercialising Economy: England 1086 to c.1300* (Manchester) 55–77

Mayhew, R. J. 1997 'Geography and literature in historical context: Samuel Johnson and eighteenth-century concepts of geography' *Oxford School of Geography Research Papers* 54

  1998 'Geography in eighteenth-century British education' *Paedagogica Historica* 34, 731–69

  1999 'Samuel Johnson's intellectual character as a traveller: a reassessment' *Age of Johnson* 10, 35–67

  2000 *Enlightenment Geography* (London)

McCloskey, D. 1994 '1780–1860: a survey' in R. Floud and D. McCloskey (eds.) *The Economic History of Britain Since 1700* Vol. I: *1700–1860* (Cambridge) 242–70

McCord, N. and Thompson, R. 1998 *The Northern Counties from AD 1000* (London)

McCrum, R., Cran, W. and MacNeil, R. 1986 *The Story of English* (London)

McKendrick, N., Brewer, J. and Plumb, J. H. 1982 *The Birth of a Consumer Society: The Commercialisation of Eighteenth-Century England* (Bloomington)

McNamee, C. 1997 *The Wars of the Bruces: Scotland, England and Ireland, 1306–1328* (East Linton)

McRae, A. 1992 'Husbandry manuals and the language of agrarian improvement' in M. Leslie and T. Raylor (eds.) *Culture and Cultivation in Early Modern England* (Leicester) 35–62

  1996 *God Speed the Plough* (Cambridge)

  1999 'The peripatetic muse, internal travel and the cultural production of space in pre-revolutionary England' in G. Mclean, D. Landry and J. P. Ward (eds.) *The Country and the City Revisited: England and the Politics of Culture, 1550–1850* (Cambridge) 41–57

Mendenhall, T. C. 1953 *The Shrewsbury Drapers and the Welsh Wool Trade in the Sixteenth and Seventeenth Centuries* (London)

Miller, E. (ed.) 1991 *The Agrarian History of England and Wales* Vol. III: *1348–1500* (Cambridge)

Miller, E. and Hatcher, J. 1995 *Medieval England: Towns, Commerce and Crafts 1086–1348* (London)

Miller, P., Botham, R., Gibson, H., Martin, R. L. and Moore, B. 2001 *Business Clusters in the UK: A First Assessment* (London)

Millward, R. and Sheard, S. 1995 'The urban fiscal problem, 1870–1914: government expenditure and finance in England and Wales' *Economic History Review* 48, 501–35

Minchinton, W. 1951 'Bristol: metropolis of the west in the eighteenth century' *Transactions of the Royal Historical Society* 4, 69–89

Mingay, G. E. 1990 *A Social History of the English Countryside* (London)

  1994 *Land and Society in England, 1750–1980* (London)

  1997 *Parliamentary Enclosure in England* (London)

Mitchell, R. and Dorling, D. 2002 'Poverty, inequality and social inclusion in the New Scotland' in C. Warhurst and G. Hassan (eds.) *Tomorrow's Scotland* (London) 168–87

Mitchell, R., Dorling, D. and Shaw, M. 2000 *Inequalities in Life and Death: What if Britain Were More Equal?* (Bristol)

Mohan, J. 1995 *A National Health Service? The Restructuring of Health Care in Britain Since 1979* (Basingstoke)

Mokyr, J. 1990 *The Lever of Riches: Technological Creativity and Economic Progress* (Oxford)

Money, J. 1977 *Experience and Identity: Birmingham and the West Midlands, 1760–1800* (Manchester)

Moran, D. 1997 'Pewtermaking in Wigan 1650–1750: urban industry before the industrial revolution' *Journal of Regional and Local Studies* 17, 1–22

Moretti, F. 1998 *Atlas of the European Novel* (London)

Morgan K. 1993 *Bristol and the Atlantic Trade in the Eighteenth Century* (Cambridge)

Morgan, V, 1979 'The cartographic image of "The Country" in early modern England' *Transactions of the Royal Historical Society* 29, 129–54

Morrill, J. 1987 'The ecology of allegiance in the English Revolution' *Journal of British Studies* 26, 461–67

Morris, R. J. 2000 'Structure, culture and society in British towns' in M. Daunton (ed.) *The Cambridge Urban History of Britain* Vol. III: *1840–1950* (Cambridge) 395–426

Morton, H. V. 1927 *In Search of England* (London)
   1942 *I saw Two Englands: The Record of a Journey Before the War and After the Outbreak of War, in the Year 1939* (London)

Muldrew, C. 1993 'Interpreting the market: the ethics of credit and community relations in early modern England' *Social History* 1, 163–83

Munro, J. H. 1991 'Industrial transformations in the northwest European textile trades, c.1290–c.1340: economic progress or economic decline?' in B. M. S. Campbell (ed.) *Before the Black Death: Studies in the 'Crisis' of the Early Fourteenth Century* (Manchester) 110–48

Munsche, P. B. 1981 *Gentlemen and Poachers* (Cambridge)

Musgrove, F. 1990 *The North of England: A History from Roman Times to the Present* (Oxford)

Musson, A. 1996 *Public Order and Law Enforcement: The Local Administration of Criminal Justice 1294–1350* (Woodbridge)

Musson, A. E. and Robinson, E. 1969a *James Watt and the Steam Revolution* (London)
   1969b *Science and Technology in the Industrial Revolution* (Manchester)

Nairn, T. 1981 *The Break-Up of Britain* (London)

Nash, T. 1781 *Collections for the History of Worcestershire* (London)

Neeson, J. M. 1993a *Commoners, Common Right, Enclosure and Social Change in England 1700–1820* (Cambridge)
   1993b 'An eighteenth-century peasantry' in J. Rule and R. Malcolmson (eds.) *Protest and Survival: Essays for E. P. Thompson* (London) 24–59

Nenadic, S. 1991 'Businessmen, the urban middle classes, and the "dominance" of manufacturers in nineteenth-century Britain' *Economic History Review* 44, 66–85

Newman, P. R. 1985 *Atlas of the English Civil War* (London)

Nichols, J. 1823 *The Progresses and Public Processions of Queen Elizabeth* (London)

Nicholson, N. 1988 *The Counties of Britain: A Tudor Atlas by John Speed* (London)

Nisbett, J. and Lascelles, G. W. 1903 'Forestry in the New Forest' in H. A. Doubleday and W. Page (eds.) *Victoria History of the County of Hampshire* Vol. II (London) 409–70

O'Brien, K. 1999 'Imperial Georgia, 1660–1789' in G. Mclean, D. Landry and J. P. Ward (eds.) *The Country and the City Revisited: England and the Politics of Culture, 1550–1850* (Cambridge) 160–79

Ogborne, M. 1998 *Spaces of Modernity: London's Geographies 1680–1780* (London)

Orel, H. (ed.) 1967 *Thomas Hardy's Personal Writings* (London)

Orton, H., Sanderson, S. and Widdowson, J. 1978 *The Linguistic Atlas of England* (London)

Orwell, G. 1962 [1937] *The Road to Wigan Pier* (Harmondsworth)

Osmond, J. 1988 *The Divided Kingdom* (London)

Overton, M. 1996 *Agricultural Revolution in England: The Transformation of the Agrarian Economy, 1500–1850* (Cambridge)

Parry, G. 1995 *The Trophies of Time: English Antiquarians of the Seventeenth Century* (Oxford)

Parsons, E. J. S. 1958 *The Map of Great Britain Circa A.D. 1360 Known as the Gough Map: An Introduction to the Facsimile* (Oxford)

Paterson, R. C. 1997 *My Wound is Deep: A History of the Later Anglo-Scots Wars 1380–1560* (Edinburgh)

Pawson, E. 1977 *Transport and the Economy: The Turnpike Roads of Eighteenth-Century Britain* (London)

1979 *The Early Industrial Revolution* (London)

Paxman, J. 1998 *The English* (London)

Pelham, R. A. 1936 'Medieval foreign trade: eastern ports' in H. C. Darby (ed.) *An Historical Geography of England before AD 1800* (Cambridge) 298–329

Pevsner, N. 1967 *The Buildings of England: Yorkshire West Riding* 2nd edn (Harmondsworth)

1983 *The Buildings of England: County Durham* 2nd edn (Harmondsworth)

Phillipps, K. C. 1984 *Language and Class in Victorian England* (Oxford)

Pocock, D. C. D. 1978 'The novelist's image of the North' *Transactions of the Institute of British Geographers* 4, 62–76

Polanyi, K. 1957 *The Great Transformation* (Boston)

Pollard, A. J. 1997 'The characteristics of the fifteenth-century North' in J. C. Appleby and P. Dalton (eds.) *Government, Religion and Society in Northern England 1000–1700* (Stroud)

Pollard, S. 1981 *Peaceful Conquest* (Oxford)

1982 *The Wasting of the British Economy* (London)

1989 *Britain's Prime and Britain's Decline: The British Economy 1870–1914* (London)

2000a *Essays on the Industrial Revolution* (Aldershot)

2000b 'Capitalism and rationality: a study of measurements in British coal mining c.1750–1850' in S. Pollard *Essays on the Industrial Revolution* (Aldershot) 296–315

Ponting, K. G. (ed.) 1969 *Aubrey's Natural History of Wiltshire* (Newton Abbot)

Poole, R. L. 1902 *Historical Atlas of Modern Europe from the Decline of the Roman Empire* (Oxford)

Porteous, J. 1977 *Canal Ports* (London)

Porter, R. 1982 *English Society in the Eighteenth Century* (London)

1994 *London: A Social History* (London)

Poster, M. (ed.) 1997 *Cultural History and Postmodernity: Disciplinary Readings and Challenges* (New York)

Postgate, M. R. 1973 'Field systems of East Anglia' in A. R. H. Baker and R. A. Butlin (eds.) *Studies of Field Systems in the British Isles* (Cambridge) 281–324

Power, J. P. and Campbell, B. M. S. 1992 'Cluster analysis and the classification of medieval demesne-farming systems' *Transactions of the Institute of British Geographers* 17, 227–45

Powicke, F. M. (ed.) 1939 *Handbook of British Chronology* (London)

Premble, J. 1987 *The Mediterranean Passion: Victorians and Edwardians in the South* (Oxford)

Pressnell, L. S. 1956 *Country Banking and the Industrial Revolution* (Oxford)

Prest, J. 1990 *Liberty and Locality: Parliament, Permissive Legislation and Ratepayers' Democracies in the Nineteenth Century* (Oxford)

Prestwich, M. 1972 *War, Politics and Finance under Edward I* (London)
    1980 *The Three Edwards: War and State in England 1272–1377* (London)

Price, R. 1999 *British Society 1680–1880* (Cambridge)

Priestley, J. B. 1934 *English Journey* (London)

Proud, L. 1994 *Consider England* (London)

Rackham, O. 1989 *The Last Forest: The Story of Hatfield Forest* (London)

Randall, A. and Charlesworth, A. (eds.) 2000 *Moral Economy and Popular Protest* (Basingstoke)

Raven, J. 1989 'British history and the enterprise culture' *Past and Present* 123, 178–204

Rawnsley, A. 2000 'Constructing "The North": space and a sense of place' in N. Kirk (ed.) *Northern Identities: Historical Interpretations of 'The North' and 'Northernness'* (Aldershot) 3–22

Read, D. 1964 *The English Provinces, c.1760–1960: A Study in Influence* (London)

Redwood, J. 1999 *The Death of Britain?* (Basingstoke)

Reed, M. and Wells, R. 1990 *Class Conflict and Protest in the English Countryside 1700–1880* (London)

Reeder, D. and Rodger, R. 2000 'Industrialisation and the city economy' in M. Daunton (ed.) *The Cambridge Urban History of Britain* Vol. III: *1840–1950* (Cambridge) 553–92

Reid, R. 1921 *The King's Council in the North* (London)

Reilly, R. 1992 *Josiah Wedgwood, 1730–1795* (London)

Rex, R. 2002 *The Lollards* (Basingstoke)

Richards, T. 1990 *The Commodity Culture of Victorian England: Advertising and Spectacle, 1851–1914* (London)

Rickman, J. 1843 'Estimated populations of England and Wales 1570–1750' *Parliamentary Papers XXII: Population/Enumeration Abstracts* (London) Preface 36–37

Rigby, S. H. 1995 *English Society in the Later Middle Ages: Class, Status and Gender* (London)

Robbins, K. 1988 *Nineteenth-Century Britain: Integration and Diversity* (Oxford)

Roberts, B. K. and Wrathmell, S. 2000 *An Atlas of Rural Settlement in England* (London)

Robson, B. T. 1973 *Urban Growth: An Approach* (London)
    1985 *Where is the North? An Essay on the North/South Divide* (Manchester)
    1990 'The years between' in R. A. Dodgshon and R. A. Butlin (eds.) *An Historical Geography of England and Wales* (London) 545–78

Roderick, G. W. and Stephens, M. D. 1982 *The British Malaise: Industrial Performance, Education and Training in Britain Today* (Falmer)

Rogaly, J. 1987 'Divided they stand' *Financial Times* 31 March

Rowe, D. J. 1990 'The north-east' in F. M. L. Thompson (ed.) *The Cambridge Social History of Britain 1750–1950* Vol. I: *Regions and Communities* (Cambridge) 414–70

Rowlands, M. B. 1975 *Masters and Men in the Small Metalware Trades of the West Midlands* (Manchester)

1987 *The West Midlands from AD 1000* (London)

Rowntree, B. S. 1941 *Poverty and Progress: A Second Social Survey of York* (London)

Rowntree, B. S. and Lavers, G. R. 1951 *Poverty and the Welfare State* (London)

Rubinstein, W. D. 1977a 'Wealth, elites and the class structure of modern Britain' *Past and Present* 76, 99–126

1977b 'The Victorian middle classes: wealth, occupation and geography' *Economic History Review* 30, 602–23

1981 *Men of Property: The Very Wealthy in Britain since the Industrial Revolution* (London)

1986 'Wealth and the wealthy' in J. Langton and R. J. Morris (eds.) 1986 *Atlas of Industrializing Britain 1780–1914* (London) 156–9

1993 *Capitalism, Culture and Decline in Britain 1750–1990* (London)

Sacks, D. H. and Kelley, D. R. (eds.) 1999 *The Historical Imagination of Early Modern Britain: History, Rhetoric and Fiction, 1500–1800* (Cambridge)

Saler, M. 1998 'Making it new: visual modernism and the "Myth of the North" in interwar England' *Journal of British Studies* 37, 419–40

Samuel, R. 1987 *Patriotism: The Making and Unmaking of British National Identity* (London)

1998 *Theatres of Memory* Vol. II: *Island Stories. Unravelling Britain* (London). See 'North and South' 153–71 and 'Unravelling Britain' 41–73

Schofield, R. E. 1963 *The Lunar Society of Birmingham: A Social History of Provincial Science and Industry in Eighteenth-Century Birmingham* (Oxford)

Schofield, R. S. 1965 'The geographical distribution of wealth in England, 1334–1649' *Economic History Review* 18, 482–510

Schuyler, R. I. 1931 *Josiah Tucker: A Selection from his Economic and Political Writings* (New York)

Schwartz, L. 1992 *London in the Age of Industrialisation* (Cambridge)

Scruton, R. 2000 *England: An Elegy* (London)

Shaw, M., Dorling, D., Gordon, D. and Davey Smith, G. 1999 *The Widening Gap: Health Inequalities and Policy in Britain* (Bristol)

Sheail, J. 1972 'The distribution of taxable population and wealth in England during the early sixteenth century' *Transactions of the Institute of British Geographers* 55, 111–26

1998 *The Regional Distribution of Wealth in England as Indicated in the 1524/5 Lay Subsidy Returns* edited by R. W. Hoyle *List and Index Society Special Series* 28 and 29 (London)

Shepherd, J. A. 1976 'Medieval village planning in northern England: some evidence from Yorkshire' *Journal of Historical Geography* 2, 3–20

Shields, R. 1991 *Places on the Margin: Alternative Geographies of Modernity* (London)

Short, B. 1989 'The de-industrialisation process: a case study of the Weald' in P. Hudson (ed.) *Regions and Industries: A Perspective on the Industrial Revolution in Britain* (Cambridge) 156–74

Skipp, V. 1978 *Crisis and Development: An Ecological Study of the Forest of Arden* (Cambridge)

Slack, P. 2002 'Perceptions and people' in P. Slack and R. Ward (eds.) *The Peopling of Britain* (Cambridge) 211–6

Sloggett, A. and Joshi, H. 1994 'Higher mortality in deprived areas: community or personal disadvantage?' *British Medical Journal* 309, 1470–4

Smith, A. 1759 *Theory of Moral Sentiments* (London)

1776 *An Inquiry into the Nature and Causes of the Wealth of Nations* (London)

Smith, D. 1989 *North and South: Britain's Economic, Social and Political Divide* (London)

Smith, K. 1989 *The British Economic Crisis* (Harmondsworth)

Smith, N. 1984 *Uneven Development: Nature, Capital and the Production of Space* (London)

Smollett, T. 1771 *The Expedition of Humphry Clinker* (London)

Snell, K. D. M. 1981 'Agricultural seasonal unemployment, the standard of living, and women's work in the south and east, 1690–1860' *Economic History Review* 34, 407–37

Sobell, D. 1998 *Longitude* (London)

Somerville, R. 1953 *History of the Duchy of Lancaster* Vol. I (London)

1972 *Officeholders in the Duchy and County Palatine of Lancaster from 1603* (London)

2000 *History of the Duchy of Lancaster* Vol. II (London)

Southall, H. 1986 'Regional employment patterns among skilled engineers in Britain, 1815–1914' *Journal of Historical Geography* 12, 268–86

1988a 'The origins of the depressed areas: unemployment, growth and regional economic structure in Britain before 1914' *Economic History Review* 41, 236–58

1988b 'Towards a geography of unionisation: the spatial organisation and distribution of early British trade unions' *Transactions of the Institute of British Geographers* 13, 466–83

1991 'Mobility, the artisan community and popular politics in early-nineteenth century England' in G. Kearns and C. W. J. Withers (eds.) *Urbanising Britain: Essays on Class and Community in the Nineteenth Century* (Cambridge) 103–30

Spring, D. 1963 *The English Landed Estate in the Nineteenth Century: Its Administration* (Baltimore)

Stacey, R. C. 1995 'Jewish lending and the medieval English economy' in R. H. Britnell and B. M. S. Campbell (eds.) *A Commercialising Economy: England 1086 to c.1300* (Manchester) 78–102

Stallybrass, P. 1989 'Time, space and unity: the symbolic discourse of the Faerie Queene' in R. Samuel (ed.) *Patriotism* Vol. III: *National Fictions* (London) 199–214

Stannard, K. 1999 'How many Italies? Process and scale in the development of the Italian space-economy' *Geography* 84, 308–18

Stedman Jones, G. 1989 'The "cockney" and the nation, 1780–1988' in D. Feldman and G. Stedman Jones (eds.) *Metropolis. London: Histories and Representations* (London) 272–324

Steed, M. 1986 'The core-periphery dimension of British Politics' *Political Geography Quarterly* 5, 4, 90–102

Stenton, F. 1958 'The roads of the Gough Map' in E. J. S. Parsons (ed.) *The Map of Great Britain Circa A.D. 1360 Known as the Gough Map: An Introduction to the Facsimile* (Oxford)

Stobart, J. 1996a 'Geography and industrialisation: the space economy of northwest England, 1701–1760' *Transactions of the Institute of British Geographers* 21, 681–96

1996b 'The spatial organisation of a regional economy: central places in northwest England in the early-eighteenth century' *Journal of Historical Geography* 22, 147–59

Stobart, J. and Lane, P. (eds.) 2000 *Urban and Industrial Change in the Midlands 1700–1840* (Leicester)

Stoyle, M. 1994 *Loyalty and Locality* (Exeter)

1996 ' "Pagans or Paragons?' Images of the Cornish during the English Civil War' *English Historical Review* 111, 300–23

Stringer, J. J. 1995 'Scottish foundations: thirteenth-century perspectives' in A. Grant and K. J. Stringer (eds.) *Uniting the Kingdom? The Making of British History* (London) 85–96

Strong, R. 2000 *The Spirit of Britain: A Narrative History of the Arts* (London)

Supple, B. 1994 'Fear of failing: economic history and the decline of Britain' *Economic History Review* 47, 441–58

Sweet, R. 1997 *The Writing of Urban Histories in the Eighteenth Century* (Oxford)

Szreter, S. and Hardy, A. 2000 'Urban fertility and mortality patterns' in M. Daunton (ed.) *The Cambridge Urban History of Britain* Vol. III: *1840–1950* (Cambridge) 629–72

Szreter, S. and Mooney, G. 1998 'Urbanisation, mortality and the standard of living debate: new estimates of life at birth in nineteenth-century British cities' *Economic History Review* 51, 84–112

Tait, J. 1908 'Political history: to the end of the reign of Henry VIII' in W. Farrer and J. Brownhill (eds.) *The Victoria History of the County of Lancaster* Vol. II (London) 175–218

Taylor, P. J. 1991 'The English and their Englishness: "a curiously mysterious, elusive and little understood people" ' *Scottish Geographical Magazine* 107, 146–61

2001 'Which Britain? Which England? Which North?' in D. Morely and K. Robins (eds.) *British Cultural Studies: Geography, Nationality and Identity* (Oxford) 127–44

Thane, P. 1990 'Government and society in England and Wales, 1750–1914' in F. M. L. Thompson (ed.) *The Cambridge Social History of Britain* Vol. III: *Social Agencies and Institutions* (Cambridge) 1–61

Theroux, P. 1983 *The Kingdom by the Sea: A Journey Round the Coast of Britain* (London)

Thirsk, J. 1961 'Industries in the countryside' in F. J. Fisher (ed.) *Essays in the Economic and Social History of Tudor and Stuart England* (Cambridge) 70–88

1978 *Economic Policy and Projects* (Oxford)

1987 *England's Agricultural Regions and Agrarian History, 1500–1750* (London)

1992 'The Crown as projector on its own estates, from Elizabeth I to Charles I' in R. Hoyle (ed.) *The Estates of the English Crown 1558–1640* (Cambridge) 297–352

Thomas, K. 1978 *Religion and the Decline of Magic* (Harmondsworth)

Thomas, P. 1990 'Belgium's north–south divide and the Walloon regional problem' *Geography* 75, 36–50

Thomas, T. 1985 'Representation of the Manchester working class in fiction, 1850–1900' in A. J. Kidd and K. W. Roberts (eds.) *City, Class and Culture: Studies of Social Policy and Cultural Production in Victorian Manchester* (Manchester) 103–216

Thompson, A. H. 1913 'Religious history' in W. Page (ed.) *The Victoria History of the County of York* Vol. III (London) 1–88

Thompson, D. 1984 *The Chartists* (London)

Thompson, E. P. 1968 *The Making of the English Working Class* (London)
1991 *Customs in Common* (London)
Thompson, F. L. M. 1963 *English Landed Society in the Nineteenth Century* (London)
Tomlin Smith, L. (ed.) 1907 *The Itinerary of John Leyland in or about the Years 1535–1543 Parts I to III* (London)
Tomlinson, J. 1996 'Inventing "decline": the falling behind of the British economy in the postwar years' *Economic History Review* 49, 731–57
Trainor, R. 2000 'The middle class patterns' in M. Daunton (ed.) *The Cambridge Urban History of Britain* Vol. III: *1840–1950* (Cambridge) 673–715
Trinder, J. B. 1973 *The Industrial Revolution in Shropshire* (Chichester)
Tuck, J. A. 1985 'War and society in the medieval North' *Northern History* 21, 33–52
Turnbull, G. 1987 'Canals, coal and regional growth during the industrial revolution' *Economic History Review* 40, 537–60
Turner, G. J. 1903 'The Justices of the Forest south of the Trent' *English Historical Review* 18, 68–72
Turner, J. 1979 *The Politics of Landscape: Rural Scenery and Society in English Poetry 1630–1660* (Harvard)
Turner, M. 1980 *English Parliamentary Enclosure* (Folkestone)
Underdown, D. 1985 *Revel, Riot and Revolution* (Oxford)
Wadsworth, A. P. and Mann, J. de L. 1965 *The Cotton Trade and Industrial Lancashire 1600–1780* (Manchester)
Waites, B. 1997 *Monasteries and Landscape in Northeast England: The Medieval Colonisation of the North York Moors* (Oakham)
Walton, J. K. 1990 'The north–west' in F. M. L. Thompson (ed.) *The Cambridge Social History of Britain 1750–1950* Vol. I: *Regions and Communities* (Cambridge) 355–414
Walvin, J. 1997 *Fruits of Empire* (London)
Ward, J. T. and Wilson, R. G. (eds.) 1971 *Land and Industry: The Landed Estate and the Industrial Revolution* (Newton Abbot)
Ward, S. 1988 *The Geography of Interwar Britain: The State and Uneven Development* (London)
Wareing, J. 1980 'Changes in the geographical distribution of the recruitment of apprentices to the London Companies 1486–1750' *Journal of Historical Geography* 6, 241–50
Warwick, G. T. 1964 'Relief and structure' in J. W. Watson (ed.) *The British Isles: A Systematic Geography* (Edinburgh) 91–109
Webb, I. 1976 'The Bradford Wool Exchange: industrial capitalism and the popularity of Gothic' *Victorian Studies* 20, 45–68
Webb, S. and Webb, B. 1894 *The History of Trade Unionism* (London)
Weiner, M. 1981 *English Culture and the Decline of the Industrial Spirit, 1850–1980* (Cambridge)
West, R. 1997 *The Life and Strange Surprising Adventures of Daniel Defoe* (London)
Westerfield, R. B. 1915 *Middlemen in English Business, Particularly Between 1660 and 1760* (Newton Abbot)
White, L. A. 1943 'Energy and the evolution of culture' *American Anthropologist* 45, 335–56
Whyman, S. E. 1999 *Sociability and Power in Late-Stuart England* (Oxford)
Wiley, M. 1998 *Romantic Geography* (London)

Williams, C. H. (ed.) 1967 *English Historical Documents Vol. V 1485–1558* (London)

Williams, R. 1973 *The Country and the City* (London)

Williamson, T. 1995 *Polite Landscapes* (Stroud)

Willis, B. 1730 *Notitia Parliamentaria: or an History of the Counties, Cities and Boroughs of England and Wales* 2nd edn (London)

Wilson, J. 1905 'Ecclesiastical history' and 'Political history' in J. Wilson (ed.) *The Victoria History of the Counties of England: Cumberland* Vol. II (London) 1–126 and 221–330

Wilson, K. 1958 'Forest Law' *Amateur Historian* 3, 305–7

Wilson, R. G. 1973 'The supremacy of the Yorkshire cloth industry in the eighteenth century' in N. B. Harte and K. G. Ponting (eds.) *Textile History and Economic History* (Manchester) 225–46

Winch, D. 1996 *Riches and Poverty: An Intellectual History of Political Economy in Britain 1750–1834* (Cambridge)

Winchester, S. 1998 *The Professor and the Madman: A Tale of Murder, Insanity and the Making of the Oxford English Dictionary* (New York)

Wilsher, P. and Cassidy, J. 1987 'Two nations: the false frontier' *Sunday Times* 11 January

Woods, R. 2000 *The Demography of Victorian England and Wales* (Cambridge)

Woods, R. and Shelton, N. 1997 *An Atlas of Victorian Mortality* (Liverpool)

Woodward, D. 1995 *Men at Work: Labourers and Building Craftsmen in the Towns of Northern England, 1450–1750* (Cambridge)

Wrigley, E. A. 1967 'A simple model of London's importance in changing England's society and economy, 1650–1750' *Past and Present* 37, 44–70.

    1987 'A simple model of London's importance in changing England's society and economy, 1650–1750' *People, Cities and Wealth* (Cambridge) 133–56 [a reprint of the 1967 paper]

    1988 *Continuity, Chance and Change: The Character of the Industrial Revolution in England* (Cambridge)

    1991 'Energy availability and agricultural productivity' in B. M. S. Campbell and M. Overton (eds.) *Land, Labour and Livestock: Historical Studies in European Agricultural Productivity* (Manchester) 323–39

    1994 'The classical economists, the stationary state and the industrial revolution' in G. D. Snooks (ed.) *Was the Industrial Revolution Necessary?* (London) 27–42

    2002 'Country and town: the primary, secondary and tertiary peopling of England in the early modern period' in P. Slack and R. Ward (eds.) *The Peopling of Britain: The Shaping of a Human Landscape* (Oxford) 217–42

Wrigley, E. A. and Schofield, R. S. 1981 *The Population History of England* (Cambridge)

Yelling, J. A. 2000 'Land, property and planning' in M. Daunton (ed.) *The Cambridge Urban History of Britain* Vol. III: 1840–1950 (Cambridge) 467–94

Zell, M. 1994 *Industry in the Countryside* (Cambridge)

Index

Cambridge Studies in Historical Geography

Titles marked with an asterisk are available in paperback.*